KNOWLEDGE CENTRE

CLASS No: 616 . 855 WHI

WITHDRAWN

D0321840

616. 855 MAH

A Cognitive Neuropsychological Approach to Assessment and Intervention in Aphasia

This book provides both a theoretical and practical reference to cognitive neuropsychological approaches for speech and language therapists working with people with aphasia. Having evolved from the activity of a group of clinicians working with people with aphasia, it is a highly practical guide that aims to interpret the theoretical literature as it relates to aphasia and link it directly to available assessment tools and therapy techniques.

The opening section of the book provides an overview of the theory underpinning the approach and how it can be applied to the assessment and interpretation of language-processing impairments. The second section offers a working explanation of different components of language processing, outlining the deficits that may arise from impairment to each component. In addition, the clinician is guided to available assessments to test out clinical hypotheses and offered interpretations of performance patterns. The final section provides a comprehensive overview of the therapy literature with systematic summaries of the therapies undertaken and a synthesis of the findings to date.

This book has been written by clinicians with hands-on experience. It will be an invaluable resource for clinicians and students of speech and language therapy and related disciplines.

Anne Whitworth is Senior Lecturer on the Speech and Language Sciences programmes at the University of Newcastle-upon-Tyne.

Janet Webster is the Co-Director of the North East Aphasia Centre at the University of Newcastle-upon-Tyne.

David Howard is Research Professor at the University of Newcastle-upon-Tyne and is co-author of the *Comprehensive Aphasia Test*.

A Cognitive Neuropsychological Approach to Assessment and Intervention in Aphasia

A clinician's guide

Anne Whitworth, Janet Webster and David Howard

Psychology Press
Taylor & Francis Group

HOVE AND NEW YORK

First published 2005
by Psychology Press
27 Church Road, Hove, East Sussex BN3 2FA

Simultaneously published in the USA and Canada
by Psychology Press Inc
270 Madison Avenue, New York NY 10016

Psychology Press is part of the Taylor & Francis Group, an Informa business

Reprinted 2006, 2007 and 2008

Copyright © 2005 Psychology Press

Typeset in Times by RefineCatch Limited, Bungay, Suffolk
Printed and bound in Great Britain by Biddles Ltd, King's Lynn
Cover design by Hybert Design

All rights reserved. No part of this book may be reprinted or
reproduced or utilised in any form or by any electronic, mechanical or
other means, now known or hereafter invented, including photocopying
and recording, or in any information storage or retrieval system,
without permission in writing from the publishers.

This publication has been produced with paper manufactured to strict
environmental standards and with pulp derived from sustainable
forests.

British Library Cataloguing in Publication Data
A catalogue record for this book is available from the British Library

Library of Congress Cataloging in Publication Data
Whitworth, Anne.
    A cognitive neuropsychological approach to assessment and
intervention in aphasia : a clinician's guide / Anne Whitworth,
Janet Webster and David Howard. – 1st ed.
        p. cm.
    Includes biographical reference and index.
    ISBN 1-84169-345-6 (hard cover)
  1. Aphasia.   2. Cognitive neuroscience.   3. Neuropsychology.
  I. Webster, Janet, 1974–   II. Howard, David, 1951–   III. Title.

    RC425.W48 2005
    616.85′52–dc22

                                                        2004013474

ISBN 978-1-84169-345-3

No method of treatment is better than the principles on which it is based, and the search for principles should concern us no less than the immediate clinical situation.

(Zangwill, 1947, p. 7)

Contents

Preface   ix
Introduction   x

PART 1
Theory and principles   1

1 A cognitive neuropsychological approach: theories
   and models   3

2 Identifying and characterising impairments: principles
   and evidence   11

PART 2
Deficits and assessment   23

3 Introduction to assessment   25

4 Auditory comprehension of spoken words   29

5 Spoken word production   45

6 Written comprehension and reading   59

7 Written word production   79

8 Object and picture recognition   97

PART 3
Therapy   105

9 Introduction to therapy   107

10 Therapy for auditory comprehension   115

viii   *Contents*

11 Therapy for word retrieval and production   135

12 Therapy for reading   187

13 Therapy for writing   227

Epilogue   259
Glossary   265
References   269
Author index   283
Subject index   289

Preface

This volume evolved from the activity of a group of speech and language therapists in Newcastle-upon-Tyne, UK, who met, and still meet, regularly to evaluate new developments in aphasia, explore new assessment tools and approaches, exchange views on management strategies, encourage clinical research and generally swap stories of working with people with aphasia. Steeped within a strong cognitive neuropsychological tradition, we decided, several years ago, to tackle the frustration that arose from the lack of accessible literature in this area for the working clinician and try to draw together what it was that we did in our daily practice. Our project benefited us all and it seemed a logical next stage for some of us to extend this and make it more comprehensive and accessible to a wider group of clinicians and students working with people with aphasia. Members of the Newcastle Aphasia Study Group who contributed to this book's antecedent are, in alphabetical order, Jennifer Bell, Helen Bird, Kirsty Bramley, Frauke Buerk, Ros Emerson, Gill Everson, Jane Giles, Liz Green, Clare Headington, Rose Hilton, Fiona Hinshelwood, Lisa Hirst, David Howard, Louise Kelly, Anne-Marie Laverty, Lucy Skelton, Susan Stewart, Jill Summersall, Sonja Turner, Julia Wade, Janet Webster, Anne Whitworth and Sheila Wight. Our many thanks to the group members for their efforts and support that allowed this book to see the light of day, and their continued enthusiasm for discussing and evaluating their work with aphasia that permeates our lively meetings. In addition, we would like to thank Lyndsey Nickels who has tirelessly read and commented on previous drafts of this volume, along with Sue Franklin and Lisa Perkins who have also given their time and wisdom to reshaping earlier ideas.

Anne Whitworth, Janet Webster and David Howard

Introduction

While a cognitive neuropsychological approach is widely used in aphasia clinics throughout the UK and other countries to assess and treat people with aphasia, there is relatively little published information that is accessible to the speech and language therapist (or speech language pathologist) that explores the application of this approach. A small number of published assessment tools, for example the Psycholinguistic Assessments of Language Processing in Aphasia (Kay, Lesser, & Coltheart, 1992) and the ADA Comprehension Battery (Franklin, Turner, & Ellis, 1992), while widely used, are not supported by accessible literature to assist the working clinician in selecting the appropriate test to use, interpreting the results and identifying intact and impaired processing systems. These are, we would argue, crucial steps in devising therapy that is, as Hatfield and Shewell (1983) put it, both rational and specific; rational in the sense that it is based on a coherent account of impaired and intact processes, and specific in that it is targeted towards the effects of the impairments for an individual.

Therapeutic application of cognitive neuropsychology also remains difficult to digest. While there is a developing literature on therapy for people with aphasia that uses therapy approaches grounded within a cognitive neuropsychological perspective, these case reports are presented in various forms that differ in their accessibility to clinicians and transparency with the theoretical models used. This book aims to link theory and practice within a cognitive neuropsychological framework, presenting the theoretical literature and relating it directly to available assessment tools and reported therapy techniques. It is intended to provide both a theoretical and practical reference for the working clinician. It does not aim to be prescriptive; it is anticipated that it will provide information that will help clinicians to use cognitive neuropsychological knowledge in the assessment and treatment of people with aphasia.

As service provision to people with aphasia often occurs within the context of healthcare systems, the terms 'person with aphasia' and 'client' are used interchangeably throughout the book.

The person with aphasia and the broader clinical context

Before embarking on our exploration of this approach, we wish, as clinicians, to state the obvious. Investigation and interpretation of communication impairments using this approach is only one facet in the holistic approach to working with people with aphasia. This approach should, we believe, only be used within a total communication framework, with the person with aphasia being central and his or her personal circumstances and partners in communication being integral to the entire process. The importance of looking at areas other than deficits, of viewing the person with aphasia as an autonomous human being, of considering communication in context and of looking outside traditional modes of service delivery, are assumed to be obvious elements of any coherent holistic approach to working with people with aphasia.

We do not, therefore, wish to imply that this approach should be used in isolation from the broader context of the person with aphasia's real-life circumstances, but we do believe that a comprehensive analysis of his or her language-processing system often forms a necessary and vital part in understanding the nature of the difficulties encountered by the person with aphasia and in directing and informing subsequent management.

Structure of the book

This volume is divided into three discrete but interconnected sections. Part 1 sets out the cognitive neuropsychological approach used within the current management of people with aphasia, placing it within both an historical and contemporary framework.

Part 2 provides a working explanation of the theoretical model, outlining the deficits that may arise from impairment to each stage of the model and discussing assessment for each stage. The areas of spoken and written word comprehension, spoken and written word production, and object recognition are explored. While strictly outside the domain of language, object and picture recognition have been included because many assessments employ picture materials; as a result, these impairments may impact on performance on language assessments. In the chapters of Part 2, we seek to provide an accessible guide to the use of assessment tools in identifying underlying impairments. This is supported by brief case studies illustrating various patterns of impairment.

Part 3 provides a selective review of the therapy literature, with detailed summaries of the therapy used. Therapy studies have been systematically reviewed to provide information on the therapy procedures employed in each study, including, for example, tasks, materials and feedback given to the client, alongside brief details of the client and the outcome of therapy. A synthesis of the therapy literature is provided for auditory comprehension, naming, reading and writing, summarising what has been gained, to date, from clinical research using a cognitive neuropsychological approach to manage communication impairment in people with aphasia. The literature reviewed here is not exhaustive, and the studies discussed are neither necessarily methodologically ideal nor are described taking the exact theoretical position of the authors of this volume. We believe, however, that they are representative of the research in the area and allow us to shed light on the utility of the theoretical models many clinicians and researchers have been applying to the management of aphasia.

Part 1
Theory and principles

1 A cognitive neuropsychological approach

Theories and models

An historical perspective

Cognitive neuropsychology first emerged as a coherent discipline in the 1970s as a reaction to the then dominant approach in neuropsychology. This earlier approach to neuropsychology (the 'classical approach') sought to characterise the performance of people with aphasia by defining them in terms of their localisation of lesion (see Shallice, 1988, for further discussion of this approach). The aim here was to understand the psychological functions of parts of the cortex by investigating the patterns of deficits shown by individuals with lesions in these areas, and identify syndromes defined in terms of deficits that frequently co-occurred. Over the last 20 years, in the UK at least, cognitive neuropsychology has expanded to become the dominant approach in neuropsychology. Part of the reason is that it moved neuropsychology from being of interest only to those concerned with brain behaviour relationships to a major source of evidence on the nature of normal processing. Another reason is that good cognitive neuropsychology pays real attention to providing accounts that address how individual people with brain lesions behave, often using sophisticated experimental methods to investigate the determinants of their performance.

The origins of cognitive neuropsychology lay in two papers on people with reading disorders by Marshall and Newcombe (1966, 1973). There were two critical features. First, Marshall and Newcombe realised that individual people with reading disorders could show qualitatively different patterns of impairment that would have been obscured by treating them as a group. They described two people who made semantic errors in single-word reading (e.g. NEPHEW → 'cousin', CITY → 'town'; a difficulty described as 'deep dyslexia'), two people who made regularisation errors (e.g. LISTEN → 'liston', ISLAND → 'izland'; 'surface dyslexia'), and two people who made primarily visually related errors (e.g. EASEL → 'aerial', PAMPER → 'paper'; 'visual dyslexia'). The second feature was that the nature of the individual's problems could be understood in terms of an information-processing model developed to account for the performance of normal individuals, in this case the 'dual-route' model of reading. Three of the essential features of cognitive neuropsychology that were to define the approach were evident here: (1) the realisation that the performance of the individual, not the average of a group, was the important evidence; (2) that the nature of errors was informative; and (3) that the explanations of individuals' performance were to be couched in terms of information models of normal language processing and not in terms of brain lesions.

The approach developed from an initial focus on reading disorders to encompass a variety of other domains. These include, in a vaguely chronological order, spelling disorders, memory impairments (including both long- and short-term memory), semantic disorders, disorders of word retrieval, disorders of object and picture recognition, word-comprehension impairments, disorders of action, executive disorders, sentence-processing impairments, number processing, and calculation. The initial focus, in terms of the people whose disorders were investigated, was on adults with acquired brain lesions, typically following stroke, head injury or, more rarely, brain infections such as herpes simplex encephalitis. The focus has now broadened to encompass developmental disorders, and those disorders found in progressive brain diseases, most prominently the dementias.

Methods have also shown a gradual change. While the early studies were in-depth investigations of single individuals, there has been an increasing use of case series designs where a series of people are investigated using the same set of tasks. The data are not, however, analysed in terms of groups, but rather the focus is on accounting for the patterns of performance of a group of people analysed individually. Here, both differences and similarities between individuals constitute the relevant evidence. Theoretical models have also evolved. While box and arrow models of cognitive architecture remain a major source of explanatory concepts, there has been increasing use of computational models, usually confined to specific domains such as reading, word retrieval or comprehension.

Finally, there has been a resurgence of interest in localisation of cognitive functions in the brain. This has been fuelled by the development of imaging methods such as positron emission tomography and functional magnetic resonance imaging that can be used to measure changes in regional blood flow (reflecting local synaptic activity) in the brain while people are engaged in cognitive tasks. These methods have allowed people to explore how and where the information-processing modules are represented in the brain (e.g. Price, 2001; Price *et al.*, 2003).

Cognitive neuropsychology as a working theoretical model

With the abandonment of theories that drew direct links between localising lesions in the brain and characterising deficits in speech and language, the replacement model drew on the components involved in processing information and the interconnections between such components. These were first illustrated in Morton and Patterson's (1980) version of the logogen model.

Morton and Patterson (1980) revised and articulated earlier versions of the logogen model (which date back to Morton, 1969) to account for both the types of errors and the factors influencing reading performance (e.g. word imageability; part of speech) in people with deep dyslexia. This model was a quintessential 'box and arrow' processing diagram that specified a number of component processes (the boxes) and how they interrelate (the arrows). The model referred to in this book is illustrated in Figure 1.1 and is (loosely) based on Patterson and Shewell's (1987) adaptation of the earlier logogen models.

While a model of this kind may appear complex, each of these components appears to be necessary to account for the processing of single words. As Coltheart, Rastle, Perry, Langdon and Ziegler (2001) argued: 'All the complexities of the model are motivated. If any box or arrow were deleted

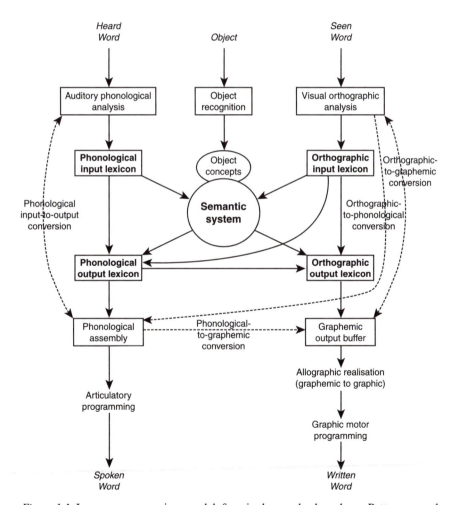

Figure 1.1 Language-processing model for single words, based on Patterson and Shewell's (1987) logogen model.

from it, the result would be a system that would fail in at least one language-processing task at which humans succeed' (p. 211).

If different modules and connections (boxes and arrows) in this model can be independently impaired, a very large number of possible patterns of performance may result from a lesion. Given this large number, one clearly cannot assume that any two people will necessarily have the same pattern of performance. The idea, therefore, that aphasia can be grouped into a limited number of identifiable and homogeneous 'syndromes' must necessarily fail. This does not, of course, mean that there will not be resemblances between the performances of different people with aphasia; to the extent that they have the same components damaged, this is precisely what we would predict. Nor does it mean that some combinations of symptoms do not appear more frequently than others. It simply means that one cannot group data from people with aphasia together as the differences between individuals are important (Shallice, 1988). Analysis of data from single individuals is the necessary consequence.

Using this kind of model to explain patterns of performance with people with aphasia involves making several assumptions, described and defended in detail by, among others, Caramazza (1986), Shallice (1988) and Coltheart (2001). Coltheart (2001) describes four assumptions:

1   *Functional modularity.* Some, at least, of the components of the cognitive system are modular, meaning that they operate independently, or relatively independently, of other components.
2   *Anatomical modularity.* Some, at least, of the modules of the cognitive system are localised in different parts of the brain. As a result, brain lesions can result in selective information-processing deficits, either by destroying the tissue responsible for particular modules or by disconnecting them. Functional modularity does not necessarily entail anatomical modularity.
3   *Universality of cognitive systems.* This simplifying assumption is that all normal people have the same cognitive systems. This is a plausible assumption for language processing, for example, but is clearly not directly applicable in domains of which some people have no experience, for example music. Note that it is not claimed here that all people will have equal experience and facility in all aspects of their cognitive system, rather that different people do not have radically different cognitive architectures for the same processes.
4   *Subtractivity.* The result of a brain lesion is to destroy, damage or impair one or more components of the normal cognitive system. Damage does not result in new information-processing systems. On the other hand, a person with brain damage may rely on different sources of information to perform a task, but these use processing systems that were available pre-morbidly. For example, a person with a severe face recognition impairment (prosopagnosia) may come to rely on a person's dress or voice to recognise them. While normal individuals may not rely on these strategies to recognise people, they can do so when necessary.

Models like that in Figure 1.1 are, in this form, radically unspecified. The diagram says nothing about how the processing in the boxes is achieved. Each of the cognitive modules will necessarily have structure and may comprise a whole set of component processes. For example, Figure 1.1 has a box called 'phonological assembly'. Levelt, Roelofs and Meyer (1999) argue that there are a number of separable processes involved in phonological assembly, including separate spell out of both the segmental and metrical structure. There is evidence that there can be separable impairments of these component processes (Nickels & Howard, 2000).

A working assumption is that any of the modules in the diagram can be lost or damaged as a result of cortical lesions. An individual with aphasia might have damage to one or several modules or the mappings between them. Because of the functional architecture of the brain, some patterns of deficits will be more frequent than others, but because lesions vary both in their precise cortical locations and in the cutting of sub-cortical white matter fibre tracts, identical patterns of deficit in any two people are unlikely. One objective in assessment can be to identify which of the modules and mappings (boxes and arrows) are damaged and which are intact, yielding a concise explanation of the pattern of performance across a range of tasks and materials.

In Chapters 4–8 we describe, in outline only, the nature of the processing in many of the components of the model. We are aware, of course, that we are not putting forward a complete, or even necessarily accurate, model of language processing even just for single words. Our fundamental claim, in the context of this book, is much more modest. It is that the model in Figure 1.1 provides a usable working model of language processing. It provides a level of description that can be used to guide a process of assessment that can identify levels of breakdown and intact and impaired processes in people with aphasia.

Competing models

There are many models of single word processing that can be, and have been, used to account for patterns of language breakdown as well as normal processing. Many of these are task-specific, dealing, for example, with spoken word production (e.g. Foygel & Dell, 2000; Levelt *et al.*, 1999; Rapp & Goldrick, 2000), spoken language comprehension (e.g. Marslen-Wilson, 1987), or semantic representation (e.g. Tyler, Moss, Durrant-Peatfield, & Levy, 2000). Evaluation of such models is beyond the scope of what this book aims to achieve. However, while these models do attempt to provide detailed accounts of representations and processes involved in particular tasks, they provide little information on how different tasks relate to each other. For example, the phonological assembly module in the lexical model of Figure 1.1 is a common output process shared by picture naming, word reading and word repetition. Impairment at this level should result in qualitatively similar patterns of impairment across all three tasks (some quantitative differences may be due to the differing nature of the input to the module). This is the pattern found in many people with phonological deficits in speech production (e.g. Caplan, Vanier, & Baker, 1986; Franklin, Buerk, & Howard, 2002).

Some models do, however, highlight the shared nature of processes and aim to account for patterns of performance across different tasks. In 1979, motivated by patterns of cross-modal repetition priming, Morton had revised the original 1969 logogen model that had a single lexicon for spoken word recognition, spoken word production, written word recognition and written word production, to have the four separate lexicons shown in Figure 1.1 (Morton, 1979a). Allport and Funnell (1981) pointed out that Morton's priming data only motivated a separation of orthographic and phonological lexicons, and, arguing against the need for the separation into input and output lexicons, suggested that a single phonological lexicon was used for both spoken word recognition and production, and a single orthographic lexicon was used for written word recognition and writing (see also Allport, 1985). There have been discussions about the explanatory adequacy of this proposal centring on a number of issues (see Howard & Franklin, 1988; Monsell, 1987). For example, there are people with deficits apparently at a lexical level in word retrieval with unimpaired recognition of the same words in spoken form (e.g. Howard, 1995) and, conversely, those with a lexical level of deficit in spoken word recognition with relatively unimpaired spoken naming (Howard & Franklin, 1988). This dissociation seems to imply separate input and output phonological lexicons. On the other hand, there have been reports of item-specific difficulties in reading and spelling that may be most easily captured by proposing impairment to a common orthographic lexicon (Behrmann & Bub, 1992).

A computational interactive activation model that also incorporated a single lexicon for word recognition and production was developed by Martin, Dell and their colleagues (Martin, Dell, Saffran, & Schwartz, 1994; Schwartz, Dell, Martin, & Saffran, 1994). In the original form of the model, word comprehension depended on exactly the same components as in word production operating in reverse. They used this to model the pattern of errors in repetition and naming in a single person who made semantic errors in repetition. However, when Dell, Schwartz, Martin, Saffran and Gagnon (1997) tried to use this model to account for the pattern of errors in naming and repetition in a group of further people with aphasia, they found that lesions that captured, with reasonable accuracy, the individuals' patterns of errors in naming, typically radically underestimated their repetition accuracy. Coupled with demonstrations that the model, in its unlesioned form, was only able to comprehend two-thirds of words correctly, was unable to repeat nonwords, and could not account for the relationships between accuracy in comprehension and production found in people with aphasia (Nickels & Howard, 1995b), Dell *et al.* (1997) abandoned this as a model of comprehension and repetition. Even its ability to account for the patterns of errors found in naming with people with aphasia has been challenged (Ruml & Caramazza, 2000). As a result of these problems, the current version of this model by

Foygel and Dell (2000) restricts its aims simply to accounting for patterns of errors in picture naming.

Finally, we need to consider the 'triangle model' developed by McClelland, Plaut, Seidenberg, Patterson and their colleagues (Plaut, McClelland, Seidenberg, & Patterson, 1996; Seidenberg & McClelland, 1989). This is a computational model of lexical processing that, like that of Allport and Funnell (1981), has only a single phonological system serving both production and comprehension of spoken words and a single orthographic system for both written input and output. The radical innovation in this model, however, is that there is no lexical representation. A set of units in phonological space, for example, encodes any possible phonological string whether word or nonword. Mappings from phonology to semantics or orthography will have been learned, using a real word vocabulary. During the process of learning, the weights in the connections between the input units and hidden units, and those between hidden units and orthography and semantics, will have been adjusted so that they achieve the correct mappings for the words used to train the model (see Plaut *et al.*, 1996, for a detailed description of this model). Knowledge of the mappings for individual words are not localised in a lexicon, but distributed across all the weights in all the connections between the domains.

The triangle model has been in development since Seidenberg and McClellands' (1989) proposal. There are two particularly notable achievements that have resulted. Plaut and Shallice (1993) showed that, at least with a limited vocabulary, a model mapping from orthography via semantics to phonology can account for most of the features found in people with deep dyslexia. Plaut *et al.* (1996) and Plaut (1999) have developed a model of the direct mapping from orthography to phonology for single-syllable words. With the right representations in both the orthographic and phonological domains, this model has enjoyed considerable success in accounting for the phenomena of normal reading and the patterns of deficit found in people with surface and phonological dyslexia. Most radically, the model shows that a single computational mechanism, trained only on a real word vocabulary, is able to generate the correct phonology for both irregular words (e.g. YACHT, PINT) and nonwords (e.g. THORK, SLINT).

Computational models of these kinds present a very interesting new way of understanding how mappings between domains might be implemented. It is important to realise, however, that the capabilities of these models depend critically on how the representations in the input and output domains are coded, as well as features of the architecture of the model such as the numbers of hidden units, and how they are connected. Models of this kind generally find it much easier to learn mappings between domains that are mostly systematic and generalisable, as in the mapping from orthography to phonology (where, for instance, the letter M at input almost always relates to a phoneme /m/ in output). This is because it finds it easiest to learn mappings where similar inputs result in similar outputs (see Plaut & Shallice, 1993).

Where, as in the mapping from orthography to semantics, there is no systematicity of this kind, the connectionist model finds this difficult to learn, although, eventually, it can succeed. Children, on the other hand, learn the mapping between new words and their meanings with extraordinary rapidity (Clark, 1993).

These models are currently limited in scope. Both of the implemented models have only feed-forward connections (that is, they use only one-directional connections between levels), although the overarching triangle model always uses bidirectional connections between domains. Since we know that the architecture of the models is critically important for how they behave, we do not know whether a model that could deal with both writing to dictation and reading aloud would behave in the same way in reading as the existing model that incorporates only connections in one direction.

One problem with connectionist models of this kind is that the way they behave is not clear until they are implemented. Given that, in the existing models, only reading aloud has been implemented, how they might extend to other tasks, such as word and nonword repetition, spoken word retrieval or writing, remains unclear. One result is that they cannot, in their present form, address the interesting associations and dissociations between tasks that are easily accommodated within the lexical model of Figure 1.1. An example of this is the fact that every person who is unable to repeat nonwords is also unable to write nonwords to dictation, but may be reasonably good at non-word reading (see Howard & Franklin, 1988, for discussion). In contrast, there are people who can repeat nonwords accurately and read them but are unable to write them to dictation (Shallice, 1981). For these reasons, at its current state of development, the triangle model's utility to the practising clinician in guiding assessment and identifying underlying deficits remains limited.

2 Identifying and characterising impairments

Principles and evidence

As we have argued, cognitive neuropsychology is based on the assumption that, as a result of a lesion, the language system can be impaired to produce identifiable patterns of impairment that can be interpreted in terms of a processing model. This is now more than an assumption; over the last 25 years, a huge volume of research has shown the utility and productivity of the approach. The goal of assessment, both for the researcher and the practising clinician, is to identify the processes that are intact and those that are impaired, and to show how these interact to produce the observed patterns of behaviour. The skill of assessment lies in the selection of the tasks and the interpretation of the data that will allow this goal to be achieved both revealingly and economically.

Looking for the evidence

The assessment process used in identifying impairments is one of forming and testing out hypotheses; the focus of these hypotheses is on testing out the relative intactness of specific components of the model. In assessing the different levels of breakdown using this model, use is usually made of three kinds of evidence. A first source of evidence is the effect of different variables (such as word length, imageability and so on) on performance. This is what Shallice (1988) describes as the 'critical variable approach' that 'seeks to establish the variables that affect the probability that a task will be correctly performed' (Nickels & Howard, 1995a, p. 1281) by a client. A second source of evidence is the nature of the errors made in different tasks. Where the tasks involve written and spoken word production, errors are made overtly, and can be classified. In comprehension tasks, the nature of possible errors is constrained by the design of the task. For example, in spoken word-to-picture matching, errors in word recognition at a lexical or pre-lexical level that result in misrecognition of a word as another phonologically related word will not be detected when the stimuli use only semantically related distractors. They would, on the other hand, be detected in word-to-picture matching using phonologically related distractors, or in a spoken word definition task.

While errors are revealing, their interpretation is not necessarily straightforward. For example, almost all clients who make semantic errors (e.g. UNCLE → 'nephew') in single-word reading ('deep dyslexics') also make visual errors (e.g. SCANDAL → 'sandal'). The obvious interpretation of these visual errors is that there is impairment in letter recognition or in the orthographic input lexicon. But, as Patterson (1979) has shown, this explanation cannot be correct (see also Coltheart, 1980; Morton & Patterson, 1980) (see the SANDAL–SCANDAL–SMANDAL paradox illustrated in Box 2.1). In general, errors of a particular kind suggest that there is an impairment at the level at which their defining feature is relevant, but as this example shows, this is not necessarily the case. Further evidence from the effects of variables and performance in related tasks is normally required.

Box 2.1 The SANDAL–SCANDAL–SMANDAL paradox

PW was a man with deep dyslexia and aphasia described by Patterson and her colleagues (Morton & Patterson, 1980; Patterson, 1978, 1979; Patterson & Marcel, 1977). PW made many semantic errors in single-word reading (e.g. SHADOW → 'dark'; SHOULDER → 'arms'; SEPULCHRE → 'tomb') – the defining symptom of deep dyslexia. Like other people with deep dyslexia, PW also made 'visual' errors in reading (e.g. TYING → 'typing'; SMOULDER → 'boulders'; APPRAISE → 'arise'). The obvious hypotheses to entertain to account for these visual errors are: (i) that there is impairment in letter recognition at the level of visual orthographic analysis; or (ii) that there is impairment to the orthographic input lexicon so that words are sometimes misrecognised as other words.

Both of these hypotheses predict that: (i) performance should be poor in visual lexical decision – that is, deciding if a letter string is a real word or not; (ii) nonwords should be misrecognised as real words and so real word errors will be made in reading nonwords; and (iii) visual errors should be equally likely on high- and low-imageability words (as imageability, a semantic variable, is not relevant to lexical and pre-lexical processing).

The results described by Patterson (1979) showed that these hypotheses had to be rejected. PW was able to perform at normal levels in lexical decision, where a person has to decide if a letter string is a real word or a nonword. Given SCANDAL, he would classify it as a word, and would judge SMANDAL to be a nonword. And, given nonwords such as SMANDAL to read, he did not say 'sandal', but 'it's not a word, I can't read it'. And, as Morton and Patterson (1980) discuss, visual errors tend to occur on lower imageability targets and the errors tend to be higher in imageability than the targets. This is sometimes called the SANDAL–SCANDAL–SMANDAL paradox. It shows clearly that the visual reading error cannot be ascribed to a difficulty in word recognition or letter perception. The semantic effects on visual errors are evidence for post-lexical levels of processing being involved.

The solution to the paradox Morton and Patterson (1980) offer is as follows:

SCANDAL activates the correct entry in the orthographic input lexicon but, because of an impairment to abstract word semantics (for which there is independent evidence), cannot activate a semantic representation. Then, the threshold on the orthographic input lexicon is reduced so that the next most active entry – SANDAL – can retrieve its (concrete) semantic representation and drive a response that results in the 'visual' error. This explanation, which relies, as in Morton's (1969, 1979a) logogen model, on lexical entries that have to reach a threshold level before they can pass activation on to other modules, might be reformulated in terms of models that allow for the cascade of information between levels, such as Coltheart and colleagues' (Coltheart, Curtis, Atkins, & Haller, 1993; Coltheart, Langdon, & Haller, 1996; Coltheart *et al.*, 2001) DRC (dual-route cascade) model. At a lexical level, SCANDAL is the most activated entry and its level of activation is sufficient to produce a correct lexical decision response. However, SANDAL also, because of its very high similarity, has a high level of activation. All of the units active in the visual input lexicon send activation to the semantic system. Because the semantics of abstract words are impaired, the semantic representation of SANDAL is more highly activated than the semantics of SCANDAL, and so the semantics of SANDAL drives the retrieval of a spoken reading response.

The third way of investigating the underlying impairment is to contrast performance on tasks that share some of their processing components. For example, in the case of PW, described above, normal performance in visual lexical decision requires, at least, letter recognition and lexical access. This finding immediately eliminates an account for visual errors at a lexical or pre-lexical level. The assumption that it reflects a central impairment to the semantic representations of abstract words predicts that PW will perform poorly in other tasks not involving visual word recognition but that do involve abstract word meaning. This can be tested using synonym judgements on spoken words. On these, as predicted, PW performs poorly with abstract words (Howard, 1985).

There are, then, three principal sources of evidence from the performance of people with aphasia that can be used to identify the nature of their underlying impairments: (1) the effects of critical variables, (2) the nature of errors and (3) convergent evidence from different tasks that use common processing components. On their own, the evidence from none of these is conclusive. Together, however, they can provide very strong evidence that allows the clinician to identify impaired processes. For this, of course, the specification of the relationships between tasks that is captured by the 'box and arrow' model in Figure 1.1 is critical.

Critical variables affecting performance

There are many factors that can be manipulated to provide information in the process of assessment. These variables give rise to error patterns from which certain assumptions can be drawn. Here we simply list some of the most commonly used variables. Others are discussed where they are relevant in Chapters 2–6.

Word frequency

Word frequency estimates derive from counting the number of occurrences of individual words. The most commonly used count is that of Kučera and Francis (1967) based on a million written words of American English of the 1960s. More recently, the CELEX database makes available much more extensive counts of British English, Dutch and German (Baayen, Piepenbrock, & Gulikers, 1995). The English count is of 16.3 million words of printed texts and 1.6 million words from spoken corpora gathered during the 1980s. This much larger corpus gives more reliable frequency counts than those provided by Kučera and Francis.

When testing for *frequency effects*, the usual method is to compare performance on a set of high-frequency words and a set of low-frequency words, matching the sets for other variables such as length, phonological complexity, imageability, and so on. When using these sets, it is important to remember that the terms high and low frequency are relative and not absolute. Across different experiments, the mean frequency of a set of high-frequency words can vary from 500 words per million (wpm) to 30 wpm, and low-frequency words from 50 to 1 wpm; one researcher's low-frequency word is another researcher's high-frequency word. This partly reflects the task used. While any high-frequency word can be used in reading, there are very few words with a frequency of more than 200 wpm that can be used in a picture-naming task.

Word frequency is strongly associated with age of acquisition (i.e. the age at which a word is likely to have been reasonably acquired) and it is difficult, although not impossible, to vary these factors independently. It has been argued that apparent word-frequency effects are really effects of age of acquisition (Ellis & Morrison, 1998). Word frequency is also very strongly related to rated familiarity. This is not surprising, as familiarity is rated in terms of how frequently a word is encountered or used.[1] There is a strong argument that rated familiarity may capture frequency differences among very low-frequency words more accurately than word frequency counts that are rather unreliable for words that occur very infrequently in the corpus (Gernsbacher, 1984).

The locus of word-frequency effects on accuracy in the model after damage is not totally clear. In almost all tasks with normal people, reaction times are shorter for high-frequency words. This has generally been attributed to either faster mapping between representations for high-frequency words (e.g. McCann & Besner, 1987; McCann, Besner, & Davelaar, 1988; the effect is in the arrows) or more accessible lexical representations (e.g. Morton, 1979b; i.e. the effect is in the boxes). In the event of impaired processing, frequency effects on accuracy have often been taken to indicate a lexical level of impairment (e.g. Lesser & Milroy, 1993). However, in semantic dementia, where the primary difficulty seems to be on a semantic level, there are very substantial frequency effects, suggesting that semantic representations corresponding to low-frequency words are more susceptible to damage (Lambon Ralph, Graham, Ellis, & Hodges, 1998). It is likely that frequency effects on accuracy with people who have language impairments may arise at lexical or semantic levels or in the mappings between them.

Imageability

When people are asked to rate words for imageability (how easily the word evokes a visual or auditory image), some words get high ratings (e.g. cat, book) and other more abstract words are judged to have low imageability (e.g. happiness, idea). Such words are used to determine the presence of an *imageability effect*. Imageability is closely related to concreteness (the concrete–abstract dimension) and, indeed, these dimensions may be impossible to distinguish (though see Marcel & Patterson, 1978, for evidence that imageability may be the determining factor). It has been suggested that imageability effects may reflect the richness of semantic representations with more imageable, concrete words having more semantic features than less imageable, abstract words (Plaut & Shallice, 1993). Another proposal is that high-imageability words have much more clearly defined and consistent meanings than low-imageability words, which tend to have meanings that are dependent on their linguistic context (Breedin, Saffran, & Coslett, 1994).

There is agreement that imageability effects occur at a semantic level. Better performance with high-imageability words than low-imageability words is a very frequent feature of aphasia (Franklin, 1989). The effects may occur at a semantic level, or in the processes of input and output from semantics (Franklin, Howard, & Patterson, 1994, 1995; Franklin, Turner, Lambon Ralph, Morris, & Bailey, 1996). There are, however, occasional people with aphasia or with progressive disorders who show the reverse effect – that is, better performance with abstract, low-imageability words than concrete, high-imageability words (e.g. Breedin *et al.*, 1994; Marshall, Chiat, Robson, & Pring, 1996; Warrington, 1975, 1981). This suggests that there may be partially independent representation of semantics for high- and low-imageability words.

Word length

Words and nonwords can be varied in their length (e.g. one-, two-, three-syllable words), while controlling for other variables such as frequency and imageability. Sets of these words are used to determine the presence of a *length effect*, where longer words and/or nonwords are repeated or accessed less accurately.

Seeking the roots of length effects is not straightforward. As words with more syllables have more phonemes, is the length effect due to the number of syllables or the number of phonemes? The obvious test is to use words that differ in their number of syllables but keeping the number of phonemes constant, for example comparing performance on four-phoneme, one-syllable words (e.g. 'trout') with four-phoneme, two-syllable words (e.g. 'poppy'). However, these words differ in their number of consonant clusters. The result is that the effects of phoneme length, syllable length and the number of clusters in a word can be very difficult to disentangle. Based on nine people who made phonological errors in production, Nickels and Howard (2004) present data that suggest that the number of phonemes is the only important factor. In contrast, Romani and Calabrese (1998) argue that phonological complexity is the determining factor for the person in their study.

With visually presented stimuli, the situation is even more complex. While in general the number of letters in a word is strongly related to the number of phonemes, this relationship is much less than perfect. For instance, ACHE has four letters but only two phonemes, whereas FLAX, also with four letters, has five phonemes. Similarly, some one-syllable words and three-syllable words have the same number of letters (e.g. PRINCE and BANANA). Differentiating between the effects of phonological and orthographic length may not, as a result, be straightforward.

These disputes may be of less importance for the clinician; in general, better performance with words with fewer phonemes suggests a problem in phonological output, most likely in the processes of phonological assembly. The rare individuals who are better at producing long words than short words (Best, 1995; Lambon Ralph & Howard, 2000) are more difficult to explain, but are most probably accounted for by a difficulty in accessing output phonology (because longer words, with fewer neighbours, are more distinctive in their phonological representations).

Word-length effects in spoken word recognition have not often been reported, perhaps because they have rarely been investigated. There are indications that people with impairments at the level of the phonological input lexicon or in access to semantics from the lexicon are better at understanding *longer* words (Franklin *et al.*, 1996; Howard & Franklin, 1988). This is probably because longer words are more distinctive in phonological space, and activate fewer similar competitors during the process of lexical access.

Word regularity

Word regularity involves comparing performance among matched sets of words with predictable or regular spelling-to-sound correspondences (e.g. MINT, RAVE) and words with less predictable spelling-to-sound correspondences (e.g. PINT, HAVE). These words are used to determine the presence of a *regularity effect* in reading, where regular words are read better than irregular words.

In English, the relationship between sound and spelling is much less predictable than the relationship of spelling to sound. For example, /pil/ can be correctly spelled as PEAL, PEEL or PELE (as in Pele Tower – a form of fortified late mediaeval farmhouse found in the North of England). But each of these can only plausibly be pronounced as /pil/. Whereas in reading most single-syllable words are regular in their spelling-to-sound correspondences (e.g. WHALE, CAUSE, FLAME), in spelling it is difficult to find many words (such as BANK, HILL, PANT) that can only be spelled in one way. When people with aphasia are better at reading or spelling regular words than irregular words, this suggests that they are using sub-lexical correspondences for the task. The implication is that lexical processing mechanisms are impaired at some point.

Lexicality

The model has processing systems that depend on lexical access; for example, reading via the orthographic input lexicon will only be possible for real words, because only familiar, known words are represented within that system. Nonwords can only be processed using routines that incorporate general rules for mapping between the input and output domains (for example, non-word reading requires the use of the process of 'orthographic to phonological conversion' that may depend on rules relating graphemes to phonemes).

Real words can be processed by the same procedure; generally this will result in correct performance, except where they are exceptions to the rules. So, for instance, all real words would be repeated correctly using 'phonological input-to-output conversion', as this mapping is completely consistent and without exceptions. In reading, in contrast, any real word with exceptional spelling-to-sound relationships (e.g. HAVE, BEAR, PINT) would be misread ('regularised') when its output is generated by the sub-lexical conversion procedure.

Comparisons of performance with real words and nonwords matched for length and phonological complexity can therefore provide useful information about how a task is performed. A *lexicality effect* is seen when performance with real words is better than with matched nonwords. Two conclusions then follow: first, that there is an impairment at some point in the sub-lexical procedure; second, lexical procedures are involved in real word processing. Better performance with nonwords than real words is a much less likely outcome but can occur, for instance, in 'surface dysgraphia' (Behrmann & Bub, 1992; Weekes, Davies, Parris, & Robinson, 2003). This means that there is an impairment at some point to the lexical procedure and thus the person is relying on sub-lexical procedures. For example, in writing to dictation, a person who relies on sub-lexical procedures will produce plausible (and therefore correct) spellings for nonwords. Real words will very often be incorrectly but plausibly spelled (e.g. spelling TRAIN as TRANE).

Word grammatical categories

These usually involve nouns, verbs, adjectives and function words, and are used to determine the presence of a *grammatical class effect*. There are systematic differences in word imageability across word classes. Nouns are typically rated as being much more imageable than verbs; adjectives are usually somewhere in between. Function words are both much less imageable and much more frequent than content words. They are also often shorter. The question of whether word class effects are real or are reducible to the effects of confounding variables such as imageability has often been raised. Allport and Funnell (1981) showed that differences between nouns and verbs in reading could disappear when word imageability was controlled. Disputes on whether all differences between nouns and verbs can be reduced to imageability differences continue (e.g. Berndt, Haendiges, Burton, & Mitchum, 2002; Bird, Howard, & Franklin, 2000).

With the contrast between content words and function words, the question of whether differences found are due to confounds with imageability or frequency is even less easily determined. Certainly, differences between content words and function words can disappear when lists matched for frequency and imageability are used (Bird, Franklin, & Howard, 2002; Howard & Franklin, 1988). One problem is that when matched lists are used for this, both the content words (very high frequency and very low imageability for content words) and the function words (very high imageability and very low frequency for function words) are atypical.

The nature of errors

In addition to these manipulated error patterns, the nature of the errors is a further source of information that may be used in seeking convergent information to identify the intact and impaired performance in processing. At a first approximation, errors suggest that there is an impairment at the level at which their defining feature is relevant. Semantic errors, for example, suggest that the underlying deficit lies in semantic representations or in the process of input to semantics or output from it. Similarly, phonological errors in production are consistent with impairment at the level of the phonological output lexicon or in more peripheral levels in phonological output. The nature of errors can never, however, by itself, be conclusive evidence of the level of underlying impairment. We have already highlighted in the SANDAL–SCANDAL–SMANDAL paradox that, in the case of PW, a person with deep dyslexia, visual errors in reading cannot be attributed to any difficulty in letter or word recognition.

There are several cautions to be noted. In many comprehension tasks, the possibility of errors is limited by the distractors used. Phonological or visual errors in word recognition will only be noticed when phonological or visual distractors are used. Similarly, semantic errors will only be made when semantically related distractors are used. Additionally, the opportunities for these errors relate directly to the number of distractors used in the relevant domain. For example, in word-to-picture matching, the rate of semantic errors will be very different if four semantically related distractors are available than if there is only one semantic distractor present. Semantic error rates may also be different when a more limited range of distractors is used in word–picture verification, where the person being assessed needs to decide whether the presented word is the name of a picture, comparing the presented name with all possible names. In comprehension, the opportunity for making diverse errors is maximised when the client is asked to define a presented word. The clinician must, therefore, select assessments carefully based on the hypotheses about the client's impairment as well as interpret performance within the context of task requirements.

In production, it is relatively straightforward to classify responses into (i) semantic errors, (ii) phonological errors and (iii) unrelated errors. Within phonological and unrelated errors, one can distinguish between real word and nonword responses. None of these classifications, however, are without their problems. For instance, how closely related does an error need to be to call the result semantically related? As there is no independent metric of semantic relatedness, the borderline is, essentially, a matter of choice. Martin *et al.* (1994) describe ATTITUDE → 'everybody has one of those days' as a semantic error. Howard and Franklin (1988) classify SHIRT → 'iron' as being unrelated.

Similarly, the degree of phonological relatedness required to classify an error as phonologically related varies radically between studies. Adopting a criterion inherited from Morton and Patterson (1980), Nickels and Howard (1995b) recognise responses as phonologically related when they share at least 50% of their phonemes with the target in approximately the same order. Martin *et al.* (1994) adopt a very much less stringent criterion – that is, a response that shares just one phoneme with the target (except for schwa) is counted as phonologically related! How errors are to be classified is, to a considerable extent, a matter of judgement. There are no correct answers that can be identified in advance. This is one reason why, in our view, errors constitute just one source of evidence about levels of breakdown. Strong conclusions about intact and impaired processes for any individual person with aphasia can only be drawn from converging evidence from the effects of critical variables and performance in related tasks together with the nature of errors made.[2]

It is also important to realise that, as Cutler (1981) pointed out, errors are multiple determined. In other words, an error can have more than one source. So, for instance, semantic errors in production may occur either when semantics are impaired or when the lexical form of the target word is unavailable (Caramazza & Hillis, 1990).

Comparisons across tasks

The comparison of performance on different tasks, where these different tasks share information-processing components, is the final critical source of evidence for identifying the locus of impairment. Much of the content of Chapters 4–8 deals with ways of making such comparisons. There are many possible ways in which this can be done, all of which depend on a task analysis that determines the processes necessary for performing a particular task. Useful comparisons are set out below.

Comparisons across modalities

Comparisons of the same tasks in spoken and written word comprehension are often used to identify whether the difficulties a person with aphasia shows are at a level common to the two modalities (when a similar level of performance, a similar distribution of errors and similar effects of psycholinguistic variables on performance should be found in the two modalities) or are specific to a single modality. Similar comparisons can be made between spoken and written naming (both necessarily involving semantic processing), or between naming, reading aloud and word repetition (all involving phonological assembly), and, when nonword reading and repetition are much more impaired than the same tasks with real words, access to the phonological output lexicon.

Comparisons of tasks tapping different levels within a modality

Franklin (1989) showed how a set of tasks that tap access to different levels of representation can be used to determine the level of breakdown in auditory word comprehension. She used: (i) nonword minimal pairs, which require access only to the output of auditory phonological analysis; (ii) auditory lexical decision, which requires access to the phonological input lexicon; and (iii) word comprehension tasks, including word-to-picture matching and synonym judgements (requiring access to semantics). Franklin argued that, if the model of Figure 1.1 is correct in the stages it postulates in spoken word comprehension, they would form a hierarchy such that impaired performance at any one level would result in impairment in all tasks tapping subsequent levels (see Table 2.1). This was the pattern she found (see client summaries in Chapter 4). This study demonstrates how careful thinking about tasks and the levels of representation that they tap can allow levels of impairment to be identified.

In word production, tasks that tap different levels without requiring processing at subsequent levels are less easily identified, although there are some comparisons of this kind that can be useful. For example, homophone judgements on pairs of written words (e.g. do SEW and SO sound the same?) require access to phonological representations without spoken output. Good

Table 2.1 The relationship between levels of impairment in spoken word comprehension and patterns of impairment in tasks tapping different levels in the processes involved (Franklin, 1989)

Task	Level of impairment			
	Auditory phonological analysis	*Phonological input lexicon*	*Access to semantics from the phonological input lexicon*	*Semantic representations*
Nonword minimal pairs	✗	✓	✓	✓
Auditory lexical decision	✗	✗	✓	✓
Spoken word comprehension	✗	✗	✗	✗
Written word comprehension	✓	✓	✓	✗

performance on homophone judgements and poor oral reading of the corresponding words suggests that the reading difficulty lies in the output processes of phonological assembly or articulatory programming. Conversely, if performance in both is impaired, it shows that the reading process is impaired at some earlier level, common to both reading aloud and homophone judgements.

Comparison of disparate tasks that share a common processing level

This point is best illustrated by example. A first example is seen in the instance of phonological assembly where, in the model of Figure 1.1, this is a process shared by picture naming, word and nonword repetition, and word and nonword reading. Where there are similar patterns of impairment across all these tasks (e.g. worse performance with words of greater phoneme length), similar errors (phonological errors identified primarily by phoneme omissions and substitutions) and similar levels of accuracy, there is strong evidence that the person's deficit is located in the processes of phonological assembly.

A second example is seen in the process of sub-lexical orthographic-to-phonological conversion being required for nonword reading. This process is also needed for nonword homophone judgements (e.g. deciding that PHAIP and FAPE are homophones) and for phonological lexical decision (deciding that KRAIT would sound like a real word when pronounced, but BRAIT would not). Similar deficits in all three tasks suggest a deficit in their common process of sub-lexical orthographic-to-phonological conversion.

A third example is apparent where, again in the model of Figure 1.1, semantic processing is required for a number of processes, including spoken and written word comprehension, and spoken and written picture naming. A common deficit in all of these tasks, with similar characteristics, suggests impairment at a semantic level (Hillis, Rapp, Romani, & Caramazza, 1990; Howard & Orchard-Lisle, 1984). It should be remembered, however, that when making a comparison between input and output tasks (comprehension and naming, in this instance), performance in the comprehension tasks may be less affected because the opportunity to make errors is limited by the distractors used.

Notes

1 Familiarity in the MRC Psycholinguistic Database (Coltheart, 1981) is derived from a subjective rating of the frequency of use of a word. In the Snodgrass and Vanderwart (1980) norms, it is a rating of the concept familiarity. These are not the same.

2 While we think converging evidence across these domains is critical for identifying intact and impaired processes, there are some who do not accept this. For example, Dell and his colleagues (Dell *et al.*, 1997; Foygel & Dell, 2000; Schwartz *et al.*, 1994) offer a model that aims to account for the pattern of errors in picture naming, but does not specify anything about the effects of psycholinguistic variables or performance in tasks other than picture naming. Their model has nothing to say about such effects.

Part 2
Deficits and assessment

3 Introduction to assessment

The following five chapters explore the model across five key domains, those of spoken word comprehension, spoken word production, reading, writing, and object and picture recognition. Each chapter focuses on a single domain, setting out the model as it relates to that aspect of the language-processing system and the deficits that may arise from disruption within that domain. Assessment is then addressed for each area, identifying:

- factors to exclude in assessment;
- general issues related to word types and effects to observe;
- indicators of impairment for each module or process within the domain;
- key areas of assessment;
- available assessment methods and tools, setting out the response types involved;
- additional assessment options;
- interpretation of the findings; and
- examples of case studies from the literature that exemplify the deficit patterns.

While each of these areas provides information for the clinician to apply throughout the assessment, the clinician needs to be strategic in his or her approach to this process.

Hypothesis testing and selectivity of tests

A hypothesis-testing approach should be taken in the assessment process, resulting in a rationalised selection of assessments. The aim of the hypothesis-testing approach is to determine the underlying cause or causes of the disruption in communication abilities – that is, which components of the model are impaired, and how these relative impairments influence each other. The clinician must be selective in deciding which assessments to use to distinguish between performance (or relative performance) on tasks contributed to by the different processing components. A clinician would not, then, attempt to assess *all* components of the model with the view to obtaining a fully comprehensive picture of performance, but would aim to identify the most defining assessments for a particular client

Drawing on observations of communication

When setting up initial hypotheses, the clinician should take into account individual information obtained on the client from initial conversational contact, such as apparent difficulties in understanding questions or clear lexical retrieval difficulties, as well as self or carer report. Consideration should also be given to observing sensory deficits, such as with vision or hearing, as these may influence the person's performance in assessment.

Refining the level of assessment

Whether the focus is on input or output processing, the whole route should be looked at initially before assessing specific processing components and refining the level of breakdown. Spoken word comprehension should be assessed, in the first instance, by tapping comprehension of a word (using a spoken word–picture matching task, for example). If this is intact, then the processes of identifying speech sounds (requiring auditory phonological analysis) and word recognition (drawing on the phonological input lexicon) can be considered to be intact. If the client has difficulty, then the component processes should be tested to establish the reasons underpinning the breakdown. That is, is auditory phonological analysis impaired? Is the phonological input lexicon impaired? Or, is it due to impairment at the semantic level?

Similarly, spoken word production should be assessed initially on a naming task that can assess the whole output route. Here, the client is required to draw on semantic representations, lexical representations, processes involved in phonological planning and assembly, as well as articulatory programming. Again, if naming is successful, assumptions can be made as to the intact nature of the component processes. If difficulties arise, the component processes can be selectively targeted for further assessment. In a naming task, the analysis of error types and the critical variables affecting performance would help to narrow down the hypotheses.

Tasks that require a more fine-tuned level of functioning may be selected first when assessing a particular processing component. For example, discrimination of minimally contrasted pairs of words may be used initially to assess a person's auditory phonological analysis skills, rather than words that have maximal contrasts. If performance is poor, it would be reasonable to then progress to maximally contrasted words to identify the level at which performance breaks down. If, however, performance was good, then it can be assumed that performance on the easier task would also be good.

Similarly, when assessing the integrity of the semantic system from auditory input, a task requiring the manipulation of heard synonyms would be more taxing than selecting from a choice of pictures in response to a heard word. Success at the former would imply success at the latter, so long as the client did not have additional difficulties related to pictorial material. Beginning with a task such as synonym judgement, however, would need to be balanced with predicted success. Where a client has semantic impairment, a word–picture matching task may expose him or her to less failure initially (while also providing an important baseline of performance); a synonym judgement task may be too high a level at which to commence assessment.

Number of test items

A further factor to consider in selecting and administering assessments is the number of items used to measure performance. A smaller number of test items may be used as the assessment process refines to establish a diagnosis; the assessor must, however, recognise that the ability of a test to detect an effect of a variable is a function of the number of items in a test (more precisely, the size of an effect that is likely to be detected depends on the square root of the number of items). Where it is important to establish whether or not a variable has an effect, a sufficiently large number of items should be used. Once component processes are identified as being impaired, however, assessment should be carried out using a sufficiently large number of items that will enable any change (or lack of it) from pre- to post-therapy to be detected. A distinction may therefore be drawn by the clinician in assessment to reach a diagnosis and assessment to monitor change following treatment.

4 Auditory comprehension of spoken words

Model of auditory comprehension of spoken words

Figure 4.1 shows the processes involved in the auditory comprehension of words. There are three stages involved in listening for meaning: auditory phonological analysis, the phonological input lexicon and the semantic system.

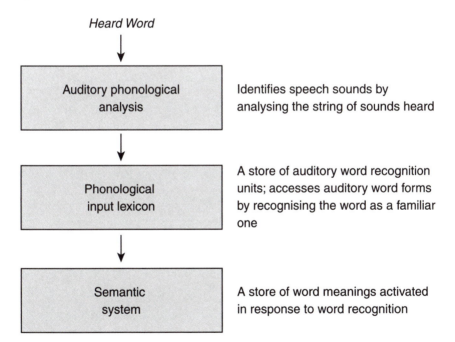

Phonological input-to-output conversion is also relevant here. This links auditory phonological analysis to phonological assembly. As this route bypasses the lexicons, it allows repetition of nonwords while also contributing to real word repetition.

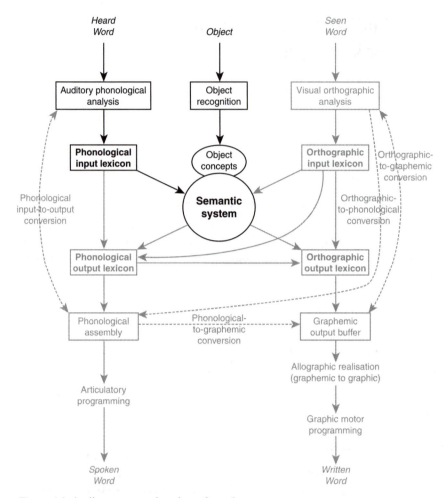

Figure 4.1 Auditory comprehension of words.

Deficits of auditory comprehension of spoken words

Auditory phonological
analysis

A deficit in auditory phonological analysis has been referred to as 'word sound deafness' (Franklin, 1989). Impairment at this level will have a profound effect on auditory comprehension, as it affects all stages of auditory verbal comprehension. It will not, however, affect the ability to discriminate between non-verbal sounds (e.g. bells) or the ability to match characteristic sounds to pictures.

As access is subsequently impaired to the phonological input lexicon, the ability to repeat real words is reduced (repetition of real words uses this route). Semantic information may, however, assist the repetition of real words by providing semantic support. As the direct route from phonological analysis to phonological assembly cannot be used, repetition of nonwords will also be impaired. Repetition of both real and nonwords may be assisted by lip-reading.

Shorter words may be harder to understand than longer words because they have more phonological neighbours with which they can be confused (Luce & Large, 2001; Luce, Pisoni, & Goldinger, 1990). 'Phonological neighbours' are other real words differing in a single phoneme. Single-syllable words usually have several, and often many, neighbours. For example, *cat* has neighbours that include *hat, rat, sat, cap, cad, can, cot, cut, kit*, and so on. Three-syllable words have many fewer neighbours: *crocodile* has none and *elephant* just two – *element* and *elegant*.

Semantics may still be accessed via reading. Comprehension may be aided by: (a) slowed speech; (b) lip-reading (which provides a visual source of phonetic information); and (c) context.

> **Phonological
> input lexicon**

A deficit in the phonological input lexicon, or access to it, has been referred to as 'word form deafness' (Franklin, 1989). As access to the lexicon (or auditory word forms) is impaired, a string of phonemes will not be recognised as a real word. Real words will be repeated as if they were nonwords. Words and nonwords can still be repeated via the direct route from phonological analysis to phonological assembly.

Frequency effects may be present – that is, high-frequency words are easier to comprehend than low-frequency words. Lexical deficits are possible, however, without frequency effects in lexical decision or auditory word comprehension (Howard & Franklin, 1988), and frequency effects do not only result from impairments at the lexical level (frequency effects have also been attributed to semantic deficits, e.g. Garrard & Hodges, 1999).

Semantics may still be accessed via reading. Reading comprehension is not affected by a deficit of the phonological input lexicon.

There is a heavy reliance on context to aid comprehension. Word recognition (in both lexical decision and naming to definition) may be better for longer words, which have fewer neighbours, than short words (e.g. Howard & Franklin, 1988).

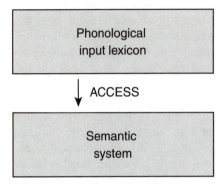

A deficit in accessing the semantic system from the phonological input lexicon has been referred to as 'word meaning deafness' (Franklin, 1989). As access to semantics is damaged, auditory comprehension is poor. Comprehension may be better for longer words than shorter words, because access to semantics is supported by more distinctive representations at a lexical level (Franklin *et al.*, 1996).

A string of phonemes is recognised as a word but not understood – that is, performance on lexical decision is good. Words and nonwords can still be repeated.

Semantics may still be accessed via reading. Again, reading comprehension is not implicated by a deficit accessing semantics from the phonological input lexicon.

```
┌─────────────────────────────┐
│        Semantic             │
│        system               │
└─────────────────────────────┘
```

Comprehension of both the auditory and written input modalities is impaired. All output modalities are also impaired (i.e. spoken and written production). Semantics is usually 'degraded' (and partially impaired) rather than totally inaccessible or destroyed.

Imageability effects are typically present – that is, words that are highly imageable (e.g. cat, book) are easier to understand than words with low imageability (e.g. happiness, idea). Reverse imageability effects with better understanding of abstract, low-imageability words than concrete, high-imageability words can occur, though rarely so.

Some people with central semantic deficits can show category effects. The most common is more impaired comprehension of words referring to animate categories – animals, plants, fruits and vegetables – than artefacts (objects). The reverse pattern also occurs, although more rarely. In addition, a variety of more selective deficits has been reported, including: selective impairment for animals with other animate categories together with objects relatively well-preserved; relative preservation of names referring to geographical features; a particular difficulty with body part names, or with proper names. Such deficits appear to be relatively uncommon, but even when they occur they may not be noticed.

People with intact object concepts but with a lexical semantic impairment will perform poorly in tasks involving words, but may perform well in non-verbal semantic tasks – for example, three-picture Pyramids and Palm Trees (Howard & Patterson, 1992; see Nickels, 2001, for discussion).

Assessments of auditory comprehension of spoken words

Preclude:

Preclude deficits of auditory acuity and higher-level auditory analysis through:

- A hearing test
- Tests using environmental sounds

General notes on assessment

Mild auditory comprehension deficits are not always evident in conversation because of the extensive use of context. Observing interaction is not therefore sufficient to rule out an auditory comprehension deficit. When assessing auditory comprehension, tests that consider the complete process (e.g. spoken word–picture matching with a variety of distractors) are a useful starting point. If performance is impaired, investigate the pattern of errors and allow this to direct further assessment. Impairment to peripheral processes (auditory phonological analysis and the phonological input lexicon) will affect subsequent processing for meaning. If performance on spoken word–picture matching is retained but comprehension deficits are still suspected, then assessment on more difficult tasks with words of lower imageability and frequency would be recommended.

It is also important to note that reading comprehension and spoken and written naming can be intact in the presence of impaired auditory comprehension, so long as the semantic system is intact. A discrepancy between spoken and written comprehension would be a key clinical indicator of auditory comprehension difficulties before the level at which semantics becomes involved.

Word types

In assessing auditory comprehension of spoken words, four types of word contrasts are useful:

1   Words with contrasting phonology, for example minimal pairs (where one phoneme in two words differs on only one distinctive feature, e.g. bat/ pat) and maximal pairs (where one phoneme has a maximal number of contrastive features across two words, e.g. bat/sat).
2   Nonwords, matched in length and phonological complexity to real words.
3   Long and short words.
4   High- and low-imageability words.

Analysis of performance on these variables allows conclusions to be drawn about three effects:

(a) A lexicality effect in minimal pair discrimination. Where nonwords are discriminated less accurately than real words of equivalent difficulty, this may imply impairment to auditory phonological analysis. Real word minimal pair discrimination can be supported by information at the lexical or semantic level.
(b) A reverse length effect where there is more accurate comprehension of long words than short words. This can result from lexical impairment (Howard & Franklin, 1988) or problems in access to semantics (Franklin *et al.*, 1996).
(c) An imageability effect. Where there is more accurate comprehension of more highly imageable words than low-imageability words, this suggests impairment to the semantic system or in access to it.

Lip-reading can improve access to phonetic information and therefore may support the client's comprehension.

> Auditory phonological
> analysis

Indicators of impairment

•   Reduced discrimination between phonemes.

General notes on assessment

The following tasks can be performed with and without lip-reading to determine whether visual information can supplement auditory information.

Key assessment areas and available methods

Area of assessment	Examples of available assessment tools	Response type
Auditory discrimination of nonword minimal pairs	PALPA 1[a]: Same/different discrimination using nonword minimal pairs	Same/different
	ADA Comprehension Battery P1 and P2[b]: Nonword minimal pairs	Same/different
Auditory discrimination of real word minimal pairs	PALPA 2: Same/different discrimination using word minimal pairs	Same/different
	PALPA 3: Minimal pair discrimination requiring written word selection	Written word selection
	PALPA 4: Minimal pair discrimination requiring picture selection	Picture selection
	ADA Comprehension Battery P3: Real word minimal pairs	Same/different
Auditory discrimination of real word maximal pairs	Maximal pairs[c]	Same/different
[a] Psycholinguistic Assessment of Language Processing in Aphasia (Kay *et al.*, 1992). [b] ADA Comprehension Battery (Franklin *et al.*, 1992). [c] Maximal Pairs (Morris, Franklin, Ellis, Turner, & Bailey, 1996).		

Additional assessment options

Area of assessment	Examples of available assessment tools	Response type
Repetition of nonwords	PALPA 8: Repetition: nonwords	Repetition
	ADA Comprehension Battery R: nonword repetition	Repetition
Repetition of words	PALPA 7: Repetition: syllable length	Repetition
	PALPA 9: Repetition: imageability × frequency	Repetition
	ADA Comprehension Battery L2: Repetition of words (length, imageability and frequency)	Repetition

Interpretation

✔ Good discrimination of words and nonwords implies that auditory phonological analysis is intact.

✗ Reduced discrimination of words and nonwords implies that auditory phonological analysis may be impaired.

✗ Reduced discrimination of nonwords relative to words (lexicality effect) implies a deficit in auditory phonological analysis with relatively intact lexical and semantic processing.

✗ Repetition of nonwords and words would also be impaired if auditory phonological analysis is implicated. Performance is characterised by phonologically related errors.

✗ Reduced performance in discriminating between minimal pairs relative to maximal pairs may provide an indication of severity.

✗ Better performance on minimal pair discrimination using written response choices (PALPA 3) than when using auditory stimuli (PALPA 1 and 2) may indicate short-term memory impairment.

Box 4.1 A case of impairment to auditory phonological analysis (word sound deafness): Client ES (Franklin, 1989)

ES was a 74-year-old male who was 3 years post-onset at the time of testing. He was an estate agent before his retirement. His aphasia resulted from a CVA. ES had fluent speech and impaired auditory comprehension. On testing, he presented with a severe phoneme discrimination deficit. His performance was characterised by severely impaired minimal pair discrimination, auditory lexical decision and auditory synonym matching. Real word repetition was as poor as nonword repetition. In terms of the discrimination of CVC words, his errors followed no pattern in terms of site or type of features contrasted. Franklin suggests that this may reflect the severity of the impairment or may be an artefact of the high number of false–positive responses on the test. ES performed significantly better on written lexical decision and written synonym matching tests than on auditory tasks.

> Phonological
> input lexicon

Indicators of impairment

• Reduced ability to recognise a word as a real word and to reject a nonword.

• Possible frequency effects (high-frequency words easier than low-frequency words).

General notes on assessment

Impaired auditory phonological analysis will impair performance on assessments of the phonological input lexicon. Consideration of performance on, for example, minimal pair tasks discussed above will be essential in determining the contribution of any impairment in auditory phonological analysis to the integrity of the phonological input lexicon.

Key assessment areas and available methods

Area of assessment	Examples of available assessment tools	Response type
Auditory lexical decision	PALPA 5: Auditory lexical decision: Imageability and frequency	Yes/no response
	ADA Comprehension Battery L1: Lexical decision	Yes/no response

Additional assessment options

Area of assessment	Examples of available assessment tools	Response type
Repetition of real words if unable to repeat nonwords	PALPA 9: Imageability and frequency repetition	Repetition
	ADA Comprehension Battery L2: Word repetition test	Repetition
Identification of spoken words using phonological distractors (written and picture response modalities)	PALPA 3: Minimal pair discrimination requiring written word selection	Written word selection
	PALPA 4: Minimal pair discrimination requiring picture selection	Picture selection
	ADA Comprehension Battery S2: Spoken word picture matching (phonological distractors)	Picture selection
Picture verification of words (phonological real word and nonword distractors)	Picture–word decision test (Howard & Franklin, 1988)	Yes/no response

Interpretation

✔ Good performance on lexical decision tasks implies that the phonological input lexicon is intact.

✗ Reduced performance on lexical decision tasks implies impairment of the phonological input lexicon.

✗ Reduced performance on picture-matching tasks and picture-verification tasks with the selection of phonological distractors may imply impairment of the phonological input lexicon.

✗ Reduced performance with low-frequency words relative to high-frequency words (frequency effect) may suggest impairment of the phonological input lexicon, but is not a necessary feature of impairment at this level.

✗ Reduced performance with low-imageability words relative to high-imageability words (imageability effect) may imply that the person is drawing on an impaired semantic system.

Box 4.2 A case of impairment to the phonological input lexicon (word form deafness): Client MK (Franklin, 1989; Howard and Franklin, 1988)

MK was a 69-year-old man who was 2 years post-onset at the time of testing. He was a consultant for an oil company. His aphasia resulted from a CVA. He had fluent speech and impaired auditory comprehension. MK was able to discriminate phonemes as well as normal controls, indicating no impairment at the level of auditory phonological analysis. He showed a mild deficit in auditory lexical decision and a moderate impairment in auditory synonym matching. His performance in written synonym matching was significantly better than his performance on the auditory version. MK made errors on a word–picture matching task with phonological distractors. He defined words he heard with definitions appropriate to phonologically related words; for example, when given the word 'pardon', he gave a definition appropriate to 'garden'. MK was unable to repeat nonwords due to an impairment in phono-logical input-to-output conversion. He was better, although still impaired at, repeating real words with imageability predicting performance; this would suggest the use of a semantically mediated route for repetition (Franklin, 1989).

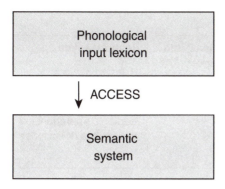

Indicators of impairment

- Ability to recognise a word as a real word but not know its meaning.
- Good access to semantics via the written modality but impaired via the auditory modality.

General notes on assessment

Impairment to auditory phonological analysis or the phonological input lexicon will also affect access to semantics. Consideration of performance on tasks assessing these components will be essential in determining any contribution that impairment in these may play in accessing semantics from the phonological input lexicon.

Key assessment areas and available methods

Area of assessment	Examples of available assessment tools	Response type
Assess semantic system	See next section	
Compare written and auditory comprehension of words	PALPA 47 and 48: Spoken and written word–picture matching (with semantic distractors)	Picture selection
	ADA Comprehension Battery S2: Spoken and written word–picture matching (with semantic distractors)	Picture selection

Additional assessment options

Area of assessment	Examples of available assessment tools	Response type
Repetition followed by spoken definition of words, with comparison to written semantic access	Informal (as described in Franklin *et al.*, 1996)	Repetition and spoken definitions versus reading comprehension and spoken definitions

Interpretation

✔ Comparable auditory performance and written performance implies input from the phonological input lexicon to semantics is intact.

✗ Reduced auditory performance relative to written performance implies input from the phonological input lexicon to semantics is impaired.

Box 4.3 A case of impairment of input to semantics from the phonological input lexicon (word meaning deafness): Client DRB (Franklin, 1989; Franklin *et al.*, 1994)

DRB was a 55-year-old man who was 2 years post-onset at the time of testing. He was a travel agent before his CVA. He had fluent speech and impaired auditory comprehension. On formal testing, he showed no impairment on minimal pair discrimination and auditory lexical decision tasks. His performance on written lexical decision was also equivalent to that of normal individuals. He showed a severe impairment on auditory synonym matching but significantly better performance on written synonym matching. He showed a significant imageability effect on the spoken version of the task but was able to access semantic information about low-imageability words from the visual word form. DRB was unable to repeat nonwords due to an impairment in phonological input-to-output conversion but was able to repeat some real words. His real word repetition was characterised by an imageability effect, suggesting the use of a semantically mediated route.

Semantic system	(comprehension)

Indicators of impairment

- If a semantic impairment, the person will have:
  - (a) impaired comprehension for both the auditory and written input modalities and
  - (b) semantic errors in both spoken and written output (but semantic errors may also indicate impairment at other levels).
- Imageability effects in all tasks requiring semantic processing.

General notes on assessment

Need to assess auditory *and* written comprehension, and spoken *and* written production, but consider effects of peripheral impairments in each modality.

Key assessment areas and available methods

Area of assessment	Examples of available assessment tools	Response type
Comprehension of spoken words – high imageability	PALPA 47: Spoken word–picture matching	Picture selection
	ADA Comprehension Battery S2: Word–picture matching	Picture selection
Comprehension of written words – high imageability	PALPA 48: Written word–picture matching	Picture selection
	ADA Comprehension Battery S2Wr: Word–picture matching	Picture selection
Comprehension of spoken words – high and low imageability	PALPA 49: Auditory synonym judgements	Same/different
	ADA Comprehension Battery S1: Synonym matching	Same/different
Comprehension of written words – high and low imageability	PALPA 50: Written synonym judgements	Same/different
	ADA Comprehension Battery S1Wr: Synonym matching – written version	Same/different

Comparison across modalities	PALPA 53: Picture naming / written naming / repetition / oral reading / written spelling	Spoken and written naming, repetition, oral reading, writing
Semantic association/ real-world knowledge	Pyramids and Palm Trees (picture and written versions) (Howard & Patterson, 1992)	Picture selection, written word selection
	PALPA 51: Word semantic association	Written word selection
Access to semantics where avoidance of pictures is necessary; comparison with single modality (spoken and written word comprehension)	PALPA 52: Spoken word- written word matching	Written word selection

Additional assessment options

Assessments that control for imageability investigate the use of the route through the semantic system. Imageability effects in tasks imply the use of semantic mediation in those tasks.

Area of assessment	Examples of available assessment tools	Response type
Imageability effect in other modalities	PALPA 9: Repetition: imageability × frequency	Repetition
	PALPA 25: Visual lexical decision: imageability × frequency	Written word selection
	PALPA 31: Oral reading: imageability × frequency	Oral reading
Convergent and divergent semantic tasks, e.g. Providing definitions and naming to definition Providing superordinate categorical information and naming from this Generative category naming (i.e. category fluency) Sorting/ categorisation tasks	See Chapey (1981)	Varied
Semantic associations	Semantic links (Bigland & Speake, 1992)	Picture selection

Interpretation

✔ Retained performance on spoken and written picture-matching and synonym judgement tasks implies an intact semantic system.

✗ Semantic errors on spoken and written picture-matching tasks alongside impaired word retrieval imply a semantic impairment.

✗ The choice of distant semantic errors on picture-matching tasks implies a more severe semantic deficit.

✗ Visually similar errors may imply a visual perceptual element.

✗ An even spread of errors may imply either (a) lack of attention or (b) severe semantic impairment.

✗ Errors on low-imageability words in spoken and written tasks but with retained performance on high-imageability words may imply a semantic impairment for low-imageability items.

Box 4.4 A case of impairment to the semantic system: Client KE (Hillis *et al.*, 1990)

KE was a 52-year-old, right-handed man. He was working as a manager in a large corporation before his CVA. A CT scan showed an infarct in the left fronto-parietal region. He was 6 months post-onset at the time of testing. KE's spontaneous speech consisted of over-learned phrases, single nouns and frequent semantic errors. In auditory comprehension, he made errors at both single word and sentence level. KE had a very limited ability to read aloud, producing mainly no responses in the reading of words and nonwords. His errors in word reading were semantically related errors (e.g. HUNGRY → 'starve') and some morphologically related errors (e.g. BUY → 'bought'). There was no evidence that orthographic-to-phonological conversion was contributing to his reading. He was at chance at matching auditory to written words. KE was able to spell some concrete nouns. His errors in writing to dictation consisted of semantic errors and mixed errors (e.g. SCREW-DRIVER → 'screwswitch'). He was unable to write nonwords and his writing showed no evidence of the use of non-lexical spelling procedures. KE was tested on the same items across oral and written picture naming, oral reading, writing to dictation and auditory and written word–picture matching. Detailed analysis of his performance showed very similar error rates and types of errors, regardless of the modality of stimulus or response. In each task, he produced a high percentage of semantic errors. There was a high degree of item consistency across modalities and in test–retest scores. There were significant differences in semantic error rates across different semantic categories that were consistent across modalities and were not predicted by frequency. The authors interpret KE's performance as evidence of selective damage to a unitary, modality-independent semantic system.

5 Spoken word production

Model of spoken word production

Figure 5.1 shows the processes involved in spoken word production during picture/object naming. There are four main stages involved in retrieving words from the semantic system (as in picture naming): the semantic system, the phonological output lexicon, phonological assembly and articulatory programming.

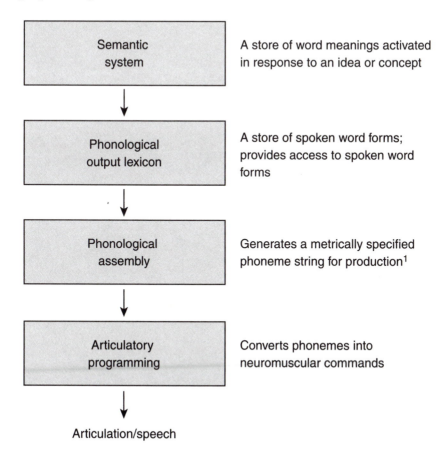

Semantic system — A store of word meanings activated in response to an idea or concept

Phonological output lexicon — A store of spoken word forms; provides access to spoken word forms

Phonological assembly — Generates a metrically specified phoneme string for production[1]

Articulatory programming — Converts phonemes into neuromuscular commands

Articulation/speech

Additional processes involved during repetition and reading words aloud are shown in Figure 5.2.

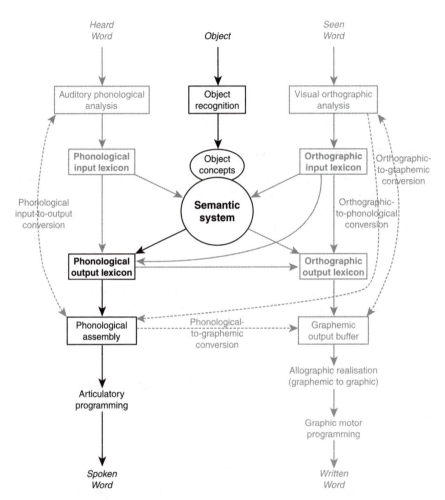

Figure 5.1 Spoken naming.

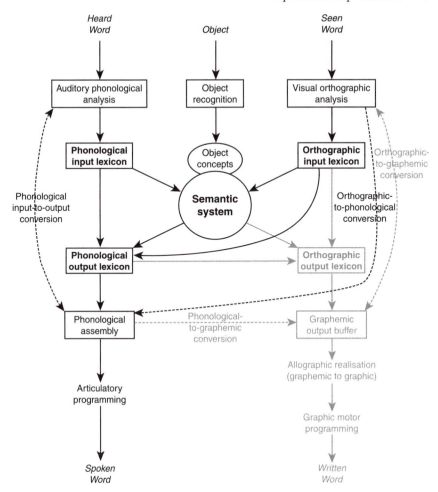

Figure 5.2 Spoken naming with reading and repetition.

Deficits of spoken word production

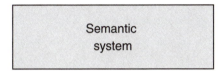

The production of both spoken and written words is impaired, together with impaired comprehension of both the auditory and written input modalities. Semantics is usually degraded rather than totally inaccessible or destroyed. Imageability effects are typically present – that is, words that are highly imageable (e.g. cat, book) are easier to produce than words with low image-ability (e.g. happiness, idea). Reverse imageability effects – better production of abstract, low-imageability words than concrete, high-imageability words – can occur, although rarely.

The production of spoken words is characterised by anomia with both failures and delays in word retrieval. Semantic errors are produced in both spoken and written naming. When cued by a phonemic cue for a semantic associate (phonemic miscueing), clients with naming disorders arising from a semantic impairment may produce a semantic associate (Howard & Orchard-Lisle, 1984). For example, when given a picture of a lion and the phoneme /t/ they produce 'tiger'.

| Phonological output lexicon | (and access to the lexicon from the semantic system) |

An impairment at this level results in impaired word retrieval in spoken naming but written word retrieval may be intact. Spoken and written comprehension are also intact. Spoken production is characterised by the following features:

1   anomia (delays and failures in word retrieval);
2   'tip of the tongue' feeling;
3   circumlocutions;
4   semantic errors (Caramazza & Hillis, 1989);
5   phonological errors or the production of word fragments;
6   a frequency effect may be present;[2]
7   if access to semantics is involved, an imageability effect may be present.

If the problem is degradation of the representations within the lexicon itself, there may be a consistent difficulty in retrieving the same items (Howard, 1995). Retrieval may be more inconsistent if the problem is in accessing the lexicon from the semantic system. In this case, retrieval of the word in repetition and/or reading aloud may be less impaired than in naming (Kay & Ellis, 1987).

| Phonological assembly |

An impairment in phonological assembly impacts all spoken production tasks (naming, reading aloud and repetition). Comprehension and written word retrieval are intact.

Spoken production is characterised by the production of phonological errors and neologisms. Clients may produce *conduite d'approche* (repeated attempts at the target word that often result in a closer approximation to the target word).

Length effects may be present, with shorter words being easier to produce than longer words.

```
Articulatory
programming
```

A deficit in articulatory programming results in an impairment to all spoken production tasks with the production of dyspraxic (phonetic) errors. Written word retrieval is intact.

```
Articulation/speech
```

Articulation difficulties result in dysarthria.

Assessments of spoken word production

Preclude:

Preclude deficits of motor speech and visual object recognition through:

- Tests for motor speech disorders to assess dysarthria and dyspraxia
- Tests for object recognition (see Chapter 8)

General notes on assessment

As word-retrieval deficits are usually evident in spontaneous speech, observation of spontaneous output will provide an important first opportunity to observe presenting patterns. When assessing spoken word production, picture-naming assessments are a useful starting point. Tests that control for a variety of contrasts (e.g. imageability and frequency) can provide some information about the possible level of any impairment. Investigations of the error types and the client's response to semantic and phonemic cues provide additional support for the diagnosis. Finally, comprehension tests and other tests of spoken word production (e.g. reading aloud and repetition) should be carried out. If performance on picture naming is not impaired but word retrieval difficulties are evident in spontaneous speech, consider carrying out tests of word retrieval that do not use picture stimuli (e.g. naming to definition, category fluency).

The specific assessment of verbs is not addressed here because the focus of this book is on word retrieval rather than sentence processing. While comparison of verb retrieval with other categories of words is often central to informing the nature of the deficit, interpretation of such behaviours is outside the scope of the theoretical model presented here.

Word types

In assessing spoken production, three types of word contrasts are useful:

1   High- and low-imageability words.
2   High- and low-frequency words.
3   Words that vary in number of phonemes/syllables.

Analysis of performance on these three variables allows conclusions to be drawn about three effects:

(a) An imageability effect. Where more highly imageable words are accessed and produced more easily than low-imageability words, this may imply impairment to the semantic system or output from the semantic system to the phonological output lexicon.
(b) A frequency effect. Where more frequent words are accessed and produced more easily than less frequent words, this may imply impairment at the level of the phonological output lexicon. Frequency effects do not only, however, result from impairments at the lexical level.[2]
(c) A length effect. Where shorter words are accessed and produced more easily than longer words, this may imply impairment in the processes of phonological assembly or articulation.

Error types

The second source of available evidence is the nature of the errors made in spoken production. These can be classified, for example, into the following categories:

1   A delay or failure to retrieve a word.
2   Semantic errors: responses that are semantically related to the target, e.g. NAIL → 'screw'.
3   Phonological errors: errors that are similar to the target in phonological form. A common criterion for phonological similarity is that at least 50% of the phonemes in the stimulus occur in the error response in approximately the same order, e.g. NAIL → /nɔɪk/. They can be words or nonwords.

4 Neologisms: nonword responses that do not share sufficient phonemes to be classified as phonological errors.

5 Semantically related circumlocutions are responses that indicate access to some intact semantic information in the absence of a phonological representation, e.g. NAIL → 'you bang it into wood'.

Key assessments of word retrieval

Naming assessment	Factors manipulated
PALPA 53: Picture naming × oral reading, repetition and written spelling	Regular and irregular words matched for word frequency, familiarity, concreteness, age of acquisition, letter length and number of syllables
PALPA 54: Picture naming × word frequency	Word frequency varied and words matched for number of syllables, letters and name agreement
Boston Naming Test (Kaplan, Goodglass, & Weintraub, 2001)	Difficulty graded
Graded Naming Test (McKenna & Warrington, 1983)	Difficulty graded
Snodgrass Pictures (Snodgrass & Vanderwart, 1980)	Information provided on name agreement, familiarity and visual complexity
Nickels' Naming Test (described in Nickels & Howard, 1994)	Word frequency and length varied, high- and low-frequency words matched for length. One-, two- and three-syllable words matched for frequency

Additional assessments of word retrieval

FAS verbal fluency (Spreen & Benton, 1977)
Naming to definition (as described by Chapey, 1981)
Note: The above assessments provide information on assessing word retrieval without picture stimuli.

```
┌─────────────────────────────────┐
│           Semantic              │          (production)
│           system                │
└─────────────────────────────────┘
```

Indicators of impairment

- If a semantic impairment, the person will have:
  - (a) impaired comprehension for both the auditory and written input modalities; and
  - (b) semantic errors in both spoken and written output (but semantic errors may also indicate impairment at other levels).
- Imageability effects in all tasks requiring semantic processing.

General notes on assessment

Need to assess spoken and written production and auditory and written comprehension but consider effects of peripheral impairments in each modality. Assess the effects of semantic cueing, phonemic cueing and phonemic miscueing.

Key assessment areas and available methods

Area of assessment	Examples of available assessment tools	Response type
Comparison across modalities	PALPA 53: Picture naming × oral reading, repetition and written spelling (see assessment of input modalities in Chapters 4 and 6)	Spoken and written naming
Error analysis of naming	As above	Picture naming

Interpretation (for the semantic system)

✔ Retained word retrieval alongside intact auditory and written comprehension implies an intact semantic system.

✗ An impairment of the semantic system is implied when a deficit is present in spoken naming in the presence of intact repetition and reading and impaired comprehension. Picture naming *requires* the semantic system, whereas repetition and oral reading do not necessarily involve semantic mediation.

✗ An impairment of the semantic system is implied when similar errors and severity of errors are present in written and spoken naming.
✗ Naming is characterised by semantic errors together with delays and failures in word retrieval, and clients may produce semantic errors in response to phonemic miscues.

See Box 4.4 in Chapter 4 describing client KE.

| Phonological output lexicon | (and access to the lexicon from the semantic system) |

Indicators of impairment

- Impaired word retrieval characterised by:

  (a) anomia with delays and failures in word retrieval;
  (b) circumlocutions;
  (c) semantic errors;
  (d) phonological errors and/or word fragments.

- Frequency effects (Caramazza & Hillis, 1989).
- Imageability effects may be present if access to semantics is involved.

General notes on assessment

Assess and analyse responses to phonemic cueing.

Key assessment areas and available methods

Area of assessment	Examples of available assessment tools	Response type
Error analysis of naming	PALPA 53: Picture naming	Picture naming
Frequency analysis of naming	PALPA 54: Picture naming × word frequency	Picture naming

Additional assessment options

Area of assessment	Examples of available assessment tools	Response type
Repetition and reading aloud of words	PALPA: PALPA 53: Picture naming × oral reading, repetition and written spelling	Repetition and reading aloud
Response to phonemic cueing	Informal	Spoken naming

Interpretation

✔ Retained picture naming, oral reading and repetition of words implies an intact phonological output lexicon.

✗ Impaired access to the phonological output lexicon or an impaired phonological output lexicon is suggested by delays and failures in word retrieval (possibly characterised by a frequency effect), circumlocutions, semantic and phonological errors, and word fragments.

✗ Impaired picture naming with better preserved repetition and reading aloud may suggest impaired access to the phonological output lexicon, rather than impairment to the word forms within the lexicon. Note, however, that repetition and reading (at least for regular words) can be done sub-lexically. Where nonword repetition or reading are good, better performance in repetition or reading than naming is probably attributable to the use of sub-lexical processes, rather than better access to lexical representations.

✗ Correct word retrieval following phonemic cueing suggests that the phonological output lexicon is intact and that access is impaired.

Box 5.1 A case of impairment to the phonological output lexicon (lexical anomia): Client EE (Howard, 1995)

EE was a 46-year-old postman who suffered a head injury falling from a ladder while painting his house. He was 4–5 years post-onset at the time of testing. His speech was fluent and grammatical, although there was evidence of word-finding difficulties. In reading aloud and writing he made errors with irregular words (surface dyslexia and dysgraphia). He scored within the normal range on the three picture and three spoken word versions of Pyramids and Palm Trees (Howard & Patterson, 1992) indicating intact recognition of pictures and intact access to semantic information. On standard assessments of naming, he presented with a severe anomia. His ability to name the pictures of the Hundred Picture Naming Test (Howard &

Franklin, 1988) was tested on three occasions to examine the consistency of retrieval, the variables affecting naming performance and the effect of different cues. EE showed a high degree of consistency in the items named correctly. (Not all clients with impairment to the phonological output lexicon show the same high degree of consistency.) His errors were mainly no responses or circumlocutions containing appropriate semantic information. He did not improve in naming with phonemic cues or extra time and semantic errors could not be elicited by phonemic miscues. His naming performance was affected by word familiarity but there was no effect of the semantic or phonological properties of words (e.g. imageability or number of phonemes). For the same one hundred items, EE showed accurate auditory lexical decision and auditory comprehension. Howard argues that EE has intact semantic information but has lost specific lexical items within the phonological output lexicon.

Phonological
assembly

Indicators during assessment

• Impaired naming, oral reading and repetition characterised by:

    (a) phonological errors/neologisms in all output tasks;
    (b) *conduite d'approche* resulting in sequences of phonological errors.

• Possible production of circumlocutions in naming.
• Length effects in all tasks requiring spoken output.

Key assessment areas and available methods

Area of assessment	Examples of available assessment tools	Response type
Error analysis of naming	PALPA 53: Picture naming	Picture naming
Effect of syllable length on repetition	PALPA 7: Repetition: syllable length	Repetition
Sub-lexical phonological input-to-output conversion	PALPA 8: Repetition: nonwords	Repetition
	ADA R: Repetition of words and nonwords	Repetition

Interpretation

✔ Retained picture naming or oral reading, or repetition of words and nonwords, implies intact phonological assembly.

✗ Impaired phonological assembly is suggested by target-oriented phonological errors in all output tasks.

✗ Reduced performance with repetition of longer words (and nonwords) relative to shorter words (and nonwords) (length effect) implies impairment of phonological assembly or subsequent processes.

✗ If repetition of nonwords is more difficult than repetition of words, this implies that the phonological assembly is more impaired than the lexicons, as the person cannot rely on lexical information to perform the task. This could also be accounted for by an impairment to sub-lexical phonological input-to-output conversion.

Box 5.2 A case of impairment to phonological assembly: Client MB (Franklin *et al.*, 2002)

MB was a retired 83-year-old lady. She had a left middle cerebral artery infarction. She was about 4 months post-onset at the time of testing. Her spontaneous speech consisted of the production of some automatic words and phrases. She produced many phonological errors and neologisms. Her auditory comprehension was functional in conversation and she had good single-word comprehension. Despite good auditory comprehension, she had difficulty on an auditory rhyme judgement, possibly indicating a specific segmentation problem. Her writing was limited and she produced many spelling errors. On formal testing of her spoken output, naming, reading aloud and repetition were all impaired, with naming being most difficult. In all tasks, she produced phonological errors consisting of both the omission and substitution of phonemes. These errors resulted in both real word and non-word errors. Some errors were repeated attempts at the target, resulting in responses that were either closer to the correct response or the correct response itself (*conduite d'approche*). There was an effect of length in all three tasks that was directly related to the number of phonemes in the word. There was no effect of frequency or imageability. MB had greater difficulty in nonword repetition and reading aloud than in the same tasks with real words. Her errors were again phonological, with a length effect for reading aloud. There was no effect of length on the repetition of nonwords, due to a floor effect. Franklin *et al.* suggest that MB has a post-lexical deficit affecting phonological assembly, specifically in phoneme encoding.

Notes

1 Some versions of this model also include a phonological output buffer that holds phoneme strings during the process of phonological assembly. It is also suggested that a phonological output buffer plays an important role in some short-term memory tasks. There is substantial evidence that the process of phonological assembly is distinct from an output buffer (see, for example, Howard & Nickels, in press; Vallar & Shallice, 1992). Impairments in short-term memory have no necessary impact on single-word phonological production (Shallice & Warrington, 1977a). Because the process of phonological assembly is clearly necessary for word production (Levelt *et al.*, 1999), and there is no clearly established need for a buffer, we have called this process 'phonological assembly'.
2 Frequency effects have been attributed to semantic deficits (Hodges, Patterson, Oxbury, & Funnell, 1992), mapping of semantics to the phonological output lexicon (Barry, Morrison, & Ellis, 1997; McCann *et al.*, 1988) and the phonological output lexicon (Howard, 1995).

6   Written comprehension and reading

Model of reading

Figure 6.1 shows the processes involved in the comprehension and reading aloud (oral reading) of written words. Three stages are involved in reading words for meaning (reading comprehension): visual orthographic analysis, the orthographic input lexicon and the semantic system.

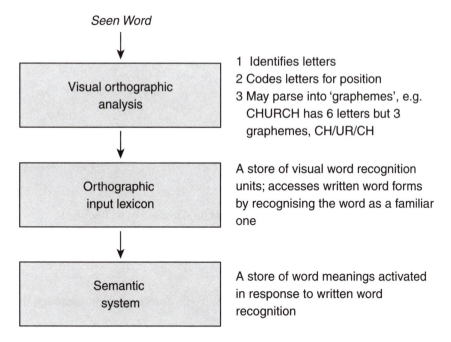

Seen Word

Visual orthographic analysis

1 Identifies letters
2 Codes letters for position
3 May parse into 'graphemes', e.g. CHURCH has 6 letters but 3 graphemes, CH/UR/CH

Orthographic input lexicon

A store of visual word recognition units; accesses written word forms by recognising the word as a familiar one

Semantic system

A store of word meanings activated in response to written word recognition

There are three routes that can be used to read words aloud. These are illustrated in Figure 6.1. The three routes for reading aloud share a varying number of components with the processes used in reading comprehension.

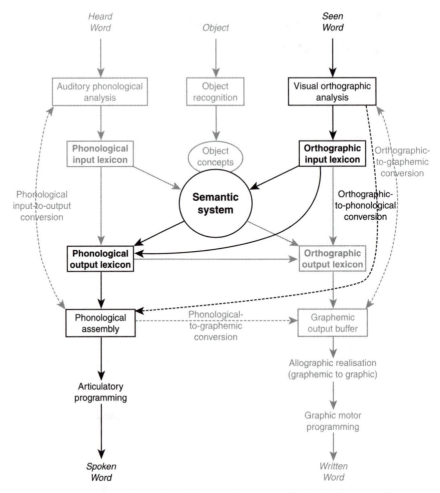

Figure 6.1 Comprehension and reading aloud (oral reading) of written words.

Semantic lexical route

This route involves reading words aloud via access to their meaning. It involves:

(a) recognition of a word in the orthographic input lexicon;
(b) access to the word's semantic representation; and
(c) retrieval of the spoken form from the phonological output lexicon.

This route can only process real, familiar words, and is not affected by spelling-to-sound regularity. It is required in the disambiguation of heterophonic homographs (words with the same spellings but different pronunciations) where the semantic context determines how the word sounds. For example:

> There was a tear in her eye.
> There was a tear in her dress.

Sub-lexical route (orthographic-to-phonological conversion)

Reading aloud via the sub-word level, orthographic-to-phonological correspondence is the 'sounding out route' or translation of visual analysis into an acoustic code that can be identified by the word recognition system. It involves:

(a) *Graphemic parsing* (within visual orthographic analysis). Dividing the letter string into units that correspond to phonemes, e.g. CH, TH, EE, A_E etc.
(b) *Grapheme-to-phoneme correspondences*. Some of these are simple correspondences between letters or graphemes (groups of letters) and sounds (e.g. B → /b/ or CH → /tʃ/), and some are context dependent (e.g. C → /s/ when followed by E or I, otherwise C → /k/).
(c) *Phonological assembly*. Blending a string of phonemes into a word.

This route allows the reading of nonwords that cannot be accessed within the lexicon. It also allows accurate reading of regular words. For irregular words, it will yield an incorrect pronunciation that will be a 'regularisation' (e.g. pronouncing PINT to rhyme with 'mint' or BEAR as 'beer').

Direct lexical route

This route involves reading aloud via a lexical but not semantic route. It involves:

(a) recognising the word in the orthographic input lexicon; and
(b) retrieving the phonology from the phonological output lexicon.

As only real, known words are represented in the lexicons, this routine can only process real words irrespective of their spelling-to-sound regularity. Words can be recognised and read aloud without semantic knowledge. For example:

> Given the written word HYENA → 'hyena ... hyena ... what in the heck is that?' (Schwartz, Saffran, & Marin, 1980, p. 261).

The routine probably works better with more familiar words, so a frequency effect may be found. As reading is not semantically mediated, variables such as word imageability or concreteness should not affect performance. There is evidence for this route from patients with dementia (Schwartz *et al.*, 1980).

Note that regular real words (e.g. MINT) will be read correctly by any of these three 'routes'. Irregular words (e.g. PINT) will be read correctly by either lexical route, but will be 'regularised' (to /pɪnt/) when read by the sub-lexical route. Nonwords that have no lexical representation can only be read using the sub-lexical route.

Deficits of reading

Deficits in reading comprehension and reading aloud depend on the location of the impairment and whether alternative routes can be utilised. Typically, routes are not wholly abolished but some routines may work less effectively than others. Reading impairments have traditionally been characterised in terms of peripheral or central dyslexias. A description of the characteristic features of the main types can be found in Table 6.1. Table 6.2 contrasts the features of the central dyslexias.

Visual orthographic
analysis

A deficit in visual orthographic analysis results in visual reading errors (as seen in neglect, attentional or visual dyslexia). Impairment to visual orthographic analysis may also result in letter by letter reading.

As visual orthographic analysis is shared in all aspects of reading, errors occur in reading comprehension and in the oral reading of words and nonwords. Real word reading is often but not necessarily better than nonword reading.

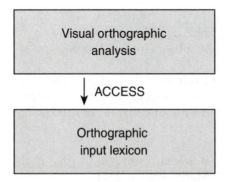

Visual orthographic
analysis

↓ ACCESS

Orthographic
input lexicon

An impairment in accessing the orthographic input lexicon will affect the recognition and comprehension of words. Impairment results in the visual error characteristics of the visual dyslexias or in letter by letter reading. If orthographic-to-phonological conversion is retained, a pattern of reading characteristic of surface dyslexia is seen. Words and nonwords are read via the sub-lexical route, resulting in accurate reading of nonwords and regular words and regularisation errors for irregular words.

Table 6.1 Characteristic features of different types of dyslexia

PERIPHERAL DYSLEXIAS

1 Neglect dyslexia (Ellis, Flude, & Young, 1987)

This peripheral dyslexia occurs as a consequence of difficulty with the visual specification of the word at the level of visual orthographic analysis. It is not a consequence of a general visual neglect.

Characteristic features:

- Spatially determined visual errors that occur consistently at either the right-hand or left-hand end of words. A neglect point can typically be discerned in reading errors. In a large proportion of the errors, all the letters will be correct on the preserved side of the neglect point, and incorrect on the impaired side of the neglect point. For example:

LOG → 'dog'   LOG → 'lot'

RIVER → 'liver'   BOOK → 'boot'

YELLOW → 'pillow'   BUCKET → 'buckle'

- Errors are typically very similar in length to the stimulus word.

2 Attentional dyslexia (Shallice & Warrington, 1977b)

This peripheral dyslexia occurs as a consequence of difficulty with the visual specification of the word at the level of visual orthographic analysis.

Characteristic feature:

- Errors involving interference/migration of letters from other words. For example:
  WIN FED → 'fin fed'

3 Visual dyslexia (Marshall & Newcombe, 1973)

This dyslexia occurs as a consequence of a difficulty identifying and recognising the visual form of the word either at the level of visual orthographic analysis or in subsequent access to the orthographic input lexicon.

Characteristic feature:

- Visual errors involving the misidentification of one word for a visually similar one (but without any strong tendency for errors to occur at one end of the word). For example:

LEND → 'land'

EASEL → 'aerial'

CALM → 'claim'

4 Letter-by-letter reading (Warrington & Shallice, 1980; Patterson & Kay, 1982)

In letter by letter reading, letters of a word cannot be identified simultaneously and in parallel, so some or all of the letters of the word will be named (and sometimes misnamed) before a response is produced. This is a consequence of impaired visual orthographic analysis. Written words are identified by a reverse operation of the intact spelling system for oral spelling (Warrington & Shallice, 1980) or by serial rather than parallel access to the input lexicon (Patterson & Kay, 1982). For example:

CHAIR → C H A I R . . . chair

TABLE → T A B . . . table

LAMP → L A N P . . . no . . . L A M . . . lamp

TOOL → F O O L . . . fool

Characteristic features:

- Very slow reading, with reading latencies increasing linearly with the word letter length.
- Occasional, more rapid responses without overt letter naming for shorter words.

Note that about 50% of people who read letter-by-letter also show the features of surface dyslexia.

CENTRAL DYSLEXIAS

1 Surface dyslexia (Marshall & Newcombe, 1973)

Surface dyslexia results from impairment to lexically mediated reading with orthographic-to-phonological conversion relatively well preserved. The lexically mediated route may be impaired at different levels: the orthographic input lexicon, access to or within the semantic system, or access to or retrieval from the phonological output lexicon.

Characteristic features:

- Regular words (e.g. MINT, FEAR) are read better than irregular words (e.g. PINT, BEAR).
- Relatively well-preserved nonword reading (although many patients are somewhat worse at reading nonwords than matched real words).

Errors in reading consist of:

- Phonologically plausible errors (mostly regularisations, e.g. YACHT → '/jætʃt/', SEW → 'sue').
- Visual errors, e.g. SUBTLE → 'sublet'.
- Errors resulting from misapplication of letter-to-sound rules, e.g. failure to apply the 'rule of E' correctly: RAGE → 'rag'.

2 Deep dyslexia (Marshall & Newcombe, 1973)

Deep dyslexia is a result of reading via an impaired semantically mediated lexical route. Orthographic-to-phonological conversion is also impaired.

Characteristic features:

- The defining symptom of deep dyslexia is the occurrence of semantic errors in single-word reading, e.g. APE → 'monkey'.
- Unable to read nonwords.
- High-imageability words are read better than low-imageability words (more impaired on abstract words).
- Content words are read better than function words (although this difference may not be found with lists matched for imageability).

Other errors that may be present include:

- Visual and/or semantic errors, e.g. CLING → 'clasp'.
- Visual errors, e.g. DOOR → 'doom'.
- Morphological errors, e.g. LOVELY → 'loving'.
- Occasional visual-then-semantic errors, e.g. SYMPATHY → 'orchestra'.
- Function word substitutions, e.g. HIM → 'was'.

3 Phonological dyslexia

Phonological dyslexia results from impaired orthographic-to-phonological conversion (the sub-lexical reading route) relative to lexical reading.

Characteristic features:

- Poor or occasionally non-existent nonword reading (and reading of unfamiliar words). Nonwords are often read as visually similar real words. For example:

  SOOF → 'soot'

  KLACK → 'slack'

- Preserved or relatively good real word reading unaffected by spelling-to-sound regularity.

If reading of words is impaired:

- High-imageability words are read better than low-imageability words (more impaired on abstract words).
- Content words may be read better than function words (although this difference may not be found with lists matched for imageability).
- Morphologically simple words are read better than morphologically complex words.

Errors in reading consist of:

- Visual errors.
- Visual and/or semantic errors.
- Morphological errors.

Note: Pure semantic errors do not occur in phonological dyslexia.

Orthographic
input lexicon

A deficit in the orthographic input lexicon results in an impairment to reading comprehension and to lexically mediated reading aloud. If

Table 6.2 Contrasting patterns of performance in different types of central dyslexia

Performance	Type of dyslexia		
	Deep dyslexia	Surface dyslexia	Phonological dyslexia
Nonword reading	✗	✓	✗
Regularity effects in reading aloud	✗	✓	✗
Imageability effects in reading aloud	✓	✗	✓ (possibly)
Grammatical class effects in reading aloud	✓	✗	✓ (possibly)
Semantic errors in reading aloud	✓	✗	✗

orthographic-to-phonological conversion is retained, a pattern of reading characteristic of surface dyslexia is seen. Words and nonwords are read via the sub-lexical route, resulting in accurate reading of nonwords and regular words and regularisation errors for irregular words.

A deficit within the lexicon results in difficulty determining whether a string of graphemes is a real word or not. Lexical decision and comprehension may occur via phonology, so irregular words are rejected (e.g. YACHT → 'that's not a word') but pseudo-homophones (e.g. BOAL JALE PHOCKS) are accepted and understood (as their corresponding real words). The meanings of real word homophones (e.g. MALE/MAIL or TWO/TO/TOO) are confused when meaning is accessed on the basis of phonology.

```
┌──────────────────────────────┐
│                              │
│         Semantic             │
│         system               │
│                              │
└──────────────────────────────┘
```

A semantic deficit results in impaired comprehension of both auditory and written words and difficulty producing both spoken and written words (see semantic impairments in Chapter 4).

Impairment to the semantic system will affect reading aloud via the semantically mediated route. Imageability effects are typically present. If orthographic-to-phonological conversion is also impaired, then reading aloud will be characteristic of either deep or phonological dyslexia.

```
┌──────────────────────────────┐
│                              │
│      Orthographic-to-        │
│   phonological conversion    │
│                              │
└──────────────────────────────┘
```

An impairment to orthographic-to-phonological conversion results in non-existent or poor reading of nonwords and novel words. Nonwords are often read as visually similar real words. Orthographic-to-phonological conversion is impaired in both deep and phonological dyslexia.

Assessments of reading

Preclude:

Preclude deficits of visual acuity and visual neglect through:

- Tests of vision (usually carried out by an optician)
- Ensuring eye glasses are worn if prescribed

- Checking influence of size of print
- Line bisection/letter cancellation/star cancellation (Behavioural Inattention Test; Wilson, Cockburn, & Halligan, 1987)

Preclude pre-morbid difficulties in literacy

General notes on assessment

When testing reading, it is important to consider both reading comprehension and reading aloud. To assess reading comprehension, a test that considers the whole process (e.g. written word to picture matching) is a useful starting point. Clients should be encouraged to read the words silently. If written word comprehension is impaired, consider the pattern of errors made. Comparing the reading aloud of regular and irregular words of varying imageability and nonwords allows the clinician to hypothesise to what extent the three reading routines are impaired and preserved. One complication is that typically these routines are not wholly abolished but some routines may be working less effectively than others. More detailed assessments will then need to be carried out to determine what specific processes are impaired.

Word types

As a first step in assessing reading aloud, three types of word lists are useful:

1   Nonwords – that is, reading aloud single-syllable nonwords. Ideally, these would be matched in terms of length and orthographic complexity to real words.
2   Regular and irregular words. These matched sets should include low-frequency irregular words, as these are the items most likely to elicit regularity effects.
3   High- and low-imageability words.

The use of these three item sets allows conclusions to be drawn about three effects:

(a)   A lexicality effect. Where nonwords are read less accurately than real words of equivalent difficulty, this implies impairment to orthographic-to-phonological conversion.
(b)   A regularity effect. Where regular words are read more accurately than irregular words, this implies that lexical reading is impaired.
(c)   An imageability effect. Where high-imageability words are read more accurately than matched low-imageability words, this implies impairment at the level of the semantic system, with some contribution of the semantically mediated route.

Error types

The second source of evidence available is the nature of the errors made in reading. These can be classified into the following categories:

1   Semantic errors: responses that are semantically related to the target, but the words are not visually related, e.g. APE → 'monkey'.
2   Visual/phonological errors: errors which are similar to the target in orthographic and/or phonological form. A common criterion for visual similarity is that at least 50% of the phonemes in the stimulus occur in the error response in approximately the same order (cf. Morton and Patterson, 1980), e.g. DOOR → 'doom'.
3   Mixed visual/semantic errors: errors that are both visually and semantically relate to the stimulus, e.g. RAT → 'cat'.
4   Morphological errors: responses that share at least the root morpheme with the stimulus, but have errors in addition, deletion or substitution of morphemes. These errors will typically be found most often with stimuli that are morphologically complex, e.g. LOVELY → 'loving'.
5   Visual-then-semantic errors: errors in which a semantic error appears to follow a visual error, e.g. SYMPATHY → 'orchestra'.
6   Phonologically plausible errors: mostly 'regularisations' but also including relatively rare 'irregularisations', e.g. SPEAR → /spɛə/.

Visual orthographic
analysis

Indicators of impairment

• Reduced ability to recognise letters.
• Impaired reading comprehension and reading aloud with visual errors.
• Length effects (shorter words easier to read than longer words).

General notes on assessment

Impaired visual orthographic analysis will affect all reading tasks.

Key assessment areas and available methods

Area of assessment	Examples of available assessment tools	Response type
Written letter recognition	PALPA 18: Mirror reversal	Letter selection
	PALPA 19: Upper-case–lower case letter matching	Letter selection

	PALPA 20: Lower-case–upper case letter matching	Letter selection
	PALPA 21: Letter discrimination: Letters in words and nonwords	Tick/correct
Auditory and written letter recognition	PALPA 23: Spoken letter–written letter matching	Letter selection

Interpretation

✔ Good performance on letter recognition, discrimination and matching tasks implies that visual orthographic analysis is intact.

✗ Impaired visual orthographic analysis is suggested by difficulty with letter recognition and the presence of visual errors in reading of words and nonwords.

Additional specific assessment options

(a) Neglect dyslexia

Area of assessment	Examples of available assessment tools	Response type
Detection of neglect errors	One, few, many bodies test (as described in Patterson & Wilson, 1990) Tests for word-centred neglect	Reading aloud
Note distribution of incorrectly read words	Informal – ask client to read passage and note the spatial distribution of the errors made Tests for page-centred neglect	Reading aloud

(b) Letter by letter reading

Area of assessment	Examples of available assessment tools	Response type
Letter naming and sounding	PALPA 22: Letter naming/ sounding	Naming/sounding letters
Length effect	PALPA 29: Letter length reading	Reading aloud

Box 6.1 A case of a letter-by-letter reader: Client CH (Patterson & Kay, 1982)

CH was an 81-year-old when he had a left CVA. He was right-handed and had worked as a chauffeur until his retirement. A CT scan showed damage in the left occipital and temporal lobes. He had a right homonymous haemianopia. He was 4 years post-onset at the time of testing. CH had normal comprehension and speech production. His spelling to dictation, both oral and written, was good although not perfect. His spelling errors were predominantly either phonologically acceptable alternatives (e.g. for 'definite' he wrote 'definate') or nearly phonologically acceptable (e.g. 'yaught' for 'yacht'). It was unclear to what extent these difficulties reflected his pre-morbid abilities. He was always able to identify words from their oral spelling. His reading was almost entirely letter by letter – that is, he named each letter before saying the word. His reading was very slow and reading latency increased linearly with word length. He had a severe deficit in naming individual letters, with a slight advantage for upper-case letters. This led to letter misidentifications resulting in reading errors (e.g. 'men' was read as 'h e n, hen'). Misidentifications between visually similar letters were most common. Other errors included the production of a word containing the same initial letter string as the target. If the letters were correctly identified and named, CH almost always produced the correct word, both words with regular and irregular spellings. Patterson and Kay propose that once CH had identified the correct letters, he used intact lexical knowledge of spelling to assign the correct pronunciation to the word.

Orthographic
input lexicon

Indicators of impairment

- Reduced ability to recognise a string of graphemes as a real word and to reject nonwords. Rejection of irregular words as nonwords and acceptance of pseudo-homophones implies reliance on orthographic-to-phonological conversion.
- Visual errors.
- Frequency effects (with high-frequency words being recognised more easily than low-frequency words).
- Regularity effects (exception words are more difficult to read aloud and regularisation errors occur, e.g. 'blewed' for blood).
- Homophone errors occur in written comprehension (e.g. BERRY → 'to put in the ground', LISTEN → 'the boxer').

General notes on assessment

Impaired visual orthographic analysis will lower performance on tests of visual lexical decision and written comprehension. Reduced access to the orthographic input lexicon may result in visual dyslexia or letter by letter reading. Impairment to the lexicon will impair reading aloud via the semantic or direct lexical route. If impairment to the orthographic input lexicon is accompanied by intact orthographic-to-phonological conversion, reading will be characteristic of surface dyslexia.

Key assessment areas and available methods

Area of assessment	Examples of available assessment tools	Response type
Written lexical decision – illegal strings	PALPA 24: Visual lexical decision with 'illegal' nonwords	Written word selection
Written lexical decision – semantic involvement	PALPA 25: Visual lexical decision: imageability × frequency	Written word selection
Written lexical decision – regularity	ADA Comprehension Battery L1Wr: Lexical decision (written version)	Yes/no response
	PALPA 27: Visual lexical decision: spelling–sound regularity	Written word selection

Interpretation

✔ Good performance on written lexical decision tasks implies that the orthographic input lexicon is intact.

✗ Reduced performance on written lexical decision tasks implies impairment to the orthographic input lexicon.

✗ Different patterns of error may be seen depending on whether the client is able to access phonological information via orthographic-to-phonological conversion. The additional options will help to confirm whether this route is intact. If intact, the client will show characteristics of surface dyslexia.

Additional specific assessment options

Area of assessment	Examples of available assessment tools	Response type
Reading nonwords	PALPA 36: Nonword reading	Reading aloud
Spelling–sound regularity effect	PALPA 35: Spelling–sound regularity and reading	Reading aloud
Access to semantics from written word form	PALPA 38: Homophone definitions and regularity	Spoken definition/ reading aloud
Access to pronunciation from written word form	PALPA 28: Homophone decision	Tick

Interpretation

✔ A regularity effect in reading and preserved reading of nonwords implies relatively intact orthographic-to-phonological conversion.

✗ If comprehension is based primarily on a phonological form, homophones will frequently be misunderstood. Where this occurs only with regular homophones (e.g. BERRY → to put in the ground) but not irregular homophones (e.g. BURY → that's not a word, /bjʊərɪ/), this suggests that the phonology on which comprehension is based is primarily sub-lexical orthographic-to-phonological conversion. Where, however, homophone errors also occur frequently with irregular homophones (e.g. BURY → grows on bushes, berry), phonology must sometimes depend on lexical and non-semantic ('direct route') recoding of orthography to phonology.

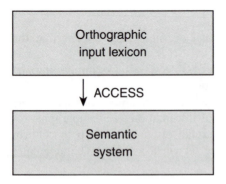

Indicators of impairment

- Written words are recognised as real words but are difficult to understand.
- Good access to semantics via the auditory modality but impaired access via the written modality.

General notes on assessment

Impairment to visual orthographic analysis or the orthographic input lexicon will also affect access to semantics. Impaired access to semantics from the orthographic input lexicon will affect reading aloud via the semantically mediated route, but both regular and irregular words may still be read via the direct lexical route.

Key assessment areas and available methods

Area of assessment	Examples of available assessment tools	Response type
Access to semantics from written word form	PALPA 38: Homophone definitions and regularity	Spoken definition/ reading aloud
Compare written and auditory comprehension of words	PALPA 47/48: Spoken and written word–picture matching	Picture selection
	ADA Comprehension Battery: Spoken and written word– picture matching	Picture selection

Interpretation

- ✔ Comparable auditory and written comprehension with retained under-standing of homophones implies input from the orthographic input lexicon to semantics is intact.
- ✗ Reduced written performance compared to auditory performance implies input to semantics from the orthographic input lexicon is impaired.
- ✗ Homophone errors in defining homophones may imply impaired access from the orthographic input lexicon to semantics, with access to seman-tics depending on a phonological code. If homophone errors occur only with regular homophones, this phonological code is generated using orthographic-to-phonological conversion. Where homophone errors occur with irregular homophones, this suggests that the phonology is sometimes derived lexically.

Box 6.2 A case of impairment to the phonological output lexicon (surface dyslexia): Client MP (Bub, Cancelliere, & Kertesz, 1985)

MP was a 62-year-old woman who was struck by a car. She sustained trauma to the skull, particularly in the region of the left temporal lobe. She was tested approximately 3 years after the accident. She presented with a severe comprehension deficit, having difficulty understanding single auditory and written words and identifying semantic associates. Her speech was characterised by anomia and jargon. Compared with her speech, her oral reading was rapid and fluent. On formal testing of her reading, her oral reading of regular words was more accurate than her reading of exception words. She showed a strong frequency effect. MP was able to read nonwords accurately. She was able to read some exception words, particularly those of high frequency; lower frequency exception words were read using general spelling-to-sound rules resulting in regularisation errors. MP was unable to identify irregular words in a lexical decision task, but on a lexical discrimination task her performance was sensitive to the regularity of letter–sound correspondence. She had particular difficulty identifying exception words as words when paired with orthographically familiar nonwords. Bub *et al.* suggest that MP was able to use some lexical knowledge to pronounce words using a route not mediated via semantics but by direct lexical connections between orthographic and phonological representations. When this route could not be accessed, she used her knowledge of spelling–sound correspondence. Due to her lexical discrimination skills, they suggest her functional impairment was located at the level of phonological retrieval rather than at the level of the orthographic representation.

Semantic
system

Indicators of impairment

- If a semantic impairment, the person will have:
  - (a) impaired comprehension for both auditory and written input modalities and
  - (b) semantic errors in both spoken and written output (but semantic errors may also indicate impairment at other levels).
- Imageability effects in all tasks requiring semantic processing.

General notes on assessment

In reading, a semantic deficit affects reading comprehension and the use of the semantically mediated route for reading aloud. If orthographic-to-phonological conversion is also impaired, the client will present with the characteristics of either deep or phonological dyslexia. The difference between the two types is the presence of pure semantic errors in deep dyslexia.

Key assessment areas and available methods

See also the assessment of semantic deficits in Chapter 4.

Area of assessment	Examples of available assessment tools	Response type
Compare written and auditory comprehension of words	PALPA 47/48: Spoken and written word–picture matching	Picture selection
	ADA Comprehension Battery: Spoken and written word–picture matching	Picture selection
Imageability effect (and interaction with frequency effect)	PALPA 31: Imageability × frequency reading	Reading aloud

Interpretation

✔ Retained performance on spoken and written comprehension and production implies intact semantics.

✗ Comparable performance on spoken and written comprehension with the choice of semantic distractors implies a semantic deficit.

✗ Errors on low-imageability items versus high-imageability items may imply a central semantic problem.

Additional specific assessment options

Area of assessment	Examples of available assessment tools	Response type
Reading nonwords	PALPA 36: Nonword reading	Reading aloud
Grammatical class effect	PALPA 33: Grammatical class reading (controlled for imageability)	Reading aloud
Morphological complexity effect	PALPA 34: Lexical morphology and reading	Reading aloud

Interpretation

✔   Retained ability to read nonwords implies intact orthographic-to-phonological conversion.

✗   Reduced ability to read nonwords implies an impairment to orthographic-to-phonological conversion.

✗   Reduced performance in reading aloud verbs and function words relative to nouns (grammatical class effects) may imply syntactic–semantic difficulties. As function words are lower in imageability, increased difficulty reading may also be due to an imageability effect.

✗   Morphological complexity effects have been found in deep dyslexia; these may be semantic in nature (Funnell, 1987).

Box 6.3 A case of impairment to semantic lexical reading and impaired orthographic-to-phonological conversion (deep dyslexia): Client GR (Marshall & Newcombe, 1966; Newcombe, Oldfield, Ratcliff, & Wingfield, 1971; Newcombe & Marshall, 1980)

GR was a 19-year-old soldier who was injured in Normandy in 1944 when a bullet penetrated his brain in the region of the left sylvian fissure and emerged in the superior parietal lobe of the left hemisphere. His speech was non-fluent and agrammatic with word finding difficulties in constrained tests and in spontaneous speech. GR's performance in reading aloud was characterised by relatively good reading of common, concrete nouns but errors on other words. His errors in reading aloud were a combination of semantic circumlocutions (e.g. for TOMATO → 'Can't pronounce it . . . don't like them myself . . . they're red') and semantic errors (e.g. ARSENIC → 'poison'). There was also evidence of semantic difficulties in other formal tests. He made a high proportion of semantic and semantic/visual errors in spoken and written word–picture matching. He had difficulty sorting written words into semantic categories and made errors when matching spoken words to written words within semantic categories. GR presented with marked difficulties in spoken naming with increased naming latencies for low-frequency words. He produced predominantly circumlocutions (described as misnaming errors). For example, for SYRINGE he produced 'a thing for pushing medicine . . . injection'.

Orthographic-to-
phonological conversion

Indicators of impairment

• Reading nonwords (i.e. pronouncing unfamiliar strings of letters) will be difficult.

General notes on assessment

Orthographic-to-phonological conversion is impaired in both deep and phonological dyslexia.

Key assessment areas and available methods

Area of assessment	Examples of available assessment tools	Response type
Reading nonwords	PALPA 36: Nonword reading	Reading aloud

Interpretation

✔ Retained ability to read nonwords implies intact orthographic-to-phonological conversion.

✗ Impaired orthographic-to-phonological conversion is suggested by a reduced ability to produce nonwords and novel words.

Box 6.4 A case of impairment to orthographic-to-phonological conversion (phonological dyslexia): Client WB (Funnell, 1983)

WB was a man who had a left hemisphere CVA at the age of 58. He was previously employed as a transport manager. His speech was non-fluent but not agrammatic and was slightly dysarthric. He presented with relatively good functional comprehension but impaired comprehension of syntactic structures. His reading aloud was characterised by an inability to read non-words, to produce the sounds for isolated letters and to read isolated suffixes. His reading aloud of words was around 90% accurate with no effect of imageability, word class, regularity or morphological complexity. He was able to read function words and suffixes when attached to appropriate or phonologically legal words. He produced very few semantic errors in real word reading. Funnell argues that WB's reading of real words was a consequence of direct word links between orthography and phonology and not semantic mediation, as he made semantic errors in the written comprehension of single words. His reading aloud of words was significantly superior to his ability to make semantic judgements about those words; although he was at chance in matching written MITTEN to GLOVE or SOCK, he could read almost all of the words correctly.

7   Written word production

Model of written production (spelling)

Figure 7.1 shows the processes involved in written word naming of objects/pictures. The processes involved in copying written words are shown in Figure 7.2. Four stages are involved in writing words to convey meaning: the semantic system, the orthographic output lexicon, the graphemic output buffer and allographic realisation.

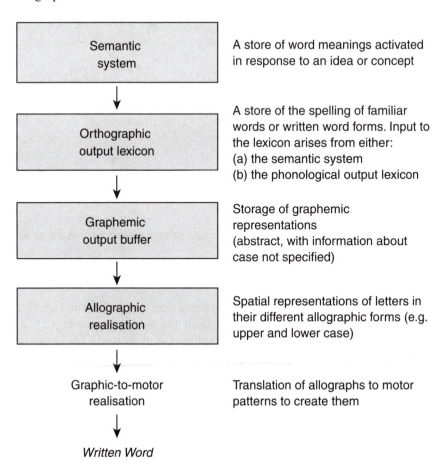

Semantic system	A store of word meanings activated in response to an idea or concept
Orthographic output lexicon	A store of the spelling of familiar words or written word forms. Input to the lexicon arises from either: (a) the semantic system (b) the phonological output lexicon
Graphemic output buffer	Storage of graphemic representations (abstract, with information about case not specified)
Allographic realisation	Spatial representations of letters in their different allographic forms (e.g. upper and lower case)
Graphic-to-motor realisation	Translation of allographs to motor patterns to create them

Written Word

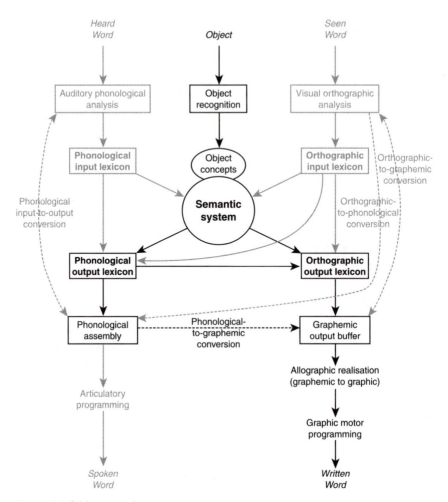

Figure 7.1 Written naming.

When writing words to dictation, there are three routes that can be used. These are illustrated in Figure 7.3.

Semantic lexical route

This route involves writing with access to meaning and is the usual spelling mechanism. It involves: (a) activation from the semantic system and (b) access to the word within the orthographic output lexicon. This route is necessary to correctly spell homophones.

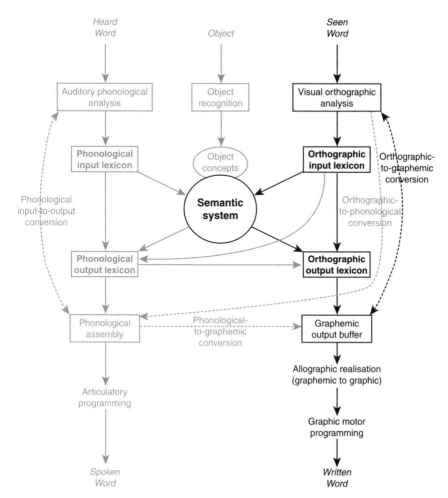

Figure 7.2 Copying written words.

Sub-lexical route (phonological-to-graphemic conversion)

Writing via phonological-to-graphemic conversion is the 'sounding out route'. It involves the segmentation of a word into phonemes and then translation of the phonemes into graphemes. This route is used for the writing to dictation of unfamiliar words and nonwords.

Direct lexical route

This route involves writing to dictation via a lexical but not semantic route. It involves: (a) retrieving the word's phonology from the phonological output lexicon and (b) activation of the word within the orthographic output lexicon. As only real, known words are represented in these lexicons, this routine can

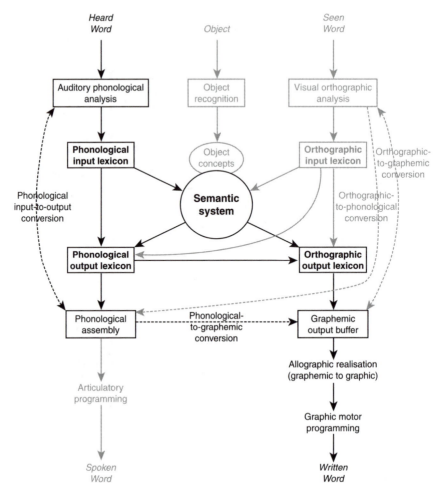

Figure 7.3 Writing to dictation

only process real words, irrespective of their sound-to-spelling regularity. This results in being able to write irregular words without semantic knowledge.

Deficits of written production (spelling)

Deficits in writing depend on the location of the impairment and whether alternative routes can be utilised. Writing impairments have traditionally been characterised in terms of deep dysgraphia, surface dysgraphia and phonological dysgraphia. Table 7.1 describes the main features of each.

Table 7.1 Characteristic features of different types of dysgraphia

DYSGRAPHIAS

1 Deep dysgraphia (Bub & Kertesz, 1982)

Deep dysgraphia results from writing via an impaired semantic route. Access to the orthographic output lexicon is impaired with an additional deficit in phonological-to-graphemic conversion.

Characteristic features:

- The defining feature of deep dysgraphia is the presence of semantic errors in writing, e.g. TIME → 'clock' in writing to dictation.
- Nonword spelling is impaired – typically impossible or close to impossible.
- High-imageability words are written more accurately than low-imageability words.
- Content words are written more accurately than function words.

2 Phonological dysgraphia (Shallice, 1981)

Phonological dysgraphia results from a difficulty in sub-lexical writing to dictation with relatively good lexical writing. The writing impairment can result from an impairment to sub-lexical phonological-to-graphemic conversion (when nonword repetition is unaffected) or in sub-lexical auditory-to-phonological conversion (when both nonword repetition and writing nonwords to dictation are impaired).

Characteristic features:

- Very poor writing of nonwords to dictation.

Real word reading may be close to perfect, but if real word reading is impaired:

- Structurally similar and morphological errors in writing to dictation.
- Better writing of high- than low-imageability words.

3 Surface dysgraphia (Beauvois & Derouesne, 1981)

Surface dysgraphia results from impairment to lexically mediated writing with phonological-to-graphemic conversion well preserved.

Characteristic features:

- Regular words and nonwords are written more accurately than irregular words.

Correct production of some high-frequency, irregular words.

- Confusion between the spelling of homophones, e.g. SAIL → 'sale'.

Errors:

(a) Regularisation errors in the spelling of irregular words, e.g. ANSWER → 'anser'.
(b) Errors involving partial knowledge of irregular words, e.g. YACHT → 'yhaght'; SWORD → 'sward'.

```
Semantic
system
```

A semantic deficit results in impaired comprehension of both auditory and written words and difficulty producing both spoken and written words (see semantic impairments in Chapter 4).

Impairment to the semantic system will affect writing to convey meaning and writing to dictation via the semantically mediated route. Imageability effects are typically present. If phonological-to-graphemic conversion is impaired, then writing will be characteristic of deep dysgraphia.

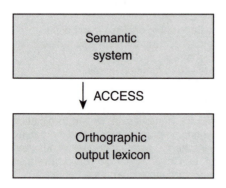

A deficit in accessing the orthographic output lexicon results in impaired writing via the semantic lexical route. Words may still be written via phonological-to-graphemic conversion or the direct lexical route. The comprehension of spoken and written words and spoken word production will be preserved. If phonological-to-graphemic conversion is also impaired, writing will be characteristic of deep dysgraphia.

```
┌─────────────────────────┐
│                         │
│       Orthographic      │
│      output lexicon     │
│                         │
└─────────────────────────┘
```

An impairment in the orthographic output lexicon results in impaired writing via the semantic lexical and the direct lexical route. If writing via phonological-to-graphemic conversion is preserved, writing will be characteristic of surface dysgraphia. A frequency effect in writing may be evident. A deficit within the orthographic output lexicon results in confusion when writing homophones.

```
┌─────────────────────────┐
│                         │
│        Graphemic        │
│      output buffer      │
│                         │
└─────────────────────────┘
```

Impairment to the graphemic output buffer results in difficulty writing words and nonwords. Written naming, writing to dictation, delayed copying, typing and oral spelling are affected.[1] As the graphemic output buffer is post-lexical, performance should not be influenced by lexical or semantic variables (e.g. word frequency, imageability, concreteness, grammatical class).

Spelling errors include: (a) additions, (b) deletions, (c) substitutions and (d) transpositions of letters. An effect of word length on spelling will be present. Letter formation is intact.

```
Allographic
realisation
```

Impairment to allographic realisation results in letter substitutions in both words and nonwords. All writing is impaired but oral spelling is retained.

Graphic-to-motor realisation

Impairment results in impaired selection of movements (Baxter & Warrington, 1986). Words can be spelt orally. Error types present in writing single letters include: (a) substitutions, (b) incomplete letters and (c) the fusion of two letters.

The ability to describe the shape of the letters is retained. Copying is unaffected (i.e. it is not an apraxic disorder). It is possible to have a selective difficulty in writing either upper-case letters (Destreri *et al.*, 2000) or lower-case letters (Patterson & Wing, 1989).

```
Phonological-to-graphemic
conversion
```

An impairment to phonological-to-graphemic conversion results in non-existent or poor writing of nonwords. Nonwords are often written as similar real words. Phonological-to-orthographic conversion is impaired in both deep and phonological dysgraphia.

Assessments of written word production

Preclude:

Preclude deficits of visual acuity, visual neglect and motor dyspraxia through:

- Tests of vision (usually carried out by optician)
- Ensuring eye glasses are worn if prescribed
- Line bisection
- Tests for motor dyspraxia
- General positioning and posture (liaise with physiotherapist)

Preclude pre-morbid difficulties in literacy

General notes on assessment

When assessing writing, written picture naming of a variety of stimuli is a useful starting point. It is important to note to what extent the client produces the word verbally before written naming. Consider the error types produced to form a hypothesis about the level of impairment. Writing to dictation of regular and irregular words of varying imageability and non-words can help to confirm the diagnosis. If an impairment to peripheral processes (graphemic output buffer, allographic realisation or graphic-to-motor realisation) is suspected, contrast written performance with copying, oral spelling and the use of a letter board/letter tiles or typing. When assessing spelling, it is important to recognise that some clients will be using their non-dominant hand and to consider pre-morbid spelling ability.

Word types

In assessing written production of words, four types of word stimuli are useful:

1   High- and low-imageability words.
2   High- and low-frequency words.
3   Regular and irregular words. These sets should include low-frequency irregular words, as these are the items most likely to elicit regularity effects.
4   Words varying in syllable length, e.g. one-, two-, three-syllable words.

In each case, it is important to ensure that the words used are within the client's pre-morbid vocabulary. Analysis of performance on these variables allows conclusions to be drawn about four effects:

(a) An imageability effect. Where high-imageability words are spelt more accurately than matched low-imageability words, this may imply impairment to the semantic system.

(b) A regularity effect. Where regular words are spelt more accurately than irregular words, this may imply impairment at the level of the orthographic output lexicon or in access to it.

(c) A frequency effect. Where high-frequency words are spelt more easily than low-frequency words, this may imply impairment at the level of the orthographic output lexicon.

(d) A length effect. Where shorter words are accessed more easily than longer words, this may imply impairment at the level of the graphemic output buffer or at another post-lexical level.

Error types

The second source of evidence available is the nature of the errors made in written production. These can be classified, for example, into the following categories:

1   Additions, e.g. TABLE → TARBLE.
2   Deletions, e.g. TABLE → TALE.
3   Substitutions, e.g. TABLE → TAPLE.
4   Transpositions of letters, e.g. TABLE → TALBE.
5   Incomplete letters.
6   The fusions of two letters.
7   Morphological errors (addition, deletion or substitution of an affix), e.g. TABLE → TABLES.
8   Semantic errors, e.g. TABLE → CHAIR.
9   Regularisation/phonologically plausible errors, e.g. TABLE → TAYBULL.

Key assessments of written naming

Naming assessment	Control factors
PALPA 53: Picture naming × oral reading, repetition and written spelling	Regular and irregular words matched for word frequency, familiarity, concreteness, age of acquisition, letter length and number of syllables
PALPA 54: Picture naming × word frequency	Word frequency varied and words matched for number of syllables, letters and name agreement

Nickels' Naming Test (described in (Nickels & Howard, 1994)	Word frequency and length varied, high- and low-frequency words matched for length. One-, two- and three-syllable words matched for frequency

Semantic system

See assessment in Chapter 4.

Indicators of impairment

* If a semantic impairment, the person will have:
    (a) impaired comprehension for both auditory and written input modalities and
    (b) semantic errors in both spoken and written output (but semantic errors may also indicate impairment at other levels).
* Imageability effects in all tasks requiring semantic processing.

General notes on assessment

In writing, a semantic impairment affects writing to convey meaning and the use of the semantic lexical route in writing to dictation. If phonological-to-graphemic conversion is also impaired, the client will present with the characteristics of deep dysgraphia. Additional assessment options are available to determine whether other characteristics are present.

Key assessment areas and available methods

Area of assessment	Examples of available assessment tools	Response type
Error analysis of naming	PALPA 53: Picture naming × oral reading, repetition and written spelling	Written naming
Imageability effect	PALPA 40: Spelling to dictation: imageability and frequency	Writing to dictation

Interpretation

✔ Retained performance on spoken and written comprehension and production implies intact semantics.

✗ Semantic errors in written naming alongside semantic errors in comprehension and spoken naming imply impairment of the semantic system.

✗ Reduced performance when spelling low-imageability words relative to high-imageability words (imageability effect) implies impairment of the semantic system.

Additional assessment options

Area of assessment	Examples of available assessment tools	Response type
Imageability effect	PALPA 40: Spelling to dictation: imageability and frequency	Writing to dictation
Grammatical class effect	PALPA 42: Spelling to dictation: grammatical class × imageability	Writing to dictation
Morphological complexity effect	PALPA 43: Spelling to dictation: morphological endings	Writing to dictation

Interpretation

✗ Reduced performance when spelling low-imageability words relative to high-imageability words (imageability effect) implies impairment of the semantic system or impaired access to the orthographic output lexicon.

✗ Reduced performance spelling verbs and function words relative to nouns (grammatical class effects) may imply syntactic-semantic difficulties. As words such as function words are lower in imageability, greater difficulty in spelling may also be due to an imageability effect.

✗ Morphological complexity effects have been found in deep dysgraphia (Badecker, Hillis, & Caramazza, 1990).

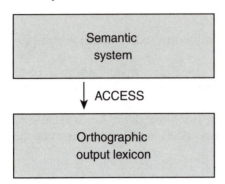

Indicators of impairment

- Semantic errors in writing without semantic errors in reading, auditory comprehension or naming.
- Imageability effects.

General notes on assessment

If access to the orthographic output lexicon is impaired alongside impaired phonological-to-graphemic conversion, writing will be characteristic of deep dysgraphia. Regular and irregular words may still be written via the direct lexical route.

Box 7.1 A case of impairment to the semantic system and phonological-to-graphemic conversion (deep dysgraphia): Client JC (Bub & Kertesz, 1982)

JC was a 21-year-old lady who suffered a left hemisphere CVA in the middle cerebral artery territory. She was 4 months post-onset at the time of testing. Her speech was non-fluent and agrammatic, with some word-finding difficulties in confrontation naming. Her comprehension of single words and short sentences was generally intact but she experienced difficulties with the comprehension of sequential commands. On formal testing of her writing, she was unable to write nonwords to dictation, producing confabulatory responses or real words that sounded similar to the target (e.g. CLIMPANY → 'balcony'). In real word writing, she produced semantic errors (e.g. TIME → 'clock'). Her writing of words was also characterised by an imageability effect (concrete nouns written more accurately than abstract nouns) and a word class effect (nouns written more accurately than verbs). She was unable to write function words. In contrast, reading and repetition of both words and nonwords was accurate.

Orthographic
output lexicon

Indicators of impairment

- Frequency effects on irregular words.
- Reduced ability to spell homophones.

General notes on assessment

If the orthographic output lexicon is impaired and phonological-to-graphemic conversion is preserved, writing will be characteristic of surface dysgraphia. Additional assessments can be used to determine the presence of a regularity effect with regularisation errors in the production of irregular words.

Key assessment areas and available methods

Area of assessment	Examples of available assessment tools	Response type
Error analysis of naming	PALPA 53: Picture naming × oral reading, repetition and written spelling	Written naming
Frequency effect	PALPA 54: Picture naming × word frequency	Written naming
	PALPA 40: Spelling to dictation: imageability and frequency	Writing to dictation
Regularity effect	PALPA 44: Spelling to dictation: regularity	Writing to dictation
Writing of homophones	PALPA 46: Spelling to dictation: disambiguated homophones	Writing to dictation

Interpretation

- ✔ Good performance in the writing of low-frequency, irregular words implies an intact orthographic output lexicon.
- ✗ Reduced performance when spelling irregular words relative to regular words (regularity effect) implies impairment at the level of the orthographic output lexicon with spared phonological-to-graphemic conversion.
- ✗ A tendency to regularise exception words may also be seen with spelling of homophones, suggesting difficulties with the orthographic output lexicon.
- ✗ Reduced performance when spelling low-frequency words relative to high-frequency words (frequency effect) implies impairment of the orthographic output lexicon.

Box 7.2 A case of impairment to the orthographic output lexicon (surface dysgraphia): Client TP (Hatfield & Patterson, 1983)

TP was a lady who had a left posterior cerebral haemorrhage at the age of 50. She was 4 months post-onset at the time of testing. Her auditory comprehension of single words and sentences was generally accurate. She had a severe naming difficulty. She was able to repeat both single words and sentences. TP's writing was characterised by many spelling errors. For example, in a picture description task she wrote 'she is stil lafing about the to men being cros' instead of 'she is still laughing about the two men being cross'. In writing to dictation, her writing of regular words was significantly better than her writing of exception words, although occasional irregular words were spelt correctly. Her spelling errors were mainly the production of phonologically plausible responses (e.g. ANSWER → 'anser'). She also sometimes confused visually similar letters (e.g. 'p' and 'b'). She was unable to disambiguate homophones in writing. Hatfield and Patterson suggest that TP's spelling reflects a reliance on a phonological spelling routine, with a minimal contribution of word-specific spelling.

Graphemic
output buffer

Indicators of impairment

* Generalised spelling errors (additions, deletions, subtractions and transpositions of letters for both words and nonwords).
* Length effects.

General notes on assessment

Impairment to the graphemic output buffer will affect all writing tasks.

Key assessment areas and available methods

Area of assessment	Examples of available assessment tools	Response type
Length effect	PALPA 39: Spelling to dictation: letter length	Writing to dictation
Real and nonword comparison	PALPA 45: Spelling to dictation: nonwords	Writing to dictation
Copying	Informal immediate and delayed copying of words and nonwords	Copying

Interpretation

✔ Preserved written naming, writing to dictation and the copying of long and short words and nonwords imply an intact graphemic output buffer.

✗ Reduced performance when spelling longer words relative to shorter words (length effect) implies impairment of the graphemic output buffer.

✗ Generalised spelling errors in the writing and copying of words and nonwords imply impairment to the graphemic output buffer.

Box 7.3 A case of impairment to the graphemic output buffer: Client FV (Miceli, Silveri, & Caramazza, 1985, 1987)

FV was 60 years old when he had a CVA. He was a lawyer. A CT scan showed a very small lesion in the uppermost portion of the angular gyrus and the lowermost portion of the superior parietal lobe with very minor involvement of the sub-cortical white matter. Initially, he presented with a mild aphasia but this resolved and he returned to work. When tested as an outpatient, he showed no aphasia but a severe writing disorder. His speech was fluent, with a varied vocabulary and a normal range of syntactic structures. He performed within the normal range on tests of spoken production and comprehension and was able to read words and nonwords correctly. His spontaneous writing was grammatical with a good vocabulary but contained frequent spelling errors. On formal testing, he was able to write single letters to dictation but made errors on sequences of letters. In written naming and writing to dictation, he made frequent spelling errors. His errors involved the substitution, omission, addition or transposition of letters, resulting in the production of nonwords. His writing accuracy was not affected by grammatical class, frequency or abstractness but was affected by length; short words were spelt more accurately than long words. He made more errors when writing nonwords than words but his errors were the same. FV often seemed to be aware of his errors and could correct about 80% of them when they were presented to him as errors. He could also identify his errors as non-words when they were presented in a lexical decision task. FV was able to copy words and nonwords accurately even following a delay of up to 10 seconds. Miceli *et al.* propose that an impairment in the graphemic output buffer could account for FV's performance in writing but cannot explain his accurate delayed copying. An impairment in phonological-to-graphemic conversion cannot explain his increased accuracy in writing words compared to nonwords. They propose a model in which the information within the graphemic output buffer is refreshed not only via phonological-to-graphemic conversion but also via the orthographic output lexicon (possibly via the phonological output lexicon).

> Allographic
> realisation

Indicators of impairment

- Substitutions of letters for both words and nonwords.

Key assessment areas and available methods

Area of assessment	Examples of available assessment tools	Response type
Comparison of oral versus written spelling	Informal – any test of spelling	Oral and written spelling
Real and nonword writing	PALPA 39: Spelling to dictation: letter length	Writing to dictation
	PALPA 45: Spelling to dictation: nonwords	Writing to dictation

Interpretation

✔ Comparable written and oral spelling implies intact allographic realisation.
✗ Reduced performance in written spelling relative to oral spelling implies impaired allographic realisation.
✗ Letter substitutions in both real words and nonwords imply impaired allographic realisation.

Graphic-to-motor realisation

Indicators of impairment

- Impaired movements and writing of single letters.

Key assessment areas and available methods

Area of assessment	Examples of available assessment tools	Response type
Spontaneous writing	Analysis of error types	Written spelling/letters
Copying ability	Ability to copy letters	Written copying

Interpretation

✔ Correct letter formation in copying and writing tasks implies intact graphic-to-motor realisation.

✗ Impaired movements during writing and impaired copying of letters, resulting in incorrect letter formation, would suggest involvement of graphic-to-motor realisation.

Phonological-to-graphemic conversion

Indicators of impairment

- Writing of nonwords will be difficult.

General notes on assessment

Phonological-to-graphemic conversion is impaired in both deep and phonological dysgraphia.

Key assessment areas and available methods

Area of assessment	Examples of available assessment tools	Response type
Writing of nonwords	PALPA 45: Spelling to dictation: nonwords	Writing to dictation

Interpretation

✔ Retained ability to write nonwords implies intact phonological-to-graphemic conversion.

✗ Impaired phonological-to-graphemic conversion is suggested by a reduced ability to write nonwords and novel words to dictation.

Box 7.4 A case of impairment to phonological-to-graphemic conversion: Client PR (Shallice, 1981)

PR was a right-handed computer salesman who had an infarction in the territory of the left middle cerebral artery in his mid-fifties. At the time of testing, his speech was fluent with varied word choice but limited grammatical constructions. He scored within the normal range on tests of auditory comprehension and naming. His reading aloud was characteristic of a mild phonological dyslexia, with slightly impaired reading of nonwords (e.g. ITE → 'it'). His spontaneous writing was slow and laboured due to slight motor and formulation difficulties and was characterised by function word and verb errors. On testing, he showed a marked difference between his ability to write matched sets of words (94% correct) and nonwords (18% correct). His errors writing nonwords were mainly no responses. When he was able to attempt nonwords, he commented that he was using a real word mediator to facilitate his spelling. He was unable to write letters to single phonemes or clusters but could write letters in response to their letter names. His errors writing real words were a combination of no responses, structurally similar errors (e.g. ABSORPTION → 'absolve') and derivational errors (e.g. ASCEND → 'ascent'). He had particular difficulty writing function words. PR was able to repeat the function words and nonwords he was unable to write. He did, however, show some impairment on tasks of phonological segmentation.

Note

1 To accommodate the presence of people with better oral spelling than written spelling, it has been suggested that there are separate output buffers for written and oral spelling (Lesser, 1990; Pound, 1996). It is unclear whether this modification to the model is necessary.

8   Object and picture recognition

Model of object and picture recognition

Several stages are involved in recognising objects from visual input (either from pictures or from the actual object). The scheme given below elaborates on our basic model in Figure 1.1.

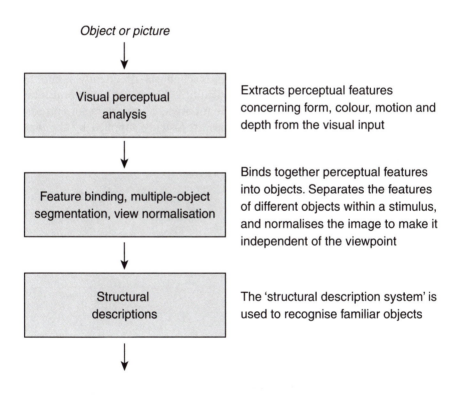

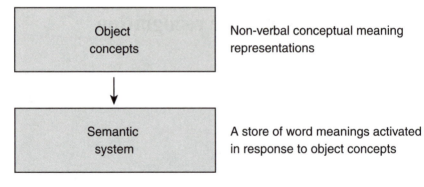

Note that objects can be recognised in other ways – that is, from touch (tactile input) or from audition – at least for objects with characteristic noises. Note also that deficits in object recognition are typically due to lesions in regions such as the occipital and inferior temporal lobes (normally supplied by the posterior cerebral artery) that are typically intact in people with aphasia due to stroke (which usually follows lesions in the territory of the middle cerebral artery) (Farah, 1990; Riddoch & Humphreys, 2001). Striking deficits in object perception are therefore unusual in this population.

The inferior temporal lobes, and particularly the fusiform gyrus and surrounding regions, are important for face recognition (De Haan, 2001). As a result, disordered face recognition (prosopagnosia) frequently occurs in conjunction with object recognition difficulties. The medial temporal lobe, particularly the hippocampus and adjacent cortex, is important for episodic memory (Parkin, 2001). These structures are usually supplied by the posterior cerebral artery and, as a result, a degree of amnesia (both retrograde and anterograde) is frequently associated with object recognition difficulties.

Deficits of object recognition

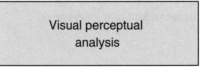

Deficits may occur in:

(a) Shape perception.
(b) Motion perception – akinetopsia.
(c) Colour perception – achromotopsia.
(d) Depth perception.

```
┌─────────────────────────────────┐
│  Feature binding, multiple-object │
│  segmentation, view normalisation │
└─────────────────────────────────┘
```

'Apperceptive' visual agnosias are deficits in object perception where elementary visual features are correctly extracted from the stimulus. The difficulties may lie in segmentation of the visual array and/or in binding together the features of objects. Recognition of pictures of objects from unusual (non-prototypical) views is typically poor. Line-by-line copying of a drawing is typically possible even where it is not recognised. Recognition of objects in other sensory modalities (e.g. by touch, sound or smell) is better than visual object recognition.

```
┌─────────────────────────────────┐
│            Structural            │
│           descriptions           │
└─────────────────────────────────┘
```

'Associative' agnosias can result from an impairment of structural descriptions. People with a deficit at this level have good performance in tasks testing more peripheral visual properties, including unusual view matching, but perform poorly in object decision (discriminating objects from non-objects). They also, typically, have difficulty in other tasks tapping stored perceptual knowledge, including object drawing to command, and answering questions about the shape of objects (e.g. does a leopard have a long tail?).

```
┌─────────────────────────────────┐
│             Object               │
│            concepts              │
└─────────────────────────────────┘
```

'Associative' agnosias may also result from an impairment of object concepts. Object decision tasks can be performed well, but people with a deficit at this level have difficulty in retrieving conceptual information about objects with all modalities of input. Semantic difficulties at this level can be category-specific. The most frequent category-specific disorders are impairment of 'animate' items (animals, plants and foods) relative to artefacts, or vice versa. Other more specific conceptual semantic disorders (e.g. of animals alone) are more rarely found (Capitani, Laiacona, Mahon, & Caramazza, 2003; Caramazza & Mahon, 2003).

Box 8.1 A case of apperceptive visual agnosia: Client HJA (Humphreys & Riddoch, 1987; Riddoch & Humphreys, 1986)

HJA was in his sixties when he suffered a stroke following an emergency operation for a perforated appendix. A CT scan showed bilateral lesions near the occipital pole, but sparing the primary visual cortex. He had a bilateral loss of the superior half of the visual fields. He had severe difficulty in recognising visually presented objects and pictures, although he was able to copy them line-by-line – showing that he could perceive them. He had lost all colour vision (achromotopsia) – a natural consequence of the lesion that affected V4, the area responsible for colour vision, bilaterally. Aside from these visual difficulties, his language was intact; he had no difficulty in naming to definition, or in naming objects from their characteristic sounds. He could read laboriously letter-by-letter, but found this exhausting and unsatisfying. Recognition of pictures was much worse when they overlapped, but improved when they were presented as silhouettes, reducing the overall complexity of the drawing. Humphreys and Riddoch describe him as having an 'integrative visual agnosia' – 'intact registration of form elements, along with an impaired ability to integrate the elements into perceptual wholes' (p.105).

Assessments of object recognition

Preclude:

Preclude deficits of visual acuity and visual neglect through:

- Test of visual acuity (usually carried out by optician)
- Line bisection (e.g. from the Behavioural Inattention Test; Wilson, Cockburn, & Halligan, 1987)

As major visual perceptual impairments are rare in post-stroke aphasia, the optimal strategy is to first test for good access to object concepts (see final section below). Only if significant impairment is found would it be worthwhile to examine earlier stages of processing.

Visual perceptual
analysis

Indicators of impairment

- Difficulty in recognising visually presented stimuli (objects, pictures) with relatively intact recognition of objects presented through other modalities.
- Difficulty in discrimination or matching of stimuli on the basis of shape, size, colour, spatial location and/or motion.

Key assessment areas and available methods

Area of assessment	Examples of available assessment tools	Response type
Shape perception	VOSP:[1] Shape detection screening test	Yes/no
	BORB:[2] Test 1: copying of elementary shapes	Drawing
Length discrimination	BORB: Test 2: length match task	Same/different
Size discrimination	BORB: Test 3: size match task	Same/different
Orientation discrimination	BORB: Test 4: orientation match task	Same/different
Spatial location	BORB: Test 5: position of gap match task	Same/different
	VOSP: Test 5: dot counting	Number
	VOSP: Test 6: position discrimination	Pointing
	VOSP: Test 7: number location	Number

[1] The Visual Object and Space Perception Battery (Warrington & James, 1991).
[2] Birmingham Object Recognition Battery (Riddoch & Humphreys, 1993).

Interpretation

- ✔ Retained object recognition implies intact shape perception.
- ✔ Retained ability to name or match colours implies that colour recognition is intact.
- ✗ Impaired recognition of visually presented objects relative to tactile presentation is necessary for an impairment at this level.

Note that poor performance on shape copying may also be due to a constructional dyspraxia (drawing impairment) or visual neglect.

Feature binding, multiple-object
segmentation, view normalisation

Indicators of impairment

- Difficulty in recognising visually presented stimuli (objects, pictures) with relatively intact recognition of objects presented through other modalities.
- Difficulty in segmentation of superimposed object drawings and/or in recognition of objects from unusual views

Key assessment areas and available methods

Area of assessment	Examples of available assessment tools	Response type
View normalisation	VOSP: Test 2: silhouettes	Name or describe object
	VOSP: Test 4: progressive silhouettes	Name or describe object
	BORB: Test 7: minimal feature view task	Pointing
	BORB: Test 8: foreshortened view task	Pointing
Object segmentation and feature binding	BORB: Test 6: overlapping figures task	Naming or matching

Interpretation

✔ Retained object recognition implies intact feature binding, object segmentation and view normalisation.

✗ Impaired recognition of visually presented objects relative to tactile presentation is necessary for an impairment at this level.

✗ Impaired recognition of unusual views and overlapping figures.

Structural
descriptions

Indicators of impairment

- Difficulty in recognising visually presented stimuli (objects, pictures) with relatively intact recognition of objects presented through other modalities.
- Difficulty in object decision and drawing from memory.

Key assessment areas and available methods

Area of assessment	Examples of available assessment tools	Response type
Object decision	BORB: Test 10: object decision	Yes/No
Drawing from memory	BORB: Test 9: drawing from memory	Drawing

Interpretation

✔ Retained object recognition implies intact structural descriptions.
✗ Impaired recognition of visually presented objects relative to tactile presentation is necessary for an impairment at this level.
✗ Impaired object decision and drawing from memory implies impaired structural descriptions.

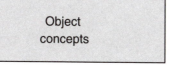

Object
concepts

Indicators of impairment

- Poor retrieval of conceptual knowledge from any stimulus modality, even when tested in tasks not requiring any (overt) language. The impairment may be category-specific.

Key assessment areas and available methods

Area of assessment	Examples of available assessment tools	Response type
Object concepts	Pyramids and Palm Trees: Pictures only version (Howard & Patterson, 1992)	Picture selection
	BORB: Test 12: associative match task	Picture selection
	BORB: Test 11: item match task	Picture selection
Category-specific disorders	The Category-Specific Names Test (McKenna, 1998)	Naming or word-to-picture matching

Interpretation

✔ Retained ability to match and name related concepts implies intact object concepts.

✗ Impaired matching of concepts (across modalities) implies difficulties with object concepts (although may be category-specific).

Part 3

Therapy

9   Introduction to therapy

There are many, very different approaches to aphasia therapy reflecting the variety of viewpoints both about the nature of the impairment in aphasia and about the aims of the therapy process (Howard & Hatfield, 1987). The diversity also reflects the great variety of symptoms present in individual clients, the varying severity and the impact that language impairments have both for the client and for their communication partners. Therapy approaches have often been classified into two main groups (Albert, Goodglass, Helm, Rubens, & Alexander, 1981; Seron, 1984) based on the underlying view held as to what aphasia is and what therapy can consequently aim to achieve. First is the belief that aphasia reflects an impairment of access to language, or damage to language processes or representations. With therapy, language functions can be restored, relearned or retrained. The second approach is based on the assumption that the impaired processes are themselves irremediable. Therapy must draw on compensatory strategies (other language and communication skills) to take over those impaired functions.

As in the preceding chapters of this volume, our discussion of therapy is presented from the theoretical viewpoint of cognitive neuropsychology. This view holds that language functions can be retrained or re-accessed through targeted intervention and will often directly target impaired processes. Based, as we have emphasised, on an analysis of both impaired and retained language-processing abilities, this approach also provides a basis for the development of therapy approaches centred on the development of compensatory strategies that draw on retained functions.

A holistic context

Within the holistic intervention offered to individual clients with aphasia, therapy motivated by a cognitive neuropsychologically based approach may be offered alongside other therapy approaches. We would agree that 'the multi-faceted nature of aphasia demands a flexible, integrated approach to therapy and support' (Pound, Parr, Lindsay, & Woolf, 2000). Therapy targeted directly at the impairment will often need to be accompanied by therapy aimed at promoting overall communication and support to deal with the psychological effects of aphasia on clients and their carers (Brumfitt, 1993). Pound *et al.* (2000), for example, describe therapy focusing on helping clients to cope with language loss and the effects of that disability on their everyday life. Holland (1982) describes methods of facilitating functional communication, while work with carers to promote the communication of the client with aphasia is described by, among others, Booth and Perkins (1999), Booth and Swabey (1999) and Lesser and Perkins (1999). These approaches are well documented elsewhere and will not be discussed here.

We believe that all treatment for aphasia should reflect an individual client's communication needs and wishes for communication and their priorities for treatment. These priorities often include therapy targeted towards the impairment in the language-processing system and cognitive neuropsychology provides a unique opportunity to identify and treat that impairment. Direct treatment for the impairment does not, however, mean that therapy is not relevant to the real-life needs of the person with aphasia or that it is focused on communication *per se*. The ultimate goal of all cognitive neuropsychologically based therapy is the use of communication skills within everyday settings and treatment should, like any other approach, employ materials and themes that are relevant and appropriate for the client. Similarly, evaluating efficacy of intervention must look beyond improvement within the language-processing system to the impact on real-life communication and the true and/or perceived benefits of improvement for the person with aphasia.

A cognitive neuropsychological perspective

Since the introduction of cognitive neuropsychology into the study of language breakdown in aphasia, there has been extensive debate about its contribution in determining therapy. Interested readers are directed to discussions in Howard and Hatfield (1987), Howard and Patterson (1989), Caramazza (1989), Basso (1989), Wilson and Patterson (1990), Hillis (1993) and Lesser and Milroy (1993). From a cognitive neuropsychological perspective, the aim of assessment is to understand the client's speech and language pattern in terms of the normal processing system, enabling targeted intervention to be developed for the individual. The assessment needs to be detailed enough to allow the identification of the impaired process or processes as well as those processing abilities that remain intact. Analysis of the surface symptoms is not sufficient to plan therapy, as the same surface symptoms may arise in various ways (Howard & Patterson, 1989). Sometimes, as Lesser and Milroy (1993) highlight, the actual therapy offered may not be radically different to traditional methods and techniques. The difference is that particular techniques targeting an aspect of the client's disorder are selected on the basis of a theoretical understanding of the underlying impairment.

Howard and Hatfield (1987) pointed out that identification of levels of breakdown and intact and impaired processes does not, in itself, *determine* the most appropriate and effective approach for therapy. It does, however, limit the range of possible treatments. As Basso and Marangolo (2000, p. 228) clearly and succinctly state:

> The most important contribution of cognitive neuropsychology to aphasia therapy lies in the massive reduction of the theoretically-motivated choices left open to the therapist. Clearly articulated and detailed hypotheses about representations and processing of cognitive functions allow rejection of all those strategies for treatment that are not theoretically justified. The more detailed the cognitive model, the narrower the spectrum of rationally motivated treatments; whereas the less fine-grained the cognitive model, the greater the number of theoretically justifiable therapeutic interventions.

The cognitive domain and mechanisms of change

It should also be acknowledged that a normal language-processing model by itself is less useful than if it were accompanied by a fully developed theory of cognitive rehabilitation (Hillis, 1993). Several researchers have identified the need for the development of a theory of therapy, and have suggested the areas it should cover (e.g. Howard & Hatfield, 1987; Byng & Black, 1995). Minimally, Hillis (1993) suggested that we need:

(a) a thorough analysis of the client's cognitive system pre- and post-therapy and a close examination of what changes have occurred;
(b) a proposed mechanism as to how change occurred; and
(c) a greater understanding as to which characteristics, both of the client and of their neurological damage, relate to the outcome of therapy.

The use of assessment procedures to analyse a client's cognitive system is covered in the preceding chapters of this volume. Mechanisms of change have received little systematic attention, at the level of determining exactly why doing some therapy task results in a specific change in a person's language system. At a broad level, one can classify a number of different therapy approaches. Table 9.1 summarises one possible set of groupings, loosely based on systems developed by Howard and Hatfield (1987) and Lesser and Milroy (1993). These include six categories of therapy approaches: (1) reactivation, (2) relearning, (3) brain reorganisation, (4) cognitive-relay, (5) substitution and (6) compensatory strategies. Further analysis of the mechanisms of change occurring in aphasia therapy was made by Whitworth (1994). The studies in the following chapters predominantly use techniques that fall under the first four categories; substitution and compensatory strategies generally assume a loss of language function, although, as stated earlier, these are not incompatible. Some of the therapy studies use a combination of therapy tasks that incorporate the use of different strategies.

Table 9.1 Summary of different therapy approaches

Approach	Aim of therapy
Reactivation	To reactivate access to impaired language and processing abilities
Relearning	Impaired language procedures or knowledge are re-acquired through learning
Brain reorganisation	To encourage alternative parts of the brain to take over the impaired language function
Cognitive-relay	To seek an alternative route or means of performing the language function, i.e. use intact components of the language system to achieve the impaired function through indirect means (Luria, 1970)
Substitution	To encourage the adoption of an external prosthesis to promote communication
Compensation	To maximise the use of retained language and communication behaviours, without focusing on the impaired functions

While this system classifies the beliefs that therapists have had about how their therapies work, we would emphasise that there is, in most cases, little or no evidence that these are the *real* mechanisms of change. One example is Melodic Intonation Therapy developed by Albert, Sparks and Helm (1973). This therapy approach is based on a rationale of using music-like speech production intended to recruit processes in the intact right hemisphere. The approach can be broadly classified as 'brain reorganisation'. Recent functional brain-imaging work, however, has found no evidence that it does recruit right-hemisphere language (Belin *et al.*, 1996). The findings suggest that intact regions within the left hemisphere are responsible for the improvements.

Hillis's third domain is that of relating the effects of therapy to the characteristics of the patient. That is, do we have a theoretical basis for distinguishing between the people with aphasia who will benefit from a treatment approach and those who will not? While this question is extremely important clinically for therapists needing to choose the most effective treatment approach, it has received little systematic attention (although see Nettleton and Lesser, 1991, for an early attempt in this direction). Howard (2003) argues that this question can be most productively addressed by using a case series approach that allows a closer examination of the nature of improvement in relation to the characteristics of the people with aphasia (see Best, Herbert, Hickin, Osborne, & Howard, 2002, for an example of this approach).

Framework for therapy evaluations: recognising the right therapy

The challenge for speech and language therapists and other professionals involved in the treatment of aphasia is to determine techniques that will be effective for the remediation of particular deficits in particular individuals. Byng and Black (1995) outline a number of critical factors that are involved in therapy and which emphasise that therapy is not just the task and the materials used but a combination of the task, the psycholinguistic concepts conveyed and the interaction between the therapist and client. The parameters used by Byng and Black (1995) to compare and contrast a range of therapies used with clients with sentence-processing difficulties form the basis of the subsequent review format. These have applicability across the spectrum of therapeutic interventions and include:

(a) the focus of therapy, i.e. the language impairment that is being worked on;
(b) the design of the task, i.e. how the task is introduced, the nature of the stimuli, the interaction between the therapist and client, and the type of feedback/facilitation given; and
(c) the hypothesised mechanism of change.

These parameters should provide sufficient detail about the therapy to allow the replication of the technique and to characterise the similarities and differences between techniques.

There is a further issue. It has been documented extensively in the literature that significant improvement in performance does not by itself show that a specific therapy technique is effective. Improvement that is a direct and specific result of therapy must be distinguished from spontaneous recovery and non-specific effects of treatment due to such influences as support, social participation and encouragement. Single case study methodology has been used to distinguish these causes of improvement, thus allowing inferences to be made about the effectiveness of treatment. Comprehensive reviews of the use and types of single case study designs can be found in Howard (1986), Willmes (1990) and Franklin (1997). The basic experimental designs are described in Table 9.2. Experimental designs are often used in combination with one another. Where the experimental design has been stated or is transparent, this is reported in the reviews.

The purpose of the reviews in the following chapters is to provide an overview of therapy techniques available for the treatment of aphasia and to allow therapists to consider and select therapy techniques that may be effective for their clients. We include studies that meet three main criteria:

1   Clients were described in sufficient detail to determine the impaired and retained processes, allowing the extent of similarity with other clients to be determined.
2   Therapy was described in sufficient detail to be replicated.

Table 9.2 Summary of single case study designs

Design	Format
Multiple baseline	Treatment is preceded and followed by testing of the process targeted in treatment and a series of other processes. The other processes may be unrelated and are expected to remain unaffected by treatment (control tasks), as well as be related and show generalised effects of treatment
	Multiple baseline designs may be across behaviours (different processes) or across tasks (same process but in different contexts)
	If treatment is effective, performance on the treated process will improve, with no or minimal improvement on the control task(s) and, where there is generalisation, improvement to some degree on those related to the targeted process
Control task	A simplified version of the multiple baseline design. Treatment is preceded and followed by testing of the process targeted in treatment and an unrelated, control process
	If treatment is effective, performance on the treated process will improve, with no or minimal improvement on the unrelated process
Repeated baseline	Treatment is preceded by repeated testing of the process to be targeted in treatment
	If treatment is effective, significant gains will be found in performance post-treatment and improvement will be significantly greater during the treatment phase than during the baseline period
Item-specific design	Treatment is preceded by testing of performance on items to be treated and untreated items
	If treatment is effective and the effects are item-specific, there will be significant gains seen on treated items, with no or minimal improvement on untreated items (unless generalisation occurs across items)
Cross-over design	Two phases of treatment preceded and followed by the testing of two processes. Process 1 treated initially followed by treatment for Process 2 (this may also involve the cross-over of items as well as different processes)
	If treatment is effective, significant gains will be found in Process 1 only (or the first set of items) following the first phase of treatment, with significant gains in Process 2 (or the second set of items) following the second phase of treatment

3   An adequate experimental design was used so that treatment efficacy could be determined.

The number of studies that unquestionably met these criteria was limited. Consequently, studies have been included that met the majority of the criteria and caveats made where information has been unavailable or extrapolated. Each study has been reviewed in the same format, the template of which is shown in Table 9.3. This aimed to facilitate comparison of studies. The

Table 9.3 Template for therapy reviews

Title, author, date and place of publication of paper

Focus of therapy
- Targeted deficit – impaired process being treated

Therapy approach
- Approach used (see Table 9.1)

Subject details

General information
- Personal information given about client, e.g. age, sex, educational background
- Details of medical history and information given about incident resulting in the aphasia

Overall pattern of language impairments and preservations
- Performance on pre-therapy assessments and author's interpretation of retained and impaired aspects of language

Length of time post-onset

Therapy

Aims of therapy
- Aims of therapy
- Duration of therapy (including frequency and length of sessions and time period)
- Therapy design to evaluate efficacy

Task
- General format and presentation of task

Materials
- Stimuli used (including psycholinguistic nature of stimuli in terms of length, frequency, regularity, etc.)

Hierarchy
- Details on the stages and progression of therapy

Feedback on error
- Therapist response or type of facilitation if the client did not produce a correct response

Feedback if correct
- Therapist response or type of facilitation if the client produced a correct response

Outcome

- Results of measures taken pre- and post-therapy
- Overall pattern of improvement seen and the extent to which the improvement is a consequence of the direct treatment received
- Improvements on task stimuli
- Across task/across stimuli
- Functional improvements
- Hypothesised mechanism of change

Other comments

- Any other relevant information
- Replications of study
- Any improvements suggested by the authors of the study
- General comments on the design of the study and the adequacy of the descriptions of the client and therapy

---

reviews are by no means an exhaustive account; this would indeed be an ambitious aim given the growing number of studies being reported in the literature. Instead, only a representative example has often been included to exemplify a particular type of therapy, or to highlight a certain variation; this is particularly true in the section looking at naming therapy, where there is a considerable number of studies. Attempts have also been made to restrict the reviews to studies that have been published and are therefore widely available. While dissertations and symposium proceedings, such as those collated for the British Aphasiology Society, provide a rich source of material, their more restricted availability has prevented them from being discussed at length here.

The studies reviewed in Chapters 10–13 are summarised at the beginning of each in a table. Detailed reviews follow in order of mention in the table (page numbers of full reviews are also reported in the summary table).

10 Therapy for auditory comprehension

Summary of auditory comprehension studies

Only a limited number of studies have used a cognitive neuropsychological framework to assess and understand auditory comprehension impairments in people with aphasia. Equally, few studies have rigorously evaluated any subsequent therapy with these clients. Those studies reviewed here are listed in Table 10.1.

Only one study (Morris *et al.*, 1996) has stringently tested the therapy used to target impaired auditory phonological analysis. This study provides a range of therapeutic activities and suggests that such a range may be necessary to maintain client motivation. A second study by Gielewski (1989) is, however, also included here, despite the narrower range of techniques used. While efficacy is not rigorously demonstrated in this second study, the author employs a Lurian approach (Luria, 1970) in diagnosis and therefore permits the diagnosis to map onto the cognitive neuropsychological model used in this book.

Grayson, Hilton and Franklin (1997) provide the sole example of an evaluated therapy study targeting the phonological input lexicon. Bastiaanse, Nijober and Taconis's (1993) therapy may also target this area, although the case reported here from this study addresses only the semantic system. Francis, Riddoch and Humphreys (2001a) describe and contrast two therapies used with a client who had problems accessing the semantic system from the phonological input lexicon. Bastiaanse *et al.* (1993) and Behrmann and Lieberthal (1989) address the semantic system from an input perspective.

There are several reasons why there is a paucity of studies of therapy for spoken word comprehension. The first is that most people with aphasia show substantial recovery in understanding single words over the first few months post-onset. As a result, there are few good candidates for therapy aimed at this level in the chronic stages. Therapy for people with substantial impairments in word comprehension is most likely to be suitable in the early stages and it is difficult to design studies that can convincingly demonstrate the specific effects of treatment during the early period when most spontaneous recovery occurs; the study by Grayson *et al.* (1997) is a notably successful exception.

Table 10.1 Summary of auditory comprehension therapy studies reviewed here

Level of impairment	Therapy studies	Therapy tasks
Auditory phonological analysis	Gielewski (1989) (p. 117)	• Spoken word–written word matching with use of visual articulograms and kinaesthetic information to increase discrimination between phonemes • Spoken word–written word matching using CVC word lists • Reinforcement tasks: rhyming tasks, spoken word–picture matching tasks with both semantic and phonological distractors
	Morris and Franklin (1995), Morris *et al.* (1996) (p. 120)	• Phoneme-to-grapheme matching • Phoneme discrimination • Spoken word–picture matching • Spoken word–written word matching • Word judgement (correct/incorrect) • CV/VC judgement (correct/incorrect) Initially lip-reading allowed, progression to free voice and then tape. Decreasing number of distinctive features different in the pairs
Phonological input lexicon	Grayson *et al.* (1997) (p. 121)	• Spoken word–picture matching (rhyming distractors) with lip-reading
Access to the semantic system (via auditory input)	Francis *et al.* (2001a) (p. 126)	Implicit auditory therapy: • Silent reading of definitions of words followed by writing of word • Silent reading and matching of written word triads (synonym judgement) Explicit auditory therapy: • Reading and listening to word definitions followed by repetition of word • Reading, listening to and matching of written word triads (synonym judgement)

Semantic system (via auditory input)	Grayson *et al.* (1997) (p. 121)	• Spoken/written word to object/ picture matching • Categorisation tasks • Matching of written word associates
	Behrmann and Lierberthal (1989) (p. 129)	• Spoken word–picture and written word–picture matching tasks used alongside discussion of distinctive features and identification from semantic cues with increasing semantic relatedness
	Bastiaanse *et al.* (1993) (p. 131)	• Spoken word–picture matching (semantic distractors) • Other semantic tasks, e.g. semantic categorisation

Secondly, therapy typically draws upon intact systems to support treatment of impaired processes. For example, treatment of word production often uses (relatively) intact input processes, such as word comprehension and word repetition, to facilitate output. While input processes can aid word production, word production cannot aid comprehension. Moreover, most people with severe difficulties in word comprehension have even more severe difficulties in output modalities because they are, typically, globally aphasic. The result is that there are normally few people with other intact abilities that could support spoken word comprehension.

The most promising possibility is written word comprehension. It is not at all uncommon for people with difficulties in understanding spoken words to have better understanding of written words, perhaps partly because written words are much less fleeting. Francis *et al.* (2001a) describe such an approach with KW, a client with word meaning deafness. He developed a strategy of visualising the written form of words, enabling him to access meaning and define words that were spoken to him. As redundancy typically aids spoken word comprehension, another possibility is to exploit this in the treatment of comprehension impairments. There are, as far as we know, no therapy studies exploiting this possibility.

EVALUATIONS OF THERAPY STUDIES

Study

Gielewski, E. J. (1989). Acoustic analysis and auditory retraining in the remediation of sensory aphasia. In C. Code and D. Muller (Eds.), *Aphasia therapy* (2nd edn.). London: Whurr Publishers.

Focus of therapy: Auditory phonological analysis (referred to as acoustic agnosia in paper).

Therapy approach: Reactivation.

Client details

General information

The client was a 45-year-old woman who had a left CVA following an overdose and which resulted in severe expressive and receptive aphasia.

Overall pattern of language impairments and preservations

Assessment data were very limited. On initial testing, the client had impaired auditory and written comprehension of sentences (no information was provided of phoneme and word level comprehension although, from the description of therapy, phoneme discrimination was considered to be impaired). Speech was predominantly jargon, with difficulties in repetition and naming. The client was able to write some individual letters but spelling ability was poor.

Time post-onset

The client was 6 weeks post-onset when therapy commenced.

Therapy

Aim

To improve auditory discrimination between phonemes within single CVC segments and within longer sequences. Therapy consisted of a one-hour session each day and continued for 5 months. The first 6 weeks of therapy are described. Progress during therapy is described but no therapy design is used to demonstrate efficacy.

Task	1. Spoken word–written word matching Matching spoken words to written word pairs presented alongside articulograms	2. Visual word lists Matching spoken words to a written word within a word list
Materials	Paired words that differed by a single phoneme or word blend	Written CVC word lists

Hierarchy	Visual clues (a) Lip-reading encouraged (b) No lip-reading	Hierarchy for visual clues and acoustic and visual similarity as in task 1
	Acoustic and visual similarity (a) Acoustically and visually different phonemes, e.g. p/s (b) Acoustically similar but visually different phonemes, e.g. p/k (c) Acoustically and visually similar sounds, e.g. p/b	**Length of List** (a) One word (b) Two words (c) Three words (d) Four words
	Position (a) Word initial (b) Word medial (c) Word final	**Presentation** (a) Provision of written list (b) No list – client must repeat words
Feedback on error	Not specified	Not specified
Feedback if correct	Not specified	Not specified

Reinforcement tasks were used alongside the auditory tasks. These consisted of rhyming tasks, including reading and writing of rhyming words and identification of non-rhyming words, and simple spoken word–picture matching tasks with increasing numbers of pictures and increasing phonological and semantic similarity.

Outcome

Initial progress during the first 6 weeks of therapy is reported. General impressions of reassessment at 3½ months post-onset are also included. Phoneme discrimination of both consonants and vowels improved at the single segment level. Auditory recall was stable up to three segments with recall of four segments not achieved. Improvement in written and auditory sentence comprehension was noted. Speech was fluent, but varied with anxiety. Spelling was good, with the client able to write sentences to dictation.

Evidence of improvement was, therefore, seen on auditory tasks along with widespread improvement on other tasks not related to auditory therapy. No explanations were given of such widespread recovery.

Other comments

While a cognitive neuropsychological framework is not used by the author, the therapy is reported to target auditory phonological analysis and the paper describes therapy in sufficient detail for this to be replicated. Unfortunately, the limited assessment and reassessment data restrict any claims made on the efficacy of the therapy. No quantitative information is provided regarding improvement. Furthermore, the client was still within a period where spontaneous recovery may be expected and such widespread gains in performance may well be a consequence of this. The inclusion of this study does, however, stress the continued clinical success of this approach and is one of the few published therapy studies targeting this area. Sound clinical efficacy studies are required to evaluate the therapy. The authors suggest that such therapy needs to be carried out daily if improvement is to be seen.

Study

Morris, J., Franklin, S., Ellis, A. W., Turner J. E., & Bailey, P. J. (1996). Remediating a speech perception deficit in an aphasic patient. *Aphasiology*, *10*, 137–158.

Focus of therapy: Auditory phonological analysis (word sound deafness).

Therapy approach: Reactivation.

Client details

General information

JS was a 73-year-old man who was a retired factory worker. He had a single left CVA resulting in a global aphasia. A CT scan showed areas of low attenuation in both hemispheres, particularly in the left basal ganglia.

Overall pattern of language impairments and preservations

JS's verbal output was restricted to the occasional single word, stereotypical phrases and neologisms. He relied predominantly on 'yes' and 'no' and non-verbal methods to communicate. Auditory comprehension was characterised by impaired pre-phonetic auditory processing as shown by impaired performance on assessments of gap detection, formant frequency discrimination, frequency modulation detection and pitch discrimination. At a phonemic level, he had impaired auditory discrimination of minimal pairs and single words. Written comprehension was also impaired, although to a lesser extent, supporting a diagnosis of central semantic impairment. The authors suggest that JS had difficulties in auditory phonological analysis (word sound deafness) with additional central semantic and output difficulties.

Time post-onset

JS was one year post-onset when this therapy commenced.

Therapy

Aim

To improve phonological discrimination. Therapy consisted of 12 sessions over a 6-week period. A multiple-baseline with control task therapy study design was used to measure efficacy.

See table on p. 122 for outline of therapy procedure.

Outcome

JS improved significantly on tasks involving minimal and maximal pair discrimination and pre-phonetic auditory discrimination tasks. There was a trend for improvement in the tests of auditory lexical decision and auditory synonym judgement. There was a significant improvement in repetition but no improvement in naming performance. No improvement was seen in the control task of written synonym judgement.

JS showed a significant improvement in his ability to discriminate speech sounds that generalised across auditory comprehension tasks. This improved discrimination also aided his repetition. Improvement was attributed to the therapy programme. No improvement was noted in unrelated tasks. No information was provided as to whether this improvement was maintained once therapy was discontinued or about improvements in functional comprehension.

Other comments

With rigorous initial assessment and reassessment data presented, this study permits a thorough evaluation of the therapy with the reported client. It is discussed in sufficient detail to replicate the therapy. JS is also described (with more details of therapy) in Morris and Franklin (1995).

Study

Grayson, E., Hilton, R., & Franklin, S. E. (1997). Early intervention in a case of jargon aphasia: efficacy of language comprehension therapy. *European Journal of Disorders of Communication, 32*, 257–276.

Focus of therapy: Phonological input lexicon and the semantic system.

	1. Phoneme–grapheme matching	2. Phoneme discrimination	3. Spoken word–picture matching	4. Spoken word–written word matching	5. Word judgement	6. Same or different judgement
Task	Matching spoken phonemes to written letters	Same–different judgements of phonemes	Matching spoken words to pictures	Matching spoken words to written words	Judge whether word matches picture	Same–different judgements of words
Materials	C + /ə/ stimuli matched to choice of three letters	Pairs of C + /ə/	CVC words. Distractors phonologically related. Differed in either initial or final consonant	CVC words. Distractors phonologically related. Differed in either initial or final consonant		CV or VC nonwords. Judged whether same or different
Hierarchy	**Phonological similarity** (a) Three distinctive features different (b) Two distinctive features different (c) One distinctive feature different	**Presentation** (a) With lip-reading (b) Free voice (c) Tape recorder	None	None	None	None
Feedback on error	Information regarding accuracy Repeated with reduced level of difficulty					
Feedback if correct	Information regarding accuracy					

Therapy approach: Reactivation.

Client details

General information

LR was a 50-year-old man and worked as a sales director. He had a CVA resulting in a dense right hemiplegia and visual agnosia. A CT scan showed an infarct in the left temporoparietal region.

Overall pattern of language impairments and preservations

LR presented with a severe auditory and written comprehension impairment at the single-word and sentence levels. His speech was characterised by English jargon and neologisms. He was unable to repeat, read aloud or write. Word retrieval did not improve with presentation of semantic or phonemic cues. On testing before the therapy, LR was significantly impaired in minimal pair discrimination, auditory lexical decision, picture matching of both spoken and written words, and general word semantics. He was also impaired in sentence comprehension. The authors hypothesised that LR had an impairment of pre-lexical processing (auditory phonological analysis), difficulty accessing the lexical form within the phonological input lexicon and a central semantic impairment. He also had an additional syntactic deficit.

Time post-onset

Therapy began 4 weeks post-onset.

Therapy

Aims

Therapy consisted of three phases, each corresponding to a separate aim:

1 To improve LR's semantic ability.
2 To continue to improve LR's semantic ability and improve auditory comprehension.
3 To increase LR's ability to process up to three key words in sentence-level therapy.

The first therapy phase consisted of a one-hour session, 5 days per week, for 4 weeks. The second phase consisted of three 15-minute sessions each week for 3 weeks. The duration and frequency of the third phase of therapy was not specified.

A cross-over design was used to evaluate treatment efficacy, where LR was reassessed following each phase of therapy.

Phase 1: semantic therapy

Task	1. Spoken/written word to object/ picture matching Sentence with key word at end. Task was to select appropriate object or picture	2. Categorisation task Sorting pictures into categories	3. Matching of written word associates Choosing associates from word lists
Materials	Common objects, pictures of objects and corresponding written words	Pictures within categories. Categories used not stated	Sheet of 10 words divided into two columns
Hierarchy	(a) Two choices, target/ unrelated distractor (b) If 80% correct, gradual increase in number of choices (up to 6) (c) Increased relatedness to target	(a) Two distant categories (b) Increasing semantic relatedness (c) Increased number of groups (d) Written words as well/instead of pictures (e) Verbal presentation with *no* written/picture stimulus	Number of items reduced if difficult
Feedback on error	(a) Repetition (b) Gesture (c) Semantic information (d) Combination of above	(a) Attention drawn to choice (b) Given name (c) Further information (d) Gesture (e) Written information (f) Combination of above	(a) Reading words (b) Additional semantic information (c) Gesture
Feedback if correct	(a) Verbal reinforcement (b) Repetition of name (c) Visual feedback – ticks	Visual feedback – ticks	Visual feedback – ticks

Phase 2: auditory training and semantic therapy

The semantic component of the therapy was the same as for the first phase but the numbers of words and pictures were increased.

Task	1. Spoken word–picture matching with rhyming foils Spoken word matched to choice of three pictures. Lip-reading encouraged	2. Spoken word–picture matching with minimal pairs Spoken word matched to choice of two pictures. Lip-reading encouraged
Materials	Hand-drawn pictures of three rhyming words. Five sets of pictures	Black and white minimal pair photographs
Hierarchy	None	None
Feedback on error	(a) Feedback regarding incorrect (b) Item repeated (c) Repetition of task until correct picture given	(a) Feedback regarding incorrect (b) Item repeated (c) Repetition of task until correct picture given
Feedback if correct	(a) Verbal reinforcement (b) Visual feedback – ticks	(a) Verbal reinforcement (b) Visual feedback – ticks

Phase 3: sentence therapy

Task	1. Selection of three named objects in a sequence Sequence of words. Clients must select corresponding objects from a choice of five. Lip-reading encouraged	2. Spoken sentence–action picture matching Spoken sentence. Match to action pictures
Materials	Unrelated objects	Action pictures
Hierarchy	(a) Increased number of distractor items (5 to 9) (b) Initial gestural support	Number of key words: (a) Two key words (b) Three key words Number of distractors: (a) Four pictures (b) Eight pictures
Feedback	Not specified	Not specified

Outcome

Following the first phase of therapy, LR showed significant improvement in written word–picture matching. Following phase 2 of therapy, significant improvement was seen in minimal pair selection and in spoken word–picture matching, but no further improvement in written word comprehension. Auditory sentence comprehension did not change significantly following phase 1 or 2 of therapy but improved significantly following phase 3.

Overall, therapy resulted in significant improvements in auditory discrimination, auditory and written single-word comprehension, and in auditory sentence comprehension. The patterns of improvement suggest specific effects of treatment. Some evidence of generalisation was noted, as effects were not item-specific. Functional comprehension was also shown to have improved. LR's speech also improved post-therapy with a reduction in neologisms and inappropriate responses. While improvement in verbal output cannot conclusively be attributed to therapy (as opposed to spontaneous recovery), the authors believe that LR's improvement in auditory to semantic processing could underlie improved expressive communication and suggest how this may be so.

Other comments

The authors suggest that the pattern of impairment, timing of therapy and therapy approach were similar to those reported by Jones (1989). The current case study was conducted by a busy clinician who acknowledged that collating pre-therapy baseline assessment data would have been useful, but difficult, given the importance of early intervention for the client. The specific effects of treatment following the three phases of the therapy programme would, however, suggest that the improvement is partly a consequence of therapy rather than spontaneous recovery alone.

Study

Francis, D. R., Riddoch, M. J., & Humphreys, G. W. (2001a). Cognitive rehabilitation of word meaning deafness. *Aphasiology*, *15*, 749–766.

Focus of therapy: Access from the phonological input lexicon to semantics (word meaning deafness).

Therapy approach: Reactivation during explicit auditory therapy. Compensation during implicit auditory therapy.

Client details

General information

KW was a 63-year-old Jamaican-born man who emigrated to England as a young adult. He was a retired bus driver who enjoyed attending further education classes. He had a CVA that resulted in a left parietal infarct.

Overall pattern of language impairments and preservations

KW was unable to understand words unless they were written down. His speech was characterised by a slight anomia and some phonemic jargonaphasia. On formal testing, he was able to match environmental sounds to pictures and to match spoken and written words. His judgement of word and non-word minimal pairs was intact. He had minor problems with lexical decision in both the spoken and written modalities, performing just outside the normal range. He scored within the normal range on the three-picture version of the Pyramids and Palm Trees Test (Howard & Patterson, 1992). He had difficulty accessing the meaning of spoken words, finding it difficult to match spoken words to pictures, to define spoken words and perform auditory synonym judgements. His auditory comprehension performance was characterised by imageability and frequency effects. His performance on tasks assessing access to semantic information from written words was significantly better than his auditory comprehension. The authors proposed that KW had word meaning deafness, with preserved early auditory processing and lexical access but impaired auditory access to meaning despite preserved orthographic access to the same information. In spelling, KW showed some of the characteristics of surface dysgraphia, with a high proportion of phonologically based errors and some confusion of homophones. He showed no regularity effect, as he was able to write some irregular words. His writing thus reflected a heavy reliance on the sub-lexical route alongside some use of a lexical writing route.

Time post-onset

KW was 4 years post-onset at the time of the current study.

Therapy

Aim

To improve the comprehension of spoken words and to contrast the effectiveness of two types of therapy: (a) implicit auditory therapy and (b) explicit auditory therapy. Implicit auditory therapy targeted auditory comprehension only indirectly via the silent reading of written words. Explicit therapy directly targeted KW's difficulty in accessing semantic information from spoken words. The therapy was carried out by KW at home using worksheets completed 3–4 times a week. Each phase of therapy lasted for 2 weeks. A cross-over item-specific design was used to demonstrate efficacy.

	Therapy 1: Implicit auditory therapy		Therapy 2: Explicit auditory therapy	
Task	**1. Reading of definitions** Silently read the definition, try to 'fix the meaning' of the word and then write the word down four times while thinking of the word's meaning	**2. Written synonym judgement** Silently read written word triads and match the treated word to another word in the triad	**3. Reading and listening to definitions** Read the definitions while listening to a taped version, try to 'fix the meaning' of the word and then repeat the word four times while thinking of the meaning	**4. Written and auditory synonym judgement** Listen to and read each triad of words and then match the treated word to another in the triad
Materials	78 words that KW was able to define from the written word but not from the spoken word. The words were divided into three matched sets of 26 words: (a) Set for therapy 1 (b) Set for therapy 2 (c) Control set			
Hierarchy	None	None	None	None
Feedback on error	Not specified	Not specified	Not specified	Not specified
Feedback if correct	Not specified	Not specified	Not specified	Not specified

Outcome

Before therapy, baseline performance in defining the spoken words was stable with comparable accuracy across the three word sets. At the end of therapy 1 (implicit therapy), improvement was seen in the definitions of the treated words but there was a significant decline in performance 2 weeks later. Following therapy 2 (explicit therapy), improvement was seen in the definitions of the treated words. No improvement was seen in performance on the control set following either therapy. During therapy, definitions were learned quicker with therapy 1 than therapy 2. When the treatment sets were compared, there was no significant difference in the degree of improvement immediately post-therapy. A significant difference was, however, seen 2 weeks post-therapy with the effects of the explicit therapy being more durable. Both therapies resulted in item-specific improvement with no generalisation to untreated words.

In contrast to the authors' predictions, explicit auditory therapy was not more effective than implicit therapy immediately post-therapy. KW improved following the implicit therapy as he adopted a compensatory strategy. The therapy involved repeated writing of the words and thus his spelling improved. During the post-therapy baseline, he was able to visualise the correct spelling enabling access to the word's meaning via the written form. The explicit therapy may have had a more durable effect, since it directly improved the link between the auditory representation of the word and its meaning. Alternatively, hearing the word alongside the written form may have enabled KW to visualise the written form when he heard the word in isolation. The improvements seen are likely to be due to therapy, as KW was a long time post-onset and performance was stable before therapy.

Other comments

Information about KW's assessment can be found in Hall and Riddoch (1997). The study shows the successful development of a strategy that compensated for KW's difficulties in accessing the meaning of words from spoken words, although this meant that the efficacy of the implicit therapy could not be assessed. It also shows that direct treatment of the impairment resulted in improvement in the auditory comprehension of a small set of words, over a very short period of therapy.

Study

Behrmann, M., & Lieberthal, T. (1989). Category-specific treatment of a lexical-semantic deficit: a single case study of global aphasia. *British Journal of Disorders of Communication*, *24*, 281–299.

Focus of therapy: Semantic system (via auditory and written comprehension).

Therapy approach: Reactivation.

Client details

General information

CH was a 57-year-old male engineer who suffered a cerebral infarct resulting in dense hemiplegia and global aphasia. A CT scan showed left middle cerebral infarct, involving the frontal, temporal and parietal lobes as well as the internal capsule.

Overall pattern of language impairments and preservations

On initial testing, CH's speech was restricted to jargon. He was unable to repeat or read words aloud. Both auditory and visual lexical decision were impaired but performance was above chance. Written and spoken single-word comprehension was impaired with selection of semantic distractors. Some ability to compute broad semantic representations was retained, but CH was impaired in tasks requiring access to more detailed semantic representations (e.g. synonym judgement). In a category sorting task, the ability to sort animals was significantly higher than chance, but performance on other categories was not significantly different from what might be expected at chance level. CH was considered to present with a semantic deficit at a single-word level.

Time post-onset

CH was at least 3 months post-onset when therapy commenced.

Therapy

Aim

To improve written and spoken comprehension of single words via category-specific rehabilitation. Therapy consisted of 15 one-hour sessions (five sessions per category) over a 6-week period, plus additional home exercises. A control task therapy study design was used to demonstrate the efficacy of therapy.

Task	1. Explain distinctive features	2. Presentation of picture alongside written/ verbal label	3. Selection of picture from semantic cues	4. Spoken–written word matching
Materials	Pictures within three categories of transport, furniture and body parts. Corresponding words.			
Hierarchy	(a) Generic (superordinate features) (b) Distinctive features		(a) Distant semantic distractors (b) Close semantic distractors	(a) Distant semantic distractors (b) Close semantic distractors
Feedback on error	Not specified	Not specified	Not specified	Not specified
Feedback if correct	Not specified	Not specified	Not specified	Not specified

Home exercises included written word–picture matching and using a dictionary to identify the semantic features of the categories and individual items within those categories.

Outcome

CH showed improved sorting of treated items into categories with some generalisation to untreated items within the treated categories of transport and body parts. Some generalisation was noted to untreated categories, but in two of the three categories it was non-significant. Significant generalisation to one untreated category was considered unrepresentative of performance. Performance improved on other semantic tasks involving wide semantic discrimination, but no improvement was recorded on narrow semantic judgements. CH's performance on the control task (syntactic comprehension) remained unchanged.

   CH's semantics, therefore, improved for the treated categories. The experimental design permits post-therapy changes to be attributed to therapy. The authors proposed that CH was able to use newly learned semantic information to sort items into categories and that he could carry over this newly acquired knowledge to items sharing class membership and semantic features. Also some changes were noted in his broad semantic knowledge and his ability to access superordinate information.

Other comments

The authors suggest that hierarchical, category-specific semantic therapy is useful in the remediation of semantic deficits, as this reflects the normal organisation of information.

Study

Bastiaanse, R., Nijober, S., & Taconis, M. (1993). The Auditory Language Comprehension Programme: a description and case study. *European Journal of Disorders of Communication*, *28*, 415–433.

Focus of therapy: Semantic system (via auditory comprehension). The programme targets access to the auditory input lexicon and semantics, but the case reported here was trained on the semantic level only.

Therapy approach: Reactivation.

Client details

General information

Mr S was a 37-year-old former teacher and a native speaker of Dutch. Involvement in a traffic accident left him with a brain contusion and a frontoparietal skull fracture. A craniectomy was performed to decompress a haematoma in the parietotemporal part of the left hemisphere, leaving Mr S with a right hemiparesis, homonymous hemianopia and aphasia.

Overall pattern of language impairments and preservations

Mr S presented with severely impaired auditory and written comprehension of single words and sentences. Errors on auditory and written comprehension tasks were predominantly semantic in nature. Expressively, Mr S was unable to retrieve single words in a naming test; responses were characterised by semantic jargon and perseverations. Spontaneous output was fluent and paragrammatic, with no communicative value. Mr S was diagnosed with a Wernicke's type aphasia with a prominent semantic deficit. In addition, the authors considered Mr S had difficulties with symbolic functions and so therapy on the ALCP was preceded by Visual Action Therapy (Helm-Estabrooks, Fitzpatrick, & Barresi, 1982).

Time post-onset

Mr S was 3 months post-onset when therapy commenced.

Therapy

Aim

To improve auditory comprehension of single words using the Auditory Language Comprehension Programme (ALCP). The ALCP is a hierarchical programme with a Base-10 format. Stages are repeated until the client performs without error. The programme has three levels:

1   Phonological level – items linked phonologically (similar vowels).
2   Semantic level – items linked semantically.
3   Complement level – items linked phonologically, via lexical-morphological correspondence or via a combination of phonological and semantic correspondence.

Mr S was treated using the semantic level and hence only the efficacy of this section is considered here.

The ALCP was used between two and five times per week for 12 weeks. In addition to the ALCP tasks, association and categorisation tasks, and training of written word comprehension, were also carried out. The frequency with which these tasks were used and their precise nature are not reported. A multiple-baseline therapy design was used to monitor efficacy.

Task	**Spoken word–picture matching task** Spoken word presented with a choice of four pictures
Materials	High-frequency, highly imageable nouns Unrelated distractors bore no relationship with either target or other distractors Semantically related distractors linked to target via coordination or collocation
Hierarchy	Semantic relatedness across four blocks: (a) Three unrelated distractors (b) Two unrelated distractors, one related distractor (c) One unrelated distractor, two related distractors (d) Three related distractors Length within each block: (a) Polysyllabic words (b) Monosyllabic words
Feedback on error	Distractor concept discussed and contrasted with target
Feedback if correct	Concept discussed via additional tasks listed as: pointing to object in room/on himself; producing/imitating corresponding gesture; giving a description; drawing/copying the object; producing the corresponding sound; visual presentation of word; or presenting characteristics of object

Outcome

Mr S completed the ALCP semantic stage, achieving 100% successful performance. Significant improvement was reported in auditory comprehension of single words, with some generalisation to untreated stimuli on a spoken word–picture matching test. Significant improvement on tests of written single-word comprehension and auditory sentence comprehension were also recorded. Spontaneous output had also significantly improved despite still being characterised by word-finding problems. Paragrammatism, while still present, had diminished. While Mr S improved on trained stimuli, the authors suggest that he still may not have access to the full meaning of the target.

Improvement was reported in all aspects of comprehension and production. The authors do not state how therapy can account for such improvement. The authors argue, however, that the increased improvement in single-word auditory comprehension, compared to sentence comprehension, is indicative of effective therapy.

Other comments

Any improvements that were due to therapy were probably a consequence of the tasks as a whole rather than just the spoken word–picture matching task; however, these are not described in sufficient detail to evaluate how therapy may have worked. Improvement may also have been a consequence of spontaneous recovery, rather than specific effects due to therapy. The therapy is, however, described in sufficient detail to replicate and evaluate the effects in a more rigorous way.

11 Therapy for word retrieval and production

Summary of naming studies

Unlike auditory comprehension, there are many studies of therapy designed to improve word retrieval. Indeed, studies targeting word retrieval form the bulk of the therapeutic literature and address a range of issues at the centre of the cognitive neuropsychology approach. The majority of studies have focused on the semantic system, the phonological output lexicon (or access to it), or a combination of these processing components, either within the same or separate therapy tasks. Although several studies do stipulate that therapy has been directed at accessing the phonological output lexicon from semantics rather than the lexicon itself, these studies are presented together here. The papers presented here also include a small number of studies that have looked at short-term facilitation of naming performance rather than therapy per se (e.g. Howard, Patterson, Franklin, Orchard-Lisle, & Morton, 1985; Le Dorze, Boulay, Gaudreau, & Brassard, 1994). These studies have been included as they use tasks that have later been developed into therapy tasks. In addition, it has been suggested that a client's response to facilitation tasks may predict their response to therapy (Hickin, Best, Herbert, Howard, & Osborne, 2002). The studies reviewed here are listed in Table 11.1.

An important distinction to be drawn in this section is between therapy that aims to treat semantic or phonological impairments and therapy that uses semantic or phonological treatment tasks (see Nickels, 2002b, for a comprehensive discussion). The first type of therapy is defined by the *underlying processing deficit* that is the focus of therapy (i.e. semantic or phonological), while the latter draws on *tasks* that employ semantic and phonological techniques. When interpreting the literature, it is essential to consider each study from each of these two perspectives. The studies reported in this chapter have therefore been set out according to both the underlying deficit targeted as well as the area targeted in therapy (see Table 11.1). It can clearly be seen that no direct relationship exists between the two aspects. While some studies stress the importance of treating semantic impairments with semantic tasks (e.g. Nettleton & Lesser, 1991) and others use phonological tasks to target phonological deficits (Miceli, Amitrano, Capasso, & Caramazza, 1996), others

Table 11.1 Summary of naming therapy studies reviewed here

Level of impairment	Therapy studies	Area targeted in therapy	Therapy tasks
Semantic system	Nettleton and Lesser (1991) (see p. 141)	Semantic	• Word-to-picture matching (name, function and written form) • Semantic judgements (category and attributes) • Categorisation
Semantic system and/or phonological output lexicon (according to client)	Howard *et al.* (1985) (p. 144) NB: Impairment for each client not specified	Semantic	• Spoken word-to-picture matching with semantic distractors • Written word-to-picture matching with semantic distractors • Yes/no question about item meaning
		Phonological	• Repetition of picture name • Phonemic cueing • Rhyme judgement
	Marshall *et al.* (1990) (p. 146)	Semantic/ phonological	• Written word-to-picture matching (with reading aloud)
	Pring *et al.* (1993) (p. 149)	Semantic/ phonological	• Word-to-picture matching (with reading aloud) • Picture-to-word matching (with reading aloud)
	Hillis and Caramazza (1994) (p. 151)	Semantic/ phonological	• Naming followed by a hierarchy of cues, including sentence completion, initial phoneme, and modelling the word. • Oral reading and word-to-picture matching
	Hillis (1989) (p. 157)	Semantic/ phonological	• Spoken naming using a cueing hierarchy
Phonological output lexicon (or access to it)	Bruce and Howard (1987) (p. 159)	Phonological	• Initial letter identification on microcomputer with repetition of computer-generated phoneme
	Nettleton and Lesser (1991) (p. 141)	Phonological	• Repetition of picture name • Naming with progressive phonological cues

Hillis and Caramazza (1994) (p. 151)	Phonological	• Teaching of orthographic-to-phonological conversion (OPC) rules • Teaching of phonological-to-orthographic conversion (POC) rules
Le Dorze et al. (1994) (p. 162)	Semantic	*Formal-semantic therapy – tasks involving semantic comprehension with spoken and written word used* • Spoken word-to-picture matching • Written word-to-picture matching • Semantic judgement – yes/no questions *Semantic therapy – tasks involving semantic comprehension where word form not presented* • Spoken definition-to-picture matching • Written definition-to-picture matching • Semantic judgement task as in formal-semantic therapy
Boyle and Coelho (1995) (p. 164)	Semantic	• Guided verbalisation of semantic features (supported by visual semantic feature chart) during picture naming
Lowell et al. (1995) (p. 167)	Semantic	• Self-generated semantic cue words read aloud by therapist • Client attempts to name picture
Miceli et al. (1996) (p. 169)	Phonological	• Reading of target items (with and without picture) • Repetition of target items • Picture naming
Howard and Harding (1998) (p. 173)	Phonological	• Use of alphabet board to retrieve spoken word
Francis et al. (2002) (p. 175)	Semantic	• Circumlocution-induced naming

Level of impairment	Therapy studies	Area targeted in therapy	Therapy tasks
	Hickin *et al.* (2002) (p. 177)	Phonological/ orthographic	• Spoken naming with progressive phonological cues • Spoken naming with progressive orthographic cues
	Nickels (2002a) (p. 179)	Phonological	• Attempted picture naming • Reading aloud • Delayed written copying of word following silent reading
Phonological (via the orthographical system)	De Partz (1986) (p. 206)	Phonological	• Generation of code word for each letter • Segmentation of initial phoneme from code word • Production of phoneme on presentation of grapheme • Phoneme blending
	Nickels (1992) (p. 209)	Phonological	• Generation of code word for each letter • Segmentation of initial phoneme from code word • Production of phoneme on presentation of grapheme • Phoneme blending
	Spencer *et al.* (2000) (p. 181)	Phonological	• Semantic and phonological cueing hierarchy using superordinate category, rhyme, phoneme and grapheme cues
Phonological assembly	Franklin *et al.* (2002) (p. 184)	Phonological assembly	• Phoneme discrimination • Self-monitoring spoken words

(e.g. Howard *et al.*, 1985) do not specify the nature of the deficit and use both types of tasks. Nettleton and Lesser (1991), however, interpreted the lack of improvement, following semantic tasks, in clients whose underlying impairment was in phonological encoding (i.e. with phonological assembly) as evidence that therapy may be driven by the model – that is, semantic impairments required semantic tasks and phonological impairments required phonological tasks. The blurring of these boundaries results in some difficulty in categorising and interpreting the outcomes of many therapies aimed at improving spoken word production.

This is confounded further by the inherent activation of semantics when working on phonology, and vice versa. While one process may not be the explicit target of therapy, it may still be intrinsically activated during a task; for example, the meaning of the word may be activated during a repetition task, particularly if repetition is carried out in the presence of a picture. Sometimes studies involve very similar therapy tasks (with very similar effects) but the tasks are described as having very different aims by the authors. Howard (2000) suggested that the overall evidence is that 'semantic' and 'phonological' therapies are effectively indistinguishable: the content of the tasks is the same – providing meaning–phonology pairings and the same patients benefit from both/either.

Few studies have attempted to tease out the impact of specific therapies on clients where authors may not expect therapy to be effective, a path which may be quite illuminating (see Nettleton & Lesser, 1991).

Because the focus of this book is on word rather than sentence processing, we have not considered therapy studies where the focus is specifically verb retrieval. This is because verb retrieval is typically targeted as part of a strategy aimed at improving sentence formulation and production. The reader is directed to cases reported, for example, by Murray and Karcher (2000) or Raymer and Ellsworth (2002) to examine the impact of therapy on verb retrieval. As mentioned earlier, interpreting the implications of verb retrieval studies requires discussion of models not outlined here.

A comment of a more general nature, although no less relevant, is that interpretation of the literature is somewhat further muddied by the nature of the assessment data reported, especially regarding the integrity of the semantic system. Good comprehension of high-imageability single words, for example, is often seen as demonstrating that the semantic system is intact and that the nature of the deficit is phonological. While this may indeed be the case for certain people, further in-depth assessment of semantics using more demanding tasks or materials (e.g. synonym judgements or comprehension of low-imageability words) may reveal some impairment of semantics (for further discussion, see Cole-Virtue & Nickels, 2004). The implication of this is that the clinician needs to be alert to a possible different underlying deficit from that reported; one solution to this would be a recommendation that semantics is reported in more depth than simply single-word comprehension using word-to-picture matching.

A final point in the interpretation of the literature is the complexity introduced by the reporting of a number of clients, within the same publication, with different underlying impairments, encountering different therapy techniques and experiencing different outcomes. Some studies of this nature have been included here and efforts have been taken to interpret the outcomes in a manner consistent with the reporting of other studies.

Despite the above caveats, there are some general pointers to emerge from the array of therapy studies addressing impaired spoken word production. Studies targeting the semantic system that have used semantic tasks, such as semantic features or cues, semantic judgements, categorisation or word-to-picture matching (e.g. Nettleton & Lesser, 1991), have shown that semantic tasks can improve semantic deficits. Studies targeting the phonological output lexicon, either the lexicon itself or access from semantics, have employed a wider range of methods and have usually ensured access to phonology by producing the spoken word form as well as, in some studies, drawing on the semantic system (e.g. Le Dorze et al., 1994; Spencer et al., 2000). The former has been via such methods as naming from phonemic cues (e.g. Nettleton & Lesser, 1991), repetition (Howard et al., 1985) and reading and repetition (e.g. Miceli et al., 1996). Outcomes of these studies generally show that production of the spoken word form in therapy by the client plays a central role in increasing spoken word production. In comparison, phonological assembly has received less attention. Franklin et al. (2002) targeted auditory phonological analysis and the client's ability to self-monitor spoken output to target phonological assembly skills. An earlier study by Cubelli, Foresti and Consolini (1988) employed a range of tasks in their efforts to improve phonemic production, including manipulating written words and syllables, producing progressively longer and more complex (in both phonological and syntactic terms) words and sentences.

The use of other routes within the processing system is also demonstrated clearly in studies where spoken naming is targeted, be it a primary or secondary target. A series of studies has drawn on the orthographic system (e.g. cueing lexical representations in the phonological output lexicon through the initial grapheme [Nickels, 1992] and teaching orthographic-to-phonological conversion (OPC) rules [De Partz, 1986]), each with the ultimate aim of improving spoken word production. These studies are reported in Chapter 12 as they sit logically with other studies addressing reading, although they are equally relevant to spoken production (for further examples of similar therapy, see Bachy-Langedock & De Partz, 1989; Bastiaanse, Bosje, & Franssen, 1996). Hillis (1989) reports a client whose therapy aimed to improve written and spoken naming using a similar approach (see this chapter with cross-reference to Chapter 12). Even when not the focus of therapy, the use of written input where the client can draw on orthographic knowledge has often been considered beneficial when working at the post-semantic stage.

A key theme to emerge from this literature is whether treatment is likely to result in item-specific effects or in generalisation to untreated items. In some studies where either semantic tasks have been employed or the deficit has been of a semantic origin, generalisation to untreated items has been reported (e.g. Boyle & Coelho, 1995; Hillis, 1989; Howard et al., 1985) (but see Howard, 2000, for a discussion of the lack of any convincing evidence for generalisation). Where the deficit is considered to relate to output phonology, generalisation to untreated items has generally been found not to occur (e.g. Miceli *et al.*, 1996); one exception is seen with client MC (Nettleton & Lesser, 1991). In addition, although many of the studies show statistically significant improvements in naming, improvement is often rather limited (in terms of the number of items learned). In aphasia, therefore, it appears that it is not just the ability to retrieve known words that is impaired, but the ability to re-learn words may also be affected. Due to the item-specific nature of improvement and the small number of words acquired, it is also very important to target the retrieval of words that are functionally useful to the client.

EVALUATIONS OF THERAPY STUDIES

Study

Nettleton, J., & Lesser, R. (1991). Therapy for naming difficulties in aphasia: Application of a cognitive neuropsychological model. *Journal of Neurolinguistics*, 6, 139–157.

Focus of therapy: Semantic system and phonological output lexicon.

Target of therapy: Semantic/phonological.

Therapy approach: Reactivation.

Client details

General information

Six clients were included in the study. All had had a CVA; only PD and NC had had CT scans, both showing left parietal region damage. PD was a 55-year-old man who had worked as a car park attendant. FF was a 68-year-old former labourer. DF was a 63-year-old housewife. MC was a 57-year-old housewife. MH was a 72-year-old woman who had previously owned a bakery. NC was a 74-year-old woman who had worked as a nursing sister.

Overall pattern of language impairments and preservations

PD had a fluent aphasia; FF had a fluent aphasia with 'empty speech' and poor auditory comprehension. DF had severe word-finding difficulties. MC was non-fluent and agrammatic. MH presented with higher level comprehension problems, fluent speech and word-retrieval difficulties. NC had moderate comprehension difficulties, fluent speech and word-finding difficulties.

The clients were allocated to one of three groups based on an analysis of errors on the Boston Naming Test (Goodglass, Kaplan, & Weintraub, 2001), their performance on spoken word-to-picture matching, and a comparison of their performance on comprehension and repetition tasks. PD and FF were considered to have a semantic impairment. They scored below the normal range on picture matching, selecting close semantic distractors. They produced mainly semantic errors on the Boston Naming Test and could be phonemically cued to produce a semantic associate of the target word which they then accepted as correct. DF and MC were considered to have an impairment of the phonological output lexicon. They scored within the normal range on picture matching and produced circumlocution errors in naming. Their repetition performance was equivalent to their performance on auditory comprehension tasks. MH and NC also scored within the normal range on picture matching. They produced phonological errors on the Boston Naming Test and presented with difficulties in repetition. They were considered to have an impairment at the level of phonological assembly (referred to by Nettleton & Lesser as the phonological output buffer).

Time post-onset

The clients varied considerably in their time post-onset. FF was 3 months, PD was 6 months, MH was 8 months, DF was 1 year, NC was 3 years and MC was 8 years post-stroke.

Therapy

Aim

To compare performance on 'model-motivated' therapy versus 'model-inappropriate' therapy. PD and FF received appropriate semantic therapy, DF and MC received appropriate phonological therapy, and MH and NC received inappropriate semantic therapy. Therapy consisted of one-hour sessions, twice a week for 8 weeks. A repeated multiple-baseline therapy design was used to compare performance on treated and untreated items.

(a) Semantic therapy

Task	Word-to-picture matching	Yes/no judgements about pictures	Categorisation
	Matching words to pictures: (a) By spoken name (b) By function (c) By written name	Making judgements based on: (a) Category information (b) Attributes	Sorting pictures into categories

Materials	Selection of object line drawings from a set of 50 treated items		
Hierarchy	Increasing semantic relatedness	None	None
Feedback	Not specified	Not specified	Not specified

(b) Phonological therapy

Task	Repetition of picture name	Rhyme judgement Judging whether the spoken name of the picture rhymes with another word	Naming with progressive phonemic cues
Materials	Names of objects from a set of 50 treated items	Selection of object line drawings from a set of 50 treated items	Selection of object line drawings from a set of 50 treated items
Hierarchy	None	None	None
Feedback	Not specified	Not specified	Not specified

Outcome

Following appropriate semantic therapy, PD showed significant improvement in his naming of the treated items. This improvement was maintained 2 months post-therapy. There was no significant change on untreated items. FF showed a non-significant trend of improvement with a qualitative change in his errors (more closely related semantic associates following therapy). Following appropriate phonological therapy, both DF and MC showed significant improvement on the treated items. MC also showed significant gains in his naming of untreated items. Following model-inappropriate semantic therapy, MH and NC showed no significant improvement on either treated or untreated items.

Appropriate semantic and phonological therapy for the four clients resulted in improvement, although this improvement was not significant for FF. The improvement seen is likely to be a consequence of therapy, as the clients were beyond the phase of spontaneous recovery and showed a relatively stable pre-therapy baseline. Inappropriate semantic therapy for the clients thought to have a difficulty at the level of phonological assembly resulted in no improvement.

Other comments

This study provides appropriate assessment data and describes the therapy in sufficient detail to replicate. The authors propose that the results of this study suggest that clients with naming difficulties should not be treated as a homogeneous group but that therapy should be motivated by an analysis of their impairment. The study suggests that semantic therapy is not appropriate for clients with phonological assembly difficulties but does not address whether semantic therapy has value for clients with phonological output difficulties.

Study

Howard, D., Patterson, K. E., Franklin, S., Orchard-Lisle, V., & Morton, J. (1985). Treatment of word retrieval deficits in aphasia: a comparison of two therapy methods. *Brain*, *108*, 817–829.

Focus of therapy: Semantic system and/or phonological output lexicon (locus not specified).

Target of therapy: Semantic/phonological.

Therapy approach: Reactivation.

Client details

General information

Twelve clients were involved in the study. All clients had specific word-finding problems as a consequence of acquired aphasia, no severe visual problems or visual agnosia, and were able to repeat single words.

Overall pattern of language impairments and preservations

On the Boston Diagnostic Aphasia Examination (Goodglass, Kaplan, & Barresi, 2001), six clients were identified as having a Broca's aphasia, four as having a mild conduction aphasia and two as having anomic aphasia.

Time post-onset

All clients were at least 6 months post-onset and usually several years post-onset.

Therapy

Aim

To compare the relative improvement in naming ability following phonological and semantic therapy. Each client received phonological and semantic therapy with 4 weeks intervening between therapy methods. Six clients had two consecutive weeks of treatment with each method and six had one week of treatment with each method. Therapy was carried out over four consecutive days in either the two weeks or the one week, depending on which group they were assigned to (i.e. the first group received therapy on 8 days). The length of the therapy session was one hour. An item-specific treatment design was used to monitor the effects of therapy.

Task	Semantic therapy	Phonological therapy
	1 Spoken word-to-picture matching with semantic distractors 2 Written word-to-picture matching with semantic distractors 3 Answering a yes/no question requiring the patient to access the meaning of the name, e.g. 'Is a cat an animal?'	1 Repeating the picture name 2 Attempting to produce the name with the aid of a phonemic cue 3 Judging whether the word rhymed with another word
Materials	300 line drawings selected from the 'Cambridge' pictures (Set A). For each picture the following were prepared: 1 A sheet containing the picture and three semantically related distractors 2 A card with the target's written name on 3 A semantic judgement for each picture, e.g. 'Is a cat an animal?' 4 A second set of different pictures of the same 300 objects (Set B)	
Hierarchy	None	
Feedback	Not specified	

Outcome

Clients were assessed on naming of their 80 test pictures by daily pre-tests, and naming of all 300 pictures, one week and 6 weeks after completion of therapy. All 12 clients showed a significant improvement in naming the treated items over naming controls in daily pre-tests. This advantage increased as treatment progressed. There was no significant difference between semantic and phonological therapy. Post-therapy, naming of the treated words improved significantly compared with the naming of the control words. There was a small but statistically reliable improvement for the clients as a group on both picture sets A and B. Eight of the 12 clients showed significant improvement, one client being able to name 40% of the pictures she couldn't previously name after only 4 hours of therapy, while four of the clients showed no change. Semantic therapy resulted in a greater improvement in the naming of treated items than phonological therapy. Improvement was not maintained 6 weeks post-therapy.

Other comments

This is a facilitation study, as different items were used across the sessions. It shows, however, that even with small amounts of therapy (4–8 hours), significant improvements in naming can be made. Improvement was unrelated to the duration of therapy, age of client, time post-onset or type of aphasia. The authors propose that the semantic representation is accessed during the course of semantic therapy. This representation is 'primed' and is more easily accessible for later naming. Phonological therapy, however, was hypothesised to act at the level of the phonological output lexicon with the effects being shorter lasting. The difference is considered to reflect the properties of these two levels of lexical representation. The authors propose that the use of good facilitating tasks such as those used here in the semantic therapy can act as a 'first stage' therapy to activate words before those words are used in a second stage therapy that maximises their communicative value. The data in this study are re-analysed in Howard (2000).

Study

Marshall, J., Pound, C., White-Thomson, M., & Pring, T. (1990). The use of picture/word matching tasks to assist word retrieval in aphasic patients. *Aphasiology*, *4*, 167–184.

Focus of therapy: Semantics and access to the phonological output lexicon.

Target of therapy: Semantic/phonological.

Therapy approach: Reactivation.

Client details

General information

Three clients are reported in this study. A further group study involving seven clients is also reported but not discussed here. RS was a 45-year-old company director who had a single left CVA. IS was a 76-year-old retired civil servant who also had a single left CVA. FW was a 76-year-old woman (no previous occupation reported) who had a left CVA and additional emotional distress which was treated unsuccessfully with anti-depressants.

Overall pattern of language impairments and preservations

RS presented with good functional comprehension. His comprehension of concrete words was retained but he had some difficulty understanding low-imageability words. He was within normal limits on the three-picture version of Pyramids and Palm Trees (Howard & Patterson, 1992). His speech was characterised by a marked anomia, particularly for verbs. In naming, he produced a lot of nil responses. He was helped by phonemic cues but could not be induced to produce semantic errors by inappropriate cues. He was able to read aloud both high- and low-imageability words accurately. It is suggested that he was unable to access the phonological output lexicon from semantics.

IS presented with functional comprehension in conversation and hesitant, non-fluent output with word-retrieval difficulties. She made errors in single-word, auditory and written comprehension tasks (selecting semantic distractors) and was outside normal limits on Pyramids and Palm Trees. In naming, she produced a combination of semantic and phonological errors. Her reading aloud of words was quite good but she was unable to read nonwords. It is suggested that her naming difficulties resulted from a combination of impaired semantics and impaired access to the phonological output lexicon.

FW had a similar pattern of performance to IS. She had impaired spoken and written comprehension alongside her naming difficulties. She produced both semantic and phonological errors in naming and was helped by phonemic and graphemic cues. Her reading aloud was not assessed. It is suggested FW had a primary semantic impairment and difficulty accessing the phonological output lexicon.

Time post-onset

RS was 10 months post-onset, IS was 3 months post-onset and FW was 5 months post-onset.

Therapy

Aim

To improve picture-naming ability through accessing semantic information. RS received 3 hours of therapy over 2 weeks, IS received 5 hours over 4 weeks (2½ hours each stage), while FW received 3½ hours over 3 weeks, which was then extended for a further 3 weeks. An item-specific therapy design was used to investigate the effects of therapy on treated and control items.

Task	**Semantic matching task** Read aloud 5 written words (target + 4 semantically related distractors) and select one to match the picture
Materials	Drawings of low-frequency words; written form of target and 4 semantically related distractors for each target
	RS: 50 drawings; 25 treated items and 25 controls (matched for equal correctness)
	IS: 100 drawings; 50 treated in two consecutive stages of 25 words; 50 controls
	FW: 50 drawings; 25 treated items and 25 controls (matched for equal correctness). Frequency higher than for other clients
Hierarchy	None
Feedback	Not specified

Outcome

RS showed significantly better naming of treated items than of untreated items immediately post-therapy. This was maintained 4 weeks later. IS also demonstrated a significant difference between improvements on both treated sets compared to performance on untreated items. Smaller gains, however, were seen with untreated items. No differences were seen between untreated and treated items for FW, although significant improvement was seen for both sets at the end of the second therapy period.

Both RS and IS made significant gains in treated items following semantic therapy despite having different underlying naming deficits, leading the authors to suggest that clients with both intact and impaired semantic systems respond to semantic therapy. Some uncertainty is highlighted by the authors, however, over the initial extent of semantic involvement in the case of IS based on the improvement seen on later testing. While RS showed no generalisation to untreated control items, small benefits were present for IS. FW made smaller gains than RS and IS; these were not treatment-specific but reflected significant overall improvement. FW's emotional state was considered to influence her performance.

Other comments

This study shows that a simple semantic task can benefit clients with different underlying impairments. Some generalisation of therapy effects is seen in IS's performance. The relationship between significant measurable gains following therapy and clinical worth, or impact to the client in a more generalised communicative sense, is discussed. Furthermore, the authors stress the distinction between studies that aim to demonstrate that therapy per se works and research that aims to evaluate methods used in therapy.

Study

Pring, T., Hamilton, A., Harwood, A., & Macbride, L. (1993). Generalisation of naming after picture/word matching tasks: only items appearing in therapy benefit. *Aphasiology*, 7, 383–394.

Focus of therapy: Semantic system and access to the phonological output lexicon.

Target of therapy: Semantic/phonological.

Therapy approach: Reactivation.

Client details

General information

Five clients were involved in the study. All had suffered a CVA. No information is provided on the age, gender, employment history or specific neurological deficits of the clients.

Overall pattern of language impairments and preservations

All clients had predominantly expressive problems with prominent word-retrieval difficulties and only mild deficits in single-word comprehension, with performance on low-imageability words more impaired than on high-imageability words. Their sentence comprehension was functional in conversation. They all showed only mild impairments in the reading aloud of high-imageability words. Four of the clients – MM, DL, BR and PB – had a Broca's type aphasia. MM and PB had deficits in verb retrieval and sentence construction. DL and BR had less severe lexical and grammatical deficits.

RH presented with severe naming difficulties and is described as having a 'recovered Wernicke's dysphasia'. In naming tasks, the clients produced omissions and circumlocutions, alongside some semantic errors.

Time post-onset

The clients were all more than 2 years post-onset. MM was more than 12 years, PB was more than 4 years, and DL, BR and RH were all between 2 and 3 years post-stroke.

Therapy

Aim

To improve naming using semantic tasks. Therapy took place (usually) daily for 2 weeks. The initial session was supervised as were sessions when a new set of items was introduced. The client carried out all other sessions unsupervised and recorded responses on a stimulus sheet. Task 1 was used in the therapist-led sessions. Task 2 was carried out independently. An item-specific design was used to measure efficacy.

Task	1. Word-to-picture matching Read aloud 4 words (target + 3 distractors) and select one to match the picture	2. Picture-to-word matching Read aloud 3 words and match each word to correct picture
Materials	72 black and white line drawings in each of three semantic categories; corresponding written (typed) words	As for task 1. Six pictures presented each time (3 targets and 3 distractors)
Hierarchy	None	None
Feedback	Not specified	Not specified

Outcome

For all clients, significant improvements were seen in treated items and related distractors following therapy; treated items, however, improved significantly more than related distractors. Related distractors improved significantly more than related unseen items, and unseen related items and controls did not differ. This study demonstrates that naming of items used in therapy tasks improved, with significant improvement seen both immediately following therapy and at follow-up one month later. Naming of treated items improved significantly more than all other items. No generalisation to unseen items occurred, regardless of whether these were in the same semantic domain or unrelated. Functional improvements were not discussed.

The tasks in this study combine phonological and semantic processing. The authors propose that the improved naming of the items used as related distractors is a consequence of the greater degree of semantic relatedness between items than in previous studies. The authors suggest that 'the use of a semantic task which explicitly draws attention to the relatedness of items may . . . be more effective' (p. 393).

Other comments

This study involved a small number of clients only and the clients were described as atypical therapy candidates with relatively mild problems. There was no clear level of deficit for each client.

Study

Hillis, A. E., & Caramazza, A. (1994). Theories of lexical processing and rehabilitation of lexical deficits. In M. J. Riddoch & G. W. Humphreys (Eds.), *Cognitive neuropsychology and cognitive rehabilitation*. London: Lawrence Erlbaum Associates Ltd.

Focus of therapy: (1) Semantic system; (2) orthographic-to-phonological conversion (OPC) and semantic system; (3) phonological-to-orthographic conversion (POC) (referred to in this book as phonological-to-graphemic conversion).

Target of therapy: (1) Semantic/phonological; (2) phonological; (3) orthographic.

Therapy approach: Reactivation with KE, JJ and HW. Cognitive-relay strategies with HW, SJD and PM.

Client details

General information

HW was a 64-year-old woman who had experienced left parietal and occipital strokes. SJD was a 44-year-old woman with a left frontoparietal infarct. PM was a 50-year-old left-handed woman with a PhD. She had a left fronto-temporal-parietal and basal ganglia stroke. KE was a 51-year-old college-educated man with a left frontoparietal infarct. JJ was a 67-year-old retired corporate executive with a left temporal and basal ganglia stroke. HW, SJD, KE and JJ were all right-handed.

Overall pattern of language impairments and preservations

HW and SJD produced fluent, grammatical speech with some morphological errors. PM's speech was grammatical but hesitant and slightly slurred. HW, SJD and PM had normal comprehension of single words but difficulty in the auditory comprehension of syntactically complex, semantically reversible sentences. HW produced semantic errors in naming and oral reading. Naming of verbs was impaired compared with nouns. In naming tasks, she responded well to phonemic cues. SJD produced semantic errors in written naming and writing to dictation. Performance was worse for verbs than nouns, with semantic and/or morphological errors. She also omitted or substituted function words in writing. PM made semantic errors in both spoken and written tasks, although performance was more accurate in spoken tasks. She was unable to read or spell nonwords or any items she could not name. KE and JJ presented with impaired single-word comprehension and produced semantic errors in all tasks. KE's naming responded well to phonemic cueing. For JJ, oral reading and writing to dictation were more accurate than naming, suggesting intact orthographic and phonological conversion mechanisms. We would interpret JJ and KE as having semantic difficulties and HW, SJD and PM as having difficulties accessing phonology.

Time post-onset

All of the clients were at least 6 months post-onset. KE was 6 months and JJ was 9 months post-stroke. HW was 2.5, SJD was 4 and PM was 2 years post-stroke.

Therapy

Aims

1   For HW, to teach orthographic-to-phonological conversion (OPC) rules and to increase activation of items for naming. She received 12 sessions on oral reading to aid verb retrieval, 5 sessions each on action and object naming via naming therapy A (see below) and 20 sessions of naming therapy B.
2   For SJD, to teach phonological-to-orthographic conversion (POC) rules as a self-monitoring strategy to block semantic errors. She received 12 sessions on POC cueing and 43 sessions on self-monitoring.
3   For PM, to teach both OPC and POC rules. She received 5 sessions on POC therapy before it was abandoned. She then received 12 sessions of OPC therapy.
4   For KE and JJ, to increase activation of items for naming. KE had 5 sessions each on object and action naming via naming therapy A. JJ had 20 sessions of naming therapy B.

A multiple-baseline across behaviours design was used to measure the effects of intervention on treated and untreated naming tasks.

Task	Teaching of POC rules (SJD, PM)	Teaching of OPC rules (HW, PM)
Materials	30 phonemes divided into three sets of 10. Each set worked on until 100% performance	Three sets of phonemes
Hierarchy	1 Point to the letter that makes the sound /phoneme/ 2 Think of a word that starts with /phoneme/ 3 A word that starts with /phoneme/ is (key word). Point to the letter that makes the first sound of (key word) 4 Write (key word). Point to the letter that makes the sound of (key word) 5 (Target letter) makes the first sound of (key word). /Phoneme/ is the first sound of (key word). (Target letter) makes the sound /phoneme/. Point to (target letter). For example, B makes the first sound of 'baby'. /b/ is the first sound of 'baby'. B makes the sound /b/. Point to B	Not specified – assumed to be similar to that of POC therapy
Feedback	Not specified	

Task	Oral reading of verbs to facilitate oral naming (HW)	Naming therapy A Picture naming using a cueing hierarchy (HW, KE)	Naming therapy B Oral reading and word-to-picture matching (HW, JJ). Word-to-picture matching involved identifying correct picture from a set of 40
Materials	40 pictures depicting transitive verbs, randomly divided into two sets A and B. When 100% performance was obtained on Set A, Set B was targeted	Pictures of 50 objects and 10 actions (items not given). When 100% performance was obtained on Set A, Set B was targeted	Set of 40 printed words and pictures of those 40 items (items not given), divided randomly into two sets for each session, one to the oral reading treatment and one to the word–picture matching treatment
Hierarchy	None	Cueing hierarchy: (a) sentence completion (b) initial phoneme (c) word itself as a spoken model When 90% performance obtained on nouns, the verb set was targeted in the same way	None
Feedback	If unable to read word, phonemic cueing or modelling used until correct response elicited		If unable to read word, phonemic cueing was used. In word-to-picture matching, items that were initially incorrect were corrected and repeated after intervening items, until a correct response was obtained

Outcome

The results are set out here sequentially according to client, including information on improvements across tasks and stimuli, functional generalisation and proposed mechanisms of change.

Client HW

HW was unable to learn OPC procedures sufficiently to aid oral production. Naming performance improved on the treated verbs (from 30% to 90% correct). In response to naming therapy A, oral naming of treated items improved (nouns from 50% to 80%, verbs from 10% to 70%). Following naming therapy B, oral reading improved naming of some items. Word-to-picture matching did not show improvement. With respect to generalised improvement across tasks and stimuli, HW was unable to blend those phonemes she could translate (see Nickels, 1992, for similar results). Verb naming improved but did not generalise to untreated items. Following therapy A, there was no generalisation to untreated items. Following therapy B, this was not tested. When considering generalised impact on daily living, those OPC rules learned by HW did not cue retrieval of phonological form (cf. Nickels, 1992). This was not stated for other treatments. The proposed mechanism of change for HW was the lowering of threshold activation for treated verb items by increasing the frequency of production. With therapy A and B, this was probably as for verb therapy above, again lowering the threshold of activation of phonological representations, because errors were hypothesised to arise at the phonological output level. The word-to-picture matching treatment was considered unsuccessful because errors were not due to a semantic level deficit.

Client SJD

SJD learned POC rules for targeted phonemes. She improved to 100% phoneme-to-grapheme translation. SJD showed a generalised effect whereby performance increased on all words. Functionally, the quantity and accuracy of written verb production in narrative improved (this was monitored each session during a paragraph-writing task). With respect to a proposed mechanism of therapy, SJD's ability to convert phonology to orthography was considered to 'block' semantic paragraphias. The ability to convert phonology to appropriate graphemes might cue access to the orthographic representation for output.

Client PM

PM was unable to learn POC rules but OPC therapy was successful. PM improved to 60% phoneme-to-grapheme translation before ceasing therapy. Grapheme-to-phoneme translation improved from about 20–30% to around

90%. PM's spelling improved only of specifically trained verbs (using a cue-ing hierarchy unstated). Grapheme-to-phoneme conversion skills allowed PM to produce phonemes to written words and hence cue accurate oral reading. Oral reading of 144 untrained items improved from 76% to 89%; however, oral naming did not improve. No functional improvement was seen with PM. Her OPC skills did not facilitate naming, because she could not retrieve the spellings of words she could not name. PM's lack of success on POC procedures might be due to differences in type or severity of deficit, even though this was postulated to be at the same locus as SJD. Success in improved reading through OPC procedures could be due to any of the many processes involved in the conversion, and it is suggested that the contrast with the lack of success in HW might be due to a difference in the precise component that is affected in the deficit or in the level of severity.

Client KE

KE improved his oral naming of all treated items from 10% to 100%. Improvement on object naming generalised to untreated items within the same semantic category. Improvement in oral naming also generalised to written naming of the same items and those of the same semantic category. Functional improvements were not stated. With KE, cueing might have provided additional activation of the target, making it available for further processing (this does not explain generalisation to other items).

Client JJ

JJ's oral reading therapy did not improve naming performance. Word-to-picture matching did, however, improve naming. As with HW, JJ's word-to-picture matching resulted in cumulative facilitation in naming; on average, one to two previously misnamed pictures were named correctly in the session following treatment. Generalisation was not tested with JJ. As with KE, func-tional improvements were also not stated. For JJ, teaching distinctions (or activating features that distinguish) between related items was the proposed mechanism of therapy because errors arise at the semantic level. Oral reading treatment was unsuccessful because errors arise before the phonological output level.

Other comments

This is a complex study that examined the efficacy of a variety of therapy techniques. The authors suggest that if the deficit is semantic, word-to-picture matching therapy can help, but not if the deficit is only at the phono-logical output level (note that semantic errors are not necessarily due to a semantic deficit). This is in contrast to many studies that have shown improvements in naming performance for clients with phonological output difficulties, following word-to-picture matching tasks and other semantic tasks (e.g. Marshall *et al.*, 1990; Le Dorze *et al.*, 1994; see discussion in Nickels, 2002b). A suggested improvement to the study would be to check for generalisation to untreated items after word-to-picture matching therapy.

Study

Hillis, A. (1989). Efficacy and generalisation of treatment for aphasic naming errors. *Archives of Physical Medicine and Rehabilitation, 70*, 632–636.

Focus of therapy: Phonological output lexicon and orthographic output lexicon.

Target of therapy: Semantic/phonological.

Therapy approach: Reactivation.

Client details

General information

Two clients are reported in this study, referred to as Patient 1 and Patient 2. Patient 1 was a 51-year-old right-handed man who had a thromboembolic stroke. A CT scan revealed a large area infarct in the left frontoparietal area. Patient 2 was a 63-year-old right-handed woman who was seen following her second CVA. A mild CVA in the left occipital area 3 years previously had left no residual speech or language difficulties. Her second CVA occurred in her left parietal area.

Overall pattern of language impairments and preservations

Patient 1 had severely impaired comprehension; yes/no responses were at chance levels. Verbal output was characterised by a low volume and perseverative syllables. While his reading comprehension was also severely impaired, written word-to-picture matching was relatively good (27/32 items), with errors being predominantly semantic. Patient 2 had intact auditory and written comprehension in the presence of severely impaired output. Spoken output was fluent with a low use of content words. Naming and repetition were profoundly impaired; errors in repetition showed semantic involvement. She was unable to name items to definition, either verbally or in writing.

Baseline assessment of naming showed that both clients made similar semantic errors in spoken naming; Patient 1 made errors in comprehension and writing as well. The homogenous pattern of semantic errors seen in Patient 1 led the authors to propose a unitary impairment in word meaning (the semantic system). Patient 2's output-specific deficits were considered to suggest two separate sources of errors for spoken and written naming – that is, a breakdown in (a) the ability to retrieve the correct phonological representation for spoken naming and (b) the ability to hold the written representation of the word while it was being written.

Time post-onset

Patient 1 was 3 months post onset at the beginning of the study, although language assessment occurred at 7 weeks post-onset. Patient 2 was 15 months post-onset from her second CVA.

Therapy

Aim

To improve written and spoken naming of nouns and verbs. Patient 1 had 1–2 hours of therapy, 5 days per week. The total number of weeks was not reported. The amount and length of therapy for Patient 2 was not reported. A multiple-baseline design across items was used to evaluate efficacy of therapy and generalisation across items and modalities.

Task	Written naming of picture set Client asked to write the name of the picture; provided with cues if unable to	Spoken naming of picture set Client asked to name the picture; provided with cues if unable to
Materials	50 black and white line drawings of familiar nouns and verbs. 10 nouns (stimulus set 1) and 10 verbs (stimulus set 2) used which client could not name (spoken or written). Other items used as controls. Baseline measures of all items were obtained over five sessions. Both tasks were carried out on set 1 (nouns) before progressing to set 2 (verbs) when 90% accuracy in naming nouns in both modalities was achieved	
Hierarchy	1 Picture stimulus (independent written name) 2 Scrambled anagram and 2 distractors 3 Scrambled anagram without distractors 4 Initial letter cue 5 Verbal name (correct writing to dictation)	1 Picture stimulus + What's this called? 2 Can you write the word? Now read it 3 What do you do with it? or What does he do? 4 Function provided 5 Written word provided 6 Verbal sentence completion

	6 Written name presented briefly (correct delayed reproduction)	6 Verbal sentence completion 7 Initial phoneme cue
Feedback on error	Proceed through hierarchy until response is successful	
Feedback if correct	When correct, present earlier cue in reverse order. Client encouraged to then say word but no feedback provided on spoken production	

Outcome

For Patient 1, both spoken and written naming improved following treatment of written naming, with generalisation in both modalities to untrained nouns in the same semantic categories. There was no generalisation from nouns to verbs. Verbs subsequently treated also showed improvement. Gains were maintained nine sessions after therapy had discontinued (length of time unreported). For Patient 2, improvement was seen following both written and spoken naming therapy, although this improvement was specific to the trained modality – that is, the simultaneous gains seen in Patient 1 following written naming therapy were not evident with the second client. There was some minor evidence to suggest a trend towards generalisation to untrained stimuli in spoken naming only. No comment was made on maintenance.

While the therapy programme had positive results for both clients, the author highlights the finding that identical treatment can improve performance of different clients for different reasons. She proposed that the contrasting results are likely to be attributed to differences in the clients' underlying deficits. The generalisation of Patient 1's improvement was considered to relate to the impairment of word meaning, while the lack of generalisation in the case of Patient 2 reflected the impairment of two distinct processes.

Other comments

The cueing hierarchies within the study were devised by observing the sorts of stimuli that sometimes elicited a correct response.

Study

Bruce, C., & Howard, D. (1987). Computer generated phonemic cueing: an effective aid for naming in aphasia. *British Journal of Disorders of Communication*, *22*, 191–201.

Focus of therapy: Phonological output lexicon.

Target of therapy: Phonological.

Therapy approach: Compensation.

Client details

General information

Five people who had suffered cortical lesions were involved in the study.

Overall pattern of language impairments and preservations

All clients were non-fluent and classified as having Broca's aphasia and word-retrieval difficulties. They had no visual agnosia or severe articulatory difficulties, and were able to repeat single concrete content words. All had failed to name more than 50 pictures in a previous study but had been able to indicate the initial letter of a significant proportion of picture names. Three clients benefited significantly from phonemic cues. The remaining two clients either named items when they were shown the initial letter or named to some extent following a cue. No information is given on comprehension abilities or the proposed location of the clients' impairments.

Time post-onset

All clients were more than 6 months post-onset.

Therapy

Aim

To evaluate the effects of a microcomputer as an aid for a cueing strategy in naming. Following pre-testing, each client had five sessions using the microcomputer with a set of 50 items that had not been named correctly (Set A). A further set of items (Set B) was compiled, not assessed and used as control items. At the conclusion of therapy, all items from both sets (A and B) were presented for naming in two sessions, one week apart. An item-specific design across tasks (with and without aid) was used with each client.

Task	**Picture naming with a computer aid for cues** Picture presented for naming, client identifies first letter and computer provides phoneme

Materials	150 drawings from Cambridge pictures, beginning with letters P C F S T B D M L. Set A had 50 treated pictures (combined with a further 50 fillers), while Set B had 50 untreated (and unseen) pictures. Apple II microcomputer with recorded digitised speech of the 9 phonemes Computer-produced phoneme + schwa
Hierarchy	(a) Clients located and then pressed the initial letter on the keyboard. The aid converted this into a phoneme (b) Clients encouraged to repeat phoneme and use this to cue word production. – For the first 3 sessions, clients had to use aid even if they could name spontaneously – In the final 2 sessions, clients used aid only when failing to name correctly in 5 seconds. In these sessions, the numbers named with and without cue were recorded
Feedback on error	If client failed to name, therapist provided phonemic cue
Feedback if correct	Not specified

Outcome

There were significant differences between the clients in their response to therapy, with different levels of benefit from the aid and between treated and untreated words seen. As a group, there was a significant effect of using the aid compared with not using the aid. A significant effect of treatment was also found, whereby better performance was recorded for naming treated Set A than untreated Set B. Aid effects generalised across Sets A and B. No significant change in performance was noted one week after testing.

When looked at individually, client-specific effects of treatment were found. All clients learned to use the aid; four clients showed significantly better naming with the aid compared with the control condition. In some cases, clients improved naming performance without the use of the aid, although they were still assisted by use of the aid (in one case, the client's improvement in unaided naming was comparable to aided performance). Clients also increased their ability to identify initial letters of words that they could not name. Therapy with the aid, therefore, had variable effects, both in increasing unaided performance of naming as well as increasing naming performance when used as a prosthetic device.

The machine-generated cue was proposed to act in the same way as a therapist-generated cue, providing extra activation to the phonological word forms within the lexicon.

Other comments

While the information available on the clients in this study is less comprehensive than for other studies, the target of therapy was clear and it showed clear benefits for some clients. A closer examination of each client's pre-therapy abilities may inform the discussion as to why clients responded differently to such an approach.

Study

Le Dorze, G., Boulay, N., Gaudreau, J., & Brassard, C. (1994). The contrasting effects of a semantic versus a formal-semantic technique for the facilitation of naming in a case of anomia. *Aphasiology, 8*, 127–141.

Focus of therapy: Access to the phonological output lexicon from the semantic system.

Target of therapy: Semantic.

Therapy approach: Reactivation.

Client details

General information

RB was a 56-year-old right-handed man who had a non-haemorrhagic single CVA, confirmed by CT scan, in the vicinity of his left carotid artery. He was a policeman before the incident. He was a bilingual speaker in French and English.

Overall pattern of language impairments and preservations

At the time of the study, RB was described as having a moderately severe, mixed aphasia. Spoken output was characterised by syntactically well-formed sentences with severe word-finding difficulties. A slight articulatory difficulty was present. On testing, he had moderately impaired picture naming. Errors consisted predominantly of no responses and some semantic errors; no phonological errors were present. Repetition was good. Good auditory and written comprehension of single words was present, although this decreased with sentences. Oral reading was mildly impaired. Writing was limited to copying.

Time post-onset

Therapy was commenced when RB was 10 months post-onset.

Therapy

Aim

To compare the relative effects of a semantic technique and a formal-semantic technique in the treatment of anomia. These techniques are discussed in the paper; the key difference between the techniques was the use of the word form in the formal-semantic technique and the use of a definition (with no usage of the word form) in the semantic technique. Therapy consisted of three one-hour therapy sessions per week for a total of 11 sessions. Therapy sessions included formal-semantic and semantic techniques rotated on each stimulus. Within each session, the naming of items treated in previous therapy sessions was tested using a maintenance test. Items to be treated within the session were tested before and after therapy. An item-specific therapy design contrasting the effects of the two treatments was used.

Task	Formal-semantic therapy Tasks involving semantic comprehension with the presentation of the word form (a) Spoken word-to-picture matching (b) Written word-to-picture matching (c) Semantic judgement – yes/ no questions	Semantic therapy Tasks involving semantic comprehension. Word form not presented (a) Matching spoken definition to picture (b) Matching written definition to picture (c) Semantic judgement task as in formal-semantic therapy
Materials	225 pictures that were named incorrectly in naming assessment. 20 stimuli were drawn from these pictures in each session. 10 pictures treated via semantic technique, 10 via formal-semantic technique. 14 stimulus cards for use in word and definition matching tasks. Each card contained 6 pictures: (a) Target (b) 3 semantic distractors (c) 2 unrelated distractors	
Hierarchy	No hierarchy	No hierarchy
Feedback on error	Not specified	Not specified
Feedback if correct	Not specified	Not specified

Outcome

Naming improved significantly for the items treated with the formal-semantic technique immediately post-therapy but the improvement was not maintained 2–3 days later. There was no change in naming for the items treated with the purely semantic technique. No change was evident on formal aphasia testing. There was, however, a reported improvement in RB's ability to convey information in a picture description task.

The authors propose that formal-semantic therapy resulted in improved naming performance immediately post-therapy but these gains were not maintained 2–3 days post-therapy. Semantic therapy resulted in no significant improvement. The authors suggest that the presentation of the word form is, therefore, critical for the facilitation of naming. No theoretical explanation is offered for the apparent generalisation to a picture description task but they suggest that the semantic technique involving use of definitions may have provided a useful model of circumlocution.

Other comments

This is a facilitation study, as different items were used across the sessions. The formal-semantic therapy is a replication of Howard and colleagues' (1985) semantic therapy.

Study

Boyle, M., & Coelho, C. A. (1995). Application of semantic feature analysis as a treatment for aphasic dysnomia. *American Journal of Speech and Language Pathology*, *4*, 94–98.

Focus of therapy: Phonological output lexicon (or access to it).

Target of therapy: Semantic.

Therapy approach: Reactivation.

Client details

General information

HW was a 57-year-old right-handed male. He was a retired postal worker with high school education. A CT scan showed a left frontoparietal ischaemic infarct.

Overall pattern of language impairments and preservations

HW presented with a Broca's type aphasia with a mild apraxic component. Spontaneous speech was characterised by frequent pauses, nonword fillers and incomplete word attempts. Picture naming was impaired. He showed retained auditory comprehension of single words. While no reference was made to HW's exact level of breakdown, he was not reported to have a primary deficit involving the semantic system.

Time post-onset

HW was 65 months post-onset when therapy started.

Therapy

Aim

To improve naming performance. Therapy consisted of 3 one-hour sessions per week, with a total of 16 sessions over 7 weeks (seven sessions Stage 1, nine sessions Stage 2). There was a one-week break between Stages 1 and 2 of therapy. A repeated-measures multiple-baseline design across tasks was used to evaluate the efficacy of therapy.

Task	**Naming and semantic feature analysis** Picture placed in centre of feature analysis chart and client attempts to name the picture. Guided verbalisation of the semantic features (group, use, action, properties, location and association)

Materials	48 Snodgrass and Vanderwart (1980) black and white line drawings divided into three groups:
	1 Treatment group (34 pictures). HW was unable to name these on 2/3 occasions. Treatment group further divided into:
	  (a) Few exemplar condition (7 pictures)
	  (b) Many exemplars condition (remaining 27 pictures)
	2 Control group – 7 pictures not named correctly on 3/3 occasions
	3 Easy Group – 7 pictures named correctly on 3/3 occasions. Easy group pictures used to provide success in therapy

Hierarchy	*Stage 1.* Few exemplars condition: training of the same 7 pictures each session with the 7 easy pictures interspersed for periodic success *Stage 2.* Many exemplars condition: 27 pictures randomised into three sets of 9 and with 7 easy pictures interspersed into each set

Feedback on error	1 Clinician provided semantic feature orally and in writing 2 If unable to name picture after all features written on chart, request for repetition of picture name and review of all features
Feedback if correct	1 Client guided through features chart even when target is named

The criterion for the transition between stages 1 and 2 and for the conclusion of treatment was 100% success over three consecutive sessions.

Outcome

HW demonstrated significant improvement in the naming of task stimuli (reaching 100% accuracy). This was maintained 2 months post-treatment. Naming performance also significantly improved for the untreated control items. There was no generalisation to connected speech (as measured by Nicholas and Brookshire's, 1993, protocol that looks at words as information-carrying units), although a clinically important functional improvement in communication was found on the Communicative Effectiveness Index (Lomas *et al.*, 1989).

Naming performance therefore improved significantly for both treated and untreated pictures. The authors propose that this improvement is a consequence of internalising the prompts in the semantic feature chart facilitating self-cueing and thus a consequence of therapy. A stable baseline had been established before therapy, although no control tasks were reported. HW was a long time post-onset and improvement was therefore unlikely to be a consequence of spontaneous recovery. No carryover into spontaneous speech was noted.

Other comments

This study reports limited assessment data on the client, making interpretation difficult. With HC's word-retrieval deficit likely to be post-semantic, input to the semantic system may well be activating access to the phonological output lexicon. The authors suggest that direct treatment of word retrieval in connected speech may be necessary to achieve improvement at that level. They further noted that functional improvement evident on the Communicative Effectiveness Index (Lomas *et al.*, 1989) may be due to either the reporter's (client's daughter) desire for improvement and for therapy to continue, or may indicate a mismatch between connected speech measures and functional measures. Generalisation of improved naming to untreated items has also been found by Hillis (1989) and Howard *et al.*

(1985). This therapy approach has been replicated by Coelho, McHugh and Boyle (2000).

Study

Lowell, S., Beeson, P. M., & Holland, A. L. (1995). The efficacy of a semantic cueing procedure on naming performance of adults with aphasia. *American Journal of Speech-Language Pathology*, *4*, 109–114.

Focus of therapy: Phonological output lexicon (or access to it).

Target of therapy: Semantic.

Therapy approach: Reactivation.

Client details

General information

This study examines three patients who all presented with aphasia following a single left CVA. BB was 74 years old, BG was 76 years old and SB was 66 years old.

Overall pattern of language impairments and preservations

BB and SB presented with a conduction-type aphasia. BG presented with an anomic aphasia. All presented with naming difficulties, despite retained single-word auditory and written comprehension and relatively unimpaired semantics.

Time post-onset

The clients were all at least 9 months post-onset when therapy was commenced. BB was 16 months post-onset, BG was 9 months post-onset and SB was 30 months post-onset.

Therapy

Aim

To improve naming of items consistently not named correctly over three pre-therapy baseline assessments. Therapy consisted of three sessions per week for 2 weeks for list 1 and then the equivalent for list 2. A multiple-baseline and cross-over design was used.

Task	1. Trained items	2. Untrained items
	Four self-generated cue words read aloud by client and therapist. Client then asked to name the picture	Client asked to name the picture
Materials	36 black and white line drawings named incorrectly on three occasions Three groups: • 12 'trained' – trained items had written cue cards • 12 'untrained' semantically related • 12 'untrained' unrelated Groups were divided into two lists for therapy (6 of each group). 18 items within each list seen 2–3 times in each session	
Hierarchy	None	None
Feedback on error	Written feedback of three written choices given and client asked to read target aloud	Written feedback of three written choices given and client asked to read target aloud
Feedback if correct	Not specified	Not specified

Therapy consisted of two tasks, one task for the 'trained' group of items and one task for the 'untrained' items. If multiple responses were given, the best response was scored. Recognisable phonological errors with one to two phonological substitutions were counted as correct. A criterion of 5/6 items named correctly in two consecutive sessions with a combined accuracy of > 50% in each of three training sessions was set for the trained items.

Outcome

Criterion was reached by BB and BG for both sets of trained items. Naming for the untrained items also improved, but only for those items which were probed on every cycle. Performance was maintained one week post-therapy. Naming performance also improved for test items not selected for treatment. SB did not reach criterion for trained items. No improvement in naming performance was evident. Performance on a control task involving the production of morphology remained unchanged for all three clients. No other post-therapy measures were reported.

Therapy resulted in improved naming performance in BB and BG. The improvement seemed to be a consequence of therapy, as the clients were stable before therapy and no improvements were noted on the control task. Similar gains in naming performance seen in the untrained items suggest that improvement may be a consequence of repeated exposure to the items and the use of the written feedback. The authors propose that the improved naming of items not selected for the 'trained' or 'untrained groups' reflects an internalisation of a semantic self-cueing strategy. No improvement was seen in SB's naming performance. The authors suggest that this lack of improvement may be a consequence of a greater impairment of semantic/phonological access and the semantic activation provided by the cues was not sufficient to overcome the deficit. SB also performed poorly on non-verbal cognitive tasks compared with BB and BG. There was no evaluation of functional improvements or carryover to spontaneous speech.

Other comments

The limited initial assessment data reported in this study means that the precise impairment of the three clients cannot be identified. The authors suggest that SB's poor performance on non-verbal cognitive tasks may be influential in the lack of improvement seen with this client and that these cognitive limitations may preclude the use of this strategy.

Study

Miceli, G., Amitrano, A., Capasso, R., & Caramazza, A. (1996). The treatment of anomia resulting from output lexical damage: analysis of two cases. *Brain and Language, 52*, 150–174.

Focus of therapy: Phonological output lexicon.

Target of therapy: Phonology.

Therapy approach: Reactivation.

Client details

General information

Two case studies are reported. RBO was a 38-year-old right-handed female who suffered a ruptured A-V malformation of the left posterior communicating artery. Following surgery, RBO presented with a global aphasia, right hemiplegia, hypoesthesia and hemianopia. A CT scan showed a large lesion involving deep and superficial structures of the left parietal and temporal lobes. RBO worked as a flight attendant. GMA was a 60-year-old right-handed male who suffered a left hemisphere stroke, leaving him with aphasia and no motor deficits. A CT scan showed involvement of the left temporal lobe. GMA had degrees in mathematics and engineering.

Overall pattern of language impairments and preservations

RMO's comprehension of isolated words remained intact with reasonable ability to convert words and nonwords (auditory and visual presentation) into verbal or written responses. Errors were phonologically or visually related to the target. Naming was severely impaired and was characterised primarily by failure to respond. Slow, mildly dysarthric output with evidence of complex grammatical structures was present; grammaticality judgements were reliable but comprehension of reversible sentences was poor. Mild buccofacial dyspraxia and reduced verbal memory were also reported. GMA presented with a similar, but milder, pattern to RBO. Comprehension was spared at the single-word level in the presence of fluent grammatically complex output. Picture naming, however, showed a mild impairment (100/120 items; nouns > verbs) and was characterised by omissions and circumlocutions, with infrequent phonological and semantic errors. Nonword transcoding tasks showed relative preservation.

Time post-onset

RBO was 18 months post-onset when the programme began. GMA was seen approximately 12 months post-onset.

Therapy

Aim

To strengthen the phonological representation and subsequent access to it through repeated reading and repetition of the word. An item-specific therapy design was used.

(a) Client RBO

Two stages of therapy were involved based on two sets of stimuli. Each stage involved 5 one-hour sessions over 5 consecutive days with 3 days in between the two stages (total period approximately 13 days).

Task	Stage 1: Reading of target items	Stage 2: Repetition of target items
Materials	90 pictures that RBO consistently failed to name but could comprehend (range of familiarity and semantic categories). Randomly assigned to three sets of 30 items (*Set 1*, 30 reading items for Stage 1; *Set 2*, 30 repetition items for Stage 2; *Set 3*, 30 untreated items). *Set 1* used	*Set 2* used
Hierarchy	Written word presented and RBO asked to read aloud. All 30 items repeated 10 times	Target word spoken by examiner and RBO asked to repeat it
Feedback on error	Corrected as many times as necessary until correct response produced	Corrected as many times as necessary until correct response produced
Feedback if correct	Not specified	Not specified

(b) Client GMO

The treatment procedure was similar to that given to RMO. Key differences were in (a) the reduced number of items (80 items), (b) the inclusion of three stages of therapy, and (c) the length of therapy in each stage being extended to 7 consecutive days with 7 days of non-treatment between each stage (total period of approximately 5 weeks).

Task	Stage 1: Reading with picture	Stage 2: Reading without picture	Stage 3: Picture naming
Materials	80 pictures that GMA could not name consistently (failed minimum 2/3 presentations) but could comprehend (range of familiarity and semantic categories). Randomly assigned to four sets of 20 items (*Set 1*, 20 items for Stage 1; *Set 2*, 20 items for Stage 2, *Set 3*, 20 items for Stage 3; *Set 4*, 20 untreated items). *Set 1* used	*Set 2* used	*Set 3* used

Hierarchy	Stimulus picture and corresponding written word presented at same time. GMA required to look at picture and read word aloud	Only written word presented and GMA required to read word aloud	Only picture presented and GMA required to name it
Feedback on error	Corrected as many times as necessary until correct response produced	Corrected as many times as necessary until correct response produced	When GMA could not name an item, a phonemic cue (initial sound, initial syllable, second syllable, etc.) was given until correct name produced. Correct response was necessary before next item introduced
Feedback if correct	Not specified	Not specified	Not specified

Outcome

For RBO, naming improved significantly for the items in both sets of treatment stimuli, regardless of modality of stimulus presentation (reading and repetition). Only treated items were named more accurately. There was no generalisation to untreated items. Improvement was maintained when tested 3 weeks after the end of treatment. As with RBO, GMA's naming improved significantly for the items in all three sets of treatment stimuli. Only treated items were named more accurately. There was no generalisation to untreated items, not even to items semantically related. Significant improvement was maintained during a 17 month follow-up period, although a decrease in response accuracy was noted over time.

The authors propose that picture-naming performance in both clients could be accounted for by selective damage to the phonological output lexicon. Improvement can be expected where exercises rely on the spoken production of words. The lexicon is therefore remediable but only on an item-specific basis. No generalisation can be expected to occur. The authors suggest that the mechanism of change may be due to one of the following:

(a) improving lexical access mechanisms;
(b) increasing activation levels of lexical representations; or
(c) repairing damage to lexical representations.

Other comments

The authors highlight the unknown but critical influence of other parameters (e.g. neuropsychological, psychological and neurological factors) and stress the need for further investigation of these.

Study

Howard, D., & Harding, D. (1998). Self-cueing of word retrieval by a woman with aphasia: why a letter board works. *Aphasiology*, *12*, 399–420.

Focus of therapy: Phonological output lexicon via input orthography.

Target of therapy: Phonology.

Therapy approach: Cognitive relay.

Client details

General information

SD was a 46-year-old woman. She had a CVA secondary to a myocardial infarction which resulted in aphasia and right hemiplegia. She had worked and studied in management but was not working at the time of her CVA.

Overall pattern of language impairments and preservations

SD presented with a severe naming impairment that was characterised by a marked improvement in her ability to retrieve the name when shown an alphabet board. Naming errors were characteristically omissions or semantic errors. Some impairment was seen in spoken comprehension, related to auditory analysis and complex sentence comprehension, but no difficulties were seen with written word comprehension (comprehension of written grammar not assessed). SD had a reading impairment consistent with deep dyslexia. She was unable to write letters independently but could copy letters and used a typewriter adeptly. When asked to write the name of objects or write words to dictation, she typed none of them accurately but was always able to write the correct initial letter. She was able to type the appropriate letter when given the phoneme but was unable to give sounds for letters. The authors suggest that SD has an impairment in mapping from semantics to the phonological output lexicon. SD was able to identify the first letter of words but was unable to form letters herself and thus the authors suggest that the alphabet board acts as a cueing strategy.

Time post-onset

SD was 20 weeks post-onset at the time of the study.

Therapy

Aims

1   To improve naming performance by providing a written cue.
2   To evaluate the effect of different conditions on cued performance.

Intervention with SD consisted of one session where an alphabet board was introduced. Subsequent sessions attempted to determine the relative benefits of a range of different cues and to systematically evaluate how the alphabet board was aiding naming.

Task	(a) **Provision of an alphabet board**
	(b) Evaluating range of cues – Extra time – Use of alphabet board – Provision of initial letter of target – Provision of spoken name of initial letter of target – Provision of phonemic cue
Materials	Alphabet board
Hierarchy	Not applicable
Feedback on error	Not specified in initial therapy. Progressed to next item in evaluation study
Feedback if correct	Not specified

Outcome

SD was able to name items that she had previously not named when provided with (a) a phonemic cue, (b) the written initial letter or (c) an alphabet board (reaching 78–96% accuracy). These cues were significantly more effective than when given extra time or the spoken letter name (achieving 14–23% correct).

SD's ability to self-cue was attributed by the authors to a lexically mediated cascade of activation from input orthography to output phonology. Her increased naming performance was possible due to her intact knowledge of the word's initial letter. A lack of benefit from the spoken name of the initial letter suggested that the written form was essential. The success of phonemic cues was explained by the likelihood that the target word was close to activation and could be, as when provided with partial orthographic information, activated with partial phonological information.

Other comments

This study represents one example of using orthography to cue word retrieval; other studies not discussed here include Bachy-Langedock and De Partz (1989) and Bastiaanse *et al.* (1996). In this case, the cognitive neuropsychological approach provides an explanation as to why a particular technique was useful to the client. It also stresses the importance of detailed assessment of a client's performance on a wide range of tasks. The authors explain the implications of this study for the logogen model of information processing, postulating different routes from the visual input lexicon to either the phonological output lexicon or a semantic lexicon as possible ways of accounting for the pattern seen in SD.

Study

Francis, D. R., Clark, N., & Humphreys, G. W. (2002). Circumlocution-induced naming (CIN): a treatment for effecting generalization in anomia? *Aphasiology*, *16*, 243–259.

Focus of therapy: Phonological output lexicon.

Target of therapy: Semantic.

Therapy approach: Reactivation.

Client details

General information

MB was a 78-year-old woman who had retired from her job as a cleaner prior to her left middle cerebral artery CVA. A CT scan also showed bilateral aneurysms of the internal carotid arteries. She had a right-sided hemiplegia.

Overall pattern of language impairments and preservations

In the initial months following her CVA, MB's initial comprehension difficulties spontaneously resolved, leaving her with specific problems in name retrieval. She produced visual, semantic and unrelated errors in naming. Francis *et al.* conclude a possible mild visual recognition deficit in the presence of more severe difficulties accessing the phonological output lexicon. She showed little evidence of spontaneous circumlocution. Both frequency and category effects were present.

Time post-onset

MB was 2–3 months post-onset at the time of the study.

Therapy

Aim

To use circumlocution as a treatment (instead of as a strategy) to improve access to naming. Therapy consisted of 13 therapy sessions over a 4-week period (3–4 sessions per week). The sessions were approximately 15–30 minutes long and conducted when MB was an inpatient. A multiple-baseline across-behaviours therapy design was used.

Task	Circumlocution-induced naming (CIN) Client attempts to name each picture. Circumlocution ('talk around the topic') is encouraged until correct name is spoken
Materials	20 black and white drawings (half animate, half inanimate, low-frequency nouns). All pictures used in each session
Hierarchy	None
Feedback	Clinician verbally reinforces information provided by client by restating what has been said. Phonological cue may be provided sparingly. Correct name not to be provided by clinician

Outcome

A small but significant improvement in spoken naming was found on untreated items (only pictures not included in therapy were reassessed). A qualitative change was seen in the type of errors produced by MB. A non-significant increase was seen in visual-semantic errors, while unrelated errors showed a significant reduction post-therapy. Circumlocutory errors did not change. Performance did not change on control measures, suggesting that improvement was a result of therapy. Treatment effects were maintained on testing 2½ weeks later.

Francis *et al.* suggest that MB's success following therapy was directly related to the client having to 'look up' items in her phonological output lexicon rather than being provided with the correct item through such methods as repetition or reading aloud. This had the effect of strengthening access to phonology from semantics, a fact reinforced by the greatest change being seen with low-frequency words rather than high-frequency words. The authors suggest that this may occur through (a) 'exercising' the impaired link between intact semantics and intact phonology, or (b) directly improving semantics through the detailed descriptions generated in circumlocution, allowing the lexical representation to be accessed more easily. They argue that, if circumlocution had only been developed as a compensatory strategy, more circumlocution would have been seen post-therapy; this did not happen.

Other comments

Francis *et al.* stress the use of a technique that is usually reserved for the generalisation phase of therapy and suggest that therapy using this method may avoid the item specificity that is usually associated with improving deficits at the level of the phonological output lexicon. Issues related to clinical research within an inpatient setting are also discussed.

Study

Hickin, J., Best, W., Herbert, R., Howard, D., & Osborne, F. (2002). Phonological therapy for word-finding difficulties: a re-evaluation. *Aphasiology*, *16*, 981–999.

Focus of therapy: Access to phonology (phonological output lexicon).

Target of therapy: Phonological and orthographic.

Therapy approach: Reactivation.

Client details

General information

Eight clients were involved in this study. All had had a single left hemisphere CVA.

Overall pattern of language impairments and preservations

The clients presented with a range of severity and aphasia types. Word retrieval was a significant component of their aphasia in the presence of no severe comprehension difficulties, or oral or verbal dyspraxia.

Time post-onset

All clients were between 2 and 8 years post-onset.

Therapy

Aims

1   To improve picture naming through phonological and orthographic cueing.
2   To examine the effects of giving a 'choice' of cues on success of naming.

While this study consisted of three phases (an assessment phase followed by two treatment phases, each lasting approximately 8 weeks), only the first treatment phase is reported in this paper. Treatment sessions were once per week over the 8 weeks and lasted between one and one and a half hours. A repeated, multiple-baseline therapy design was used; clients were assessed on two occasions before therapy and once after therapy.

Task	Picture naming with phonological cueing	Picture naming with orthographic cueing
Materials	100 words (drawn from assessment of 200) divided into two sets of 50 words matched for baseline naming accuracy. 50 words were used for phonological cueing and 50 words used for orthographic cueing. 20 additional client-selected (high functional impact) words were orthographically cued. All 120 items were presented once per session, either phonological cued words followed by orthographic cued words, or vice versa	
Hierarchy	Cueing hierarchy: (a) Initial phoneme of the target word (with schwa) and an unrelated distractor (b) The first syllable of target and distractor (c) The whole word of target and distractor (d) Repetition of the target word Number of distractors increased from one (first 2 sessions) to two (next 2 sessions) to three (final 4 sessions)	Cueing hierarchy: (a) Initial grapheme of the target word and an unrelated distractor (b) The first syllable written of target and distractor (c) The whole word written of target and distractor (d) Repetition of the target word Number of distractors increased from one (first 2 sessions) to two (next 2 sessions) to three (final 4 sessions)
Feedback on error	Proceed through hierarchy until response is successful	Proceed through hierarchy until response is successful
Feedback if correct	Not specified	Not specified

Outcome

Significant improvement in spoken naming of the original 200 items was found in seven of the eight clients. Five of the clients who showed overall improvement improved significantly more on treated items than untreated items. Of these five clients, one client improved significantly on untreated items, suggesting some generalisation, while the other four clients showed item-specific improvement. The two other clients who improved showed no significant difference between treated and untreated items, one of whom may have shown some generalisation effects.

There were no significant differences between the effects of phonological and orthographic treatment for any participant, although one participant showed a non-significant trend towards benefiting more from phonological cues. Seven clients showed some improvement in naming self-selected words with the change for three reaching statistical significance. Individual responses to therapy are discussed in the light of pre-therapy assessment findings.

The authors suggest that the effectiveness of the different cueing approaches may be due to the client being required to make a choice at each stage. Against this is their finding that in the facilitation study there was no effect of making a choice of cue. The study design does not, however, exclude whether this may simply be due to repeated practice.

The item-specific benefits of phonological therapy seen in previous studies are reinforced by this study and are considered to result from activation of 'individual mappings from semantics to phonological representations'.

Other comments

The authors discuss the relationship between facilitation and treatment in relation to the eight clients and show that short-term benefits may predict response to therapy. The facilitation part of the study is reported in Best *et al.* (2002).

Study

Nickels, L. A. (2002a). Improving word finding: practice makes (closer to) perfect? *Aphasiology*, *16*, 1047–1060.

Focus of therapy: Phonological output lexicon.

Target of therapy: Phonology.

Therapy approach: Reactivation.

Client details

General information

JAW was a 60-year-man who worked, until his CVA, as a carpenter. A CT scan showed a left middle cerebral artery infarct.

Overall pattern of language impairments and preservations

JAW had a fluent aphasia, characterised by impaired naming. Auditory comprehension was poor, with an impairment considered to be present at a pre-lexical level of processing. Semantic processing was within normal limits for high-imageability words but was impaired for abstract and low-imageability words. A severe naming deficit showed significant frequency effects and consistent but non-significant length effects. These difficulties were considered to arise from a phonological processing deficit. Written naming was also poor but considered to arise from problems with the graph-emic output buffer. Given his auditory processing and phonological output difficulties, repetition was poor. Reading was also impaired, in particular his ability to read using the orthographic-to-phonological conversion route.

Time post-onset

JAW was over 12 months post-onset.

Therapy

Aims

1   To improve picture naming through repeated presentation of the same stimulus items.
2   To determine any differences between the three tasks of (a) attempted naming, (b) reading aloud and (c) delayed copying in improving naming performance.

Three treatment phases were completed with JAW, each corresponding to six consecutive days of therapy and one day of assessment. Between each week of therapy, JAW had a one-week non-therapy period.

Task	**Attempted naming** Naming pictures	**Reading aloud** Reading words	**Delayed copying** Read word, turn over page and silently write picture name
Materials	102 pictures divided into three sets of 34 (a Naming set, a Reading set and a Copying (control) set – matched for baseline spoken naming accuracy and approximately for length and frequency. The Reading and Copying sets were presented as written words		
Hierarchy	None	None	None
Feedback	No feedback or correction	No feedback or correction	No feedback or correction

Outcome

Significant improvement in spoken naming was found following each of the three treatment phases. Improvement was item-specific and was maintained 2 weeks after the end of the final therapy period. Written naming did not improve following attempted naming but did show significant improvement following reading aloud and delayed copying. Maintenance was tested for reading aloud and was found to be present.

Nickels argues that improvement was due, first, to the variability in JAW's naming abilities; his inconsistency in naming reduced as the lexical item was activated over and over again. Second, successful naming of the word led to 'long-term priming of subsequent retrieval' of that word. Priming of mapping from semantics to phonology is common to each of these tasks, although the two tasks of reading aloud and delayed copying have the added advantage of also accessing phonology via spelling.

This study reports the benefits involved in word finding even when a word is attempted but not named. It further reports success in the absence of any feedback or correction being given. Finally, it proposes that practice is a powerful component of subsequent word-finding success.

Other comments

This study reinterprets Howard and colleagues' (1985) conclusions of generalisation of naming success to control items as related to practice – that is, repeated opportunities to say the names of the items.

Study

Spencer, K. A., Doyle, P. J., McNeil, M. R., Wambaugh, J. L., Park, G., & Carroll, B. (2000). Examining the facilitative effects of rhyme in a patient with output lexicon damage. *Aphasiology, 14*, 567–584.

Focus of therapy: Access to the phonological and orthographic output lexicons.

Target of therapy: Phonology.

Therapy approach: Reactivation.

Client details

General information

NR was a 47-year-old right-handed native English-speaking woman with aphasia following a left parietal haemorrhage. She had completed a two-year art degree.

Overall pattern of language impairments and preservations

NR presented with a conduction aphasia. She had relatively intact single-word comprehension but impaired sentence comprehension. Naming, repetition and oral reading were impaired with phonological errors and neologisms, particularly as word length increased. She was unable to repeat or read non-words. NR was unable to do rhyme judgement tasks involving pictures but performed better on tasks involving written words, relying on the orthographic similarity of the words. NR's difficulties were interpreted as insufficient access to phonological information and faulty encoding of the phonological representations retrieved from the lexicon. Similarly in writing, written naming and writing to dictation of words and nonwords were impaired, with errors of letter substitution, insertion and deletion. This was interpreted as an inability to access and manipulate orthographic representations.

Time post-onset

NR was 12 months post-onset when therapy began.

Therapy

Aim

To provide partial phonological information and thereby enhance access to the phonological output lexicon and the orthographic output lexicon. NR received daily therapy totalling 110 sessions over 7 months. A multiple-baseline and item-specific design was used.

Task	**Semantic category rhyme therapy (SCRT)** Naming using a systematic cueing hierarchy 1 Client provided with superordinate semantic category and rhyming word and asked to name the target (e.g. 'Name a four-legged animal that rhymes with course') 2 Rhyme pair repeated by client 3 Written word presented and client asked to copy word 4 Word produced verbally again by client
Materials	Four lists of 17 pairs of rhymed words (each list from 4 different semantic categories – four-legged animals, household items, carpenter's tools, articles of clothing). The first member of each pair provided the phonological cue, and the second was the target for oral and written naming 12 of each set were targeted for treatment and 5 were not treated (control items) (with the exception of tools where no control items were present)
Hierarchy	None
Feedback on error	1 Phonemic cue provided with a 5-second response time permitted 2 Graphemic cue, with a 5-second response time 3 Therapist says the rhyme–target pair and provides written target word. Client asked to say the word pair, copy the target word, and say the word pair once more
Feedback if correct	1 After correct verbal response, response confirmed by the therapist and the rhyme pair repeated by the client ('horse/course') 2 After correct written response, client asked to repeat the word pair again

The hierarchy for presentation and feedback is clearly documented diagrammatically in the article.

Outcome

Results were analysed using both visual inspection and statistical evaluation. NR demonstrated significantly improved oral and written naming for treated items, with continued improvement following the cessation of therapy and generalisation to untreated items. Improvement was better than would be expected if only maintenance of skills had occurred. Improvement was also seen in naming, nonword repetition and in the percentage of correct information units in connected speech (an index of accurate, relevant and informative words in connected speech, as described in Nicholas and Brookshire, 1993).

No change was recorded on the control task that measured auditory sentence comprehension.

In normal processing, activation of the semantic system following input to the phonological input lexicon would activate the corresponding phonological representation in the output lexicon. Damage to the phonological output lexicon would diminish or prevent this activation. The authors proposed that improvement in accessing the target words was facilitated by providing a rhyme, where activation of the phonological representation of the rhyme word spread to other entries in the output lexicon with similar sounds. Furthermore, by providing semantic information at the start of each therapy task in addition to the rhyme, stronger activation of the target word's phonological and orthographic representation was also facilitated. The pattern of delayed generalisation was explained by the authors as possibly resulting from 'retrieval inhibition' or 'lateral inhibition'.

Other comments

The number of control items in this study ($n = 5$) was small, making any interpretation of treatment effects on untreated items difficult.

Study

Franklin, S., Buerk, F., & Howard, D. (2002). Generalised improvement in speech production for a subject with reproduction conduction aphasia. *Aphasiology*, *16*, 1087–1114.

Focus of therapy: Phonological assembly (phonological encoding).

Target of therapy: Assembly of phonology.

Therapy approach: Reactivation via a strategy of self-monitoring.

Client details

General information

MB was an 83-year-old retired lady. She suffered a left middle cerebral artery infarction.

Overall pattern of language impairments and preservations

MB presented with a reproduction conduction aphasia. Spontaneous speech was characterised by the production of automatic words, phonological errors and neologisms. She had retained single-word comprehension and auditory matching span. Naming, repetition and oral reading were all impaired with phonological errors, particularly with longer words. There was no effect of frequency or imageability. She made repeated attempts at the target word (*conduite d'approche*). Production of nonwords was less accurate than real word production. MB's impairment was located at the level of phonological assembly, specifically a problem of phoneme retrieval during phonological encoding. She also presented with impaired auditory rhyme judgement and some sentence-level difficulties in written comprehension.

Time post-onset

MB was about 6 months post-onset when therapy began.

Therapy

Aim

To improve MB's perceptual processing and monitoring skills as a strategy for improving the detection and correction of errors in speech production. It was hypothesised that spoken word production would improve for both treated and untreated words. Therapy consisted of a total of 21 sessions (7 sessions in Phase 1, 14 sessions in Phase 2) of around 30–45 minutes. Sessions were twice weekly. A multiple-baseline therapy design across tasks, materials and time was used.

Task	Phoneme discrimination Hearing spoken sounds/words and matching them to written material	Self-monitoring Hearing spoken words and judging whether the productions are correct/ incorrect. Then to identify the location of the error within the word
Materials	65 words from the Nickels Naming Test (set matched to an untreated set of 65 items)	20 words each session taken from treated 65 item set
Hierarchy	(a) Deciding whether spoken words are long/short (b) Spoken-to-written phoneme matching (c) Identification of initial phoneme (d) Identification of final phoneme (e) Identification of rhyming word	(a) External monitoring (examiner off-line) – therapist produces word for MB to judge (b) Indirect monitoring (off-line) – MB names picture and recorded response is played back to her for monitoring (c) Direct internal monitoring (on-line) – MB names picture and is immediately asked to judge production

Feedback on error	Not stated	Once errors identified, production of correct target word
Feedback if correct	Not specified	

Outcome

Following Phase 1, there was a significant improvement in naming. A further significant improvement in naming was seen following Phase 2. The improvement was maintained 4 months post-therapy. There was no significant difference between treated and untreated items. Following therapy, there was an overall decrease in MB's *conduite d'approche*, and when multiple responses were produced they more often resulted in correct productions.

Therapy resulted in significant improvement in the naming of both treated and untreated words. Improvement was also seen in the repetition and reading aloud of both words and nonwords. Generalisation to spontaneous speech was seen with a significant increase in the production of phonologically accurate words. MB had stable naming performance before therapy and there was no change on a control task of written sentence comprehension, so naming improvement is unlikely to be due to spontaneous recovery.

The authors suggest that therapy resulted in an improved ability to select phonemes during phonological encoding. It is proposed that improvement was not due to improved self-monitoring skills.

Other comments

With rigorous initial and reassessment data, this is a thorough evaluation of the therapy. Therapy is discussed in sufficient detail to replicate the study but it is not clear what aspect of therapy is responsible for the improvements seen.

12 Therapy for reading

Summary of reading studies

Reading therapies are a relatively recent development in aphasia despite the dyslexias providing the initial impetus for developments in cognitive neuropsychology in the 1960s and 1970s. The influence of the developmental literature is probably seen more in reading than other processing domains. The development of normal reading skills and the management of developmental dyslexia have informed a number of studies reported in this chapter (for examples of discussion of reading models in the acquisition of literacy, see Chall, 1983; Frith, 1986; Gough, 1996; Metsala & Ehri, 1998; Shankweiler & Liberman, 1989; Share & Stanovich, 1995).

For many clinicians working with people with aphasia, reading and writing impairments have taken a lower profile against the more visible (and possibly better understood) deficits of auditory comprehension and spoken production. Those studies reported in the literature tend to group around a small number of impaired processes, with the individual differences of the clients reported giving rise to variations on a theme. The studies reviewed here are listed in Table 12.1.

Studies targeting visual orthographic analysis have generally aimed to improve letter-by-letter reading. This has often involved some form of kinaesthetic input. For example, Lott, Friedman and Linebaugh (1994) required their client to trace letters on the palm of the hand, while Maher, Clayton, Barrett, Schober-Peterson and Rothi (1998) encouraged their client to copy each letter onto any hard accessible surface. Other strategies reported by the latter authors involving, for example, semantic prompts, proved unsuccessful. Maher *et al.* (1998) argue that using a cognitive neuropsychological approach does not, in itself, dictate the appropriate therapy, but that a thorough assessment based on this approach does allow a comprehensive picture to emerge of the client's impaired and residual skills, and contributes to any therapeutic decision making.

Greenwald and Rothi's (1998) client, MR, also had problems at the pre-lexical level but, unlike other alexic people reported in the literature, she was unable to use a letter-by-letter strategy. Identifying retained skills – in this

Table 12.1 Summary of reading therapy studies reviewed here

Level of impairment	Therapy studies	Therapy tasks
Visual orthographic analysis	Greenwald and Rothi (1998) (see p. 190)	• Spoken naming of written letters
	Maher *et al.* (1998) (see p. 192)	• Semantic access strategy • Motor cross-cueing strategy (kinaesthetic input)
Orthographic input lexicon (surface dyslexia)	Coltheart and Byng (1989) (see p. 195)	• Reading of irregular words using picture and symbol mnemonics
	Francis *et al.* (2001b) (see p. 198)	• Simultaneous oral spelling of irregular words • Simultaneous oral spelling of irregular words using client's own phonetic reading in a phrase with correct pronunciation
Orthographic input lexicon and access to semantics (surface dyslexia)	Scott and Byng (1989) (see p. 202)	• Comprehension of homophones via computer-presented sentence completion task. Homophonic and orthographically similar word foils
Semantic system	Byng (1988) (see p. 204)	• Picture-to-written word matching tasks for abstract words. • Dictionary work to generate synonyms for abstract words
Orthographic-to-phonological conversion[1] (phonological dyslexia and/or deep dyslexia)	De Partz (1986) (see p. 206) Nickels (1992) (see p. 209) Berndt and Mitchum (1994) (see p. 212)	All studies based on de Partz (1986): • Generation of code word for each letter • Segmentation of initial phoneme from code word • Production of phoneme on presentation of grapheme • Phoneme blending
	Conway *et al.* (1998) (see p. 214)	• Phonological awareness using the Auditory Discrimination in Depth (ADD) program
	Kendall *et al.* (1998) (see p. 218)	• Teaching of the 'c-rule' and the 'g-rule'
	Francis *et al.* (2001b) (see p. 198)	• Identifying letters • Linking letters to phonemes • Blending consonant clusters
	Friedman and Lott (2002) (see p. 220)	• Bigraph–phoneme correspondences
	Yampolsky and Waters (2002) (see p. 223)	• Grapheme–phoneme correspondences • Phoneme blending • Phonological awareness using the Wilson reading system

[1] The treatment of grapheme–phoneme correspondence may result in: (a) a reduction of semantic and visual errors by using the sub-lexical route to support lexical reading; (b) improvement in naming if the client's written naming is superior to oral naming. Clients are encouraged to visualise name and then read aloud.

case, a striking ability to name a word when it was spelled aloud – was central to determining an effective treatment approach for MR. Delving further into this retained skill – that is, how the word was pronounced after being spelled aloud – enabled the authors to hypothesise where exactly in the language-processing system the impairment was located and how MR might respond to therapy. Teaching letter-by-letter reading was still considered an appropriate therapy approach to use, but this decision was directly related to an assessment of her retained skills. It should also be noted that this approach did produce significant improvement, highlighting the potential for very severely impaired alexic patterns to change with individualised therapy.

A limited number of studies have looked at the orthographic input lexicon, with only one study (Scott & Byng, 1989) looking at access to semantics from the lexicon. Targeting semantics via written input has also received little attention, although see Byng (1988). Those studies focusing on the orthographic input lexicon raise some of the same issues of generalisation seen in output phonology whereby therapy effects show a tendency to be item specific, unless other processes become involved in the change process.

A number of studies have reported attempts to remediate the orthographic-to-phonological conversion route, a process impaired in both deep and phonological dyslexia, through re-teaching correspondence between graphemes and phonemes. The first study reported by De Partz (1986) successfully re-educated a person in using grapheme-to-phoneme correspondence rules; SP, a young client with a Wernicke-type aphasia, had intact lexical knowledge which mediated the process. Several other studies have replicated this approach and met with varying levels of success. Berndt and Mitchum (1994) reported less success with their client, LR, an older man with global aphasia, who improved to some extent but had difficulties blending combinations of phonemes longer than two in length (e.g. CVC combinations). An impairment in short-term memory was given as a possible reason for this. Nickels (1992) reported a similarly low level of improvement with TC, a middle-aged man with a Wernicke-type aphasia, until a semantic component was introduced to the intervention protocol and reading improved.

Blending of phonemes had also been reported by Nickels (1992) to be an area of difficulty for her client, although the length of intervention with TC was considerably shorter than de Partz's earlier client. Friedman and Lott (2002) attempted to address the area of blending phonemes by requiring their clients, LR and KT, to learn *bigraphs* (e.g. a VC or CV combination) rather than individual graphemes. They reported greater success with blending. Those clients for whom higher rates of success using this type of approach have been reported have also received a correspondingly longer period of intervention, raising issues of practicality with respect to provision of therapy services. There is also an issue of the utility of this approach. While the number of graphemes (letters or groups of letters standing for a single phoneme, e.g. C, T, TH, EA) in English is relatively limited, the number of bigraphs is very large. If there was generalisation to untrained but related bigraphs – for instance, learning that AT is /æt/ and EM is /ɛm/ might help a client to deduce the pronunciation of AM – this might not be a problem. Friedman and Lott (2002), however, found no evidence of improvement to bigraphs that were not treated.

An issue highlighted by Greenwald and Rothi (1998) relates to the importance of feedback. MR would not, they believe, have made the same gains if she had been left to herself to practise letter naming; the feedback, both when correct and in error, was vital to behaviour change. Interestingly, they also discuss the potential for feedback being delivered by a carer, friend or a computer program, thereby reducing the time required of an experienced professional and potentially making long-term intervention more viable.

The terminology may vary between studies, with some studies referring to *alexia* and others *dyslexia*. As the terms *aphasia* and *dysphasia* may be used synonymously in the literature by some authors and considered to differentiate partial from total language loss by others, this is also the case in the reading literature. Throughout this chapter, terms used by the respective authors have been retained with no inferences drawn regarding the authors' orientation. This also applies in the following chapter with respect to *agraphia* and *dysgraphia*.

EVALUATIONS OF THERAPY STUDIES

Study

Greenwald, M. L., & Rothi, L. J. G. (1998). Lexical access via letter naming in a profoundly alexic and anomic patient: a treatment study. *Journal of the International Neuropsychological Society*, *4*, 595–607.

Focus of therapy: Visual orthographic analysis.

Therapy approach: Cognitive relay strategy using letter-by-letter reading.

Client details

General information

MR was a 72-year-old right-handed retired clerical worker who reported no developmental reading difficulties. She had a left CVA resulting in severe alexia with agraphia, a right homonymous hemianopia, anomia, some apraxia and Gertmann's syndrome. An MRI scan showed occipital lobe damage that extended to the temporal-parietal-occipital junction.

Overall pattern of language impairments and preservations

MR's language performance was consistent with an anomic aphasia characterised by fluent output, lexical retrieval difficulties, preserved repetition and relatively spared auditory comprehension. Her anomia was considered to be due to both impaired semantics and access to phonology from semantics.

MR was unable to read aloud words or nonwords, or use a letter-by-letter strategy. Successful attempts at naming letters and phonemes were probably due to chance. Severe naming difficulties contrasted with two preserved abilities: (1) an intact ability to name a word when a word was orally spelled to her (100% success) and (2) an ability to name environmental sounds (75% success). With respect to the former ability, her success in pronouncing both regular and exception words, nonwords and words of low imageability and frequency, suggested that her ability to encode letters and access phonology were intact via orally spelled words and that her problems related to an impaired ability to decode graphemic cues from the written form. She was unable to perform any pre-lexical or lexical tasks when printed.

Time post-onset

MR was 13 months post-onset at the time of the study.

Therapy

Aim

To teach reading using a letter-by-letter strategy of letter naming. Treatment was provided in two phases. During both of these phases, treatment was given twice each day, 5 days a week over 5 weeks (2½ weeks for each set of training items). The session involved approximately 15 min treatment and 5–15 min probing behaviours. A multiple baseline design across behaviours was used to examine the efficacy of therapy.

Task	Phase 1: Letter naming Shown a letter and asked to name	Phase 2: Letter identification Identification of letter from a large sample
Materials	Two sets of 8 letters. Each item trained four times each session. Order of items was randomised. 88% success criterion over two consecutive sessions or 24 sessions before moving to set 2	Larger sample of letters

Hierarchy	None	Additional practice with letters named incorrectly
Feedback on error	Incorrect response acknowledged and client asked to finger trace the letter once or twice and re-attempt to name the letter. On second error, the incorrect response was again acknowledged and the clinician provided the letter name, traced the letter and provided a description of the shape of the letter. The client was asked to finger trace the letter and repeat the name three times	
Feedback if correct	Positive response acknowledged and client asked to finger trace the letter while repeating the letter name three times	

Outcome

During phase 1, naming of the first set of letters improved significantly (although this was not robust from session to session). There was a significantly better naming performance with the second set of letters when these were introduced. During phase 2, when both sets were treated together, significant improvement continued for both sets of letters. No generalisation was seen to oral reading of words for those untreated letters, or to oral naming of Arabic numerals or written symbols. MR reported some carryover of her success in therapy to daily life, being able to read (or attempt) functional signs and labels.

Improvement was maintained when tested one week post-therapy. At 6–12 months post-therapy, MR demonstrated a higher success rate with upper-case letters than lower-case letters, a possible influence of therapy, together with improved abilities in letter formation, again possibly due to tracing the written letter shapes during the period of intervention.

Other comments

MR is also reported in Greenwald, Raymer, Richardson and Rothi (1995), where her naming impairment is the focus of therapy. Greenwald and Rothi stress the value of assessing how orally spelled words are pronounced, an influential factor in deciding to use the spoken system in the therapy reported here.

Study

Maher, L. M., Clayton, M. C., Barrett, A. M., Schober-Peterson, D., & Rothi, L. J. G. (1998). Rehabilitation of a case of pure alexia: exploiting residual abilities. *Journal of the International Neuropsychological Society, 4*, 636–647.

Focus of therapy: Visual orthographic analysis.

Therapy approach: Reactivation (described by authors as 'restitutive') using a semantic access strategy. Cognitive-relay (described by authors as 'substitutive') using a motor cross-cueing strategy to reactivate access to letters.

Client details

General information

VT was a 43-year-old right-handed woman who had a CVA that resulted in alexia, a dense right homonymous hemianopia, dysarthria (described as 'confusion' with articulation) and some memory loss. An MRI scan showed a large left hemisphere occipital infarct, in the territory supplied by the posterior cerebral artery, and some cerebellar involvement. A second CVA had not resulted in further symptoms. VT had a university degree. Before her CVA, she had worked as a chemist and laboratory supervisor.

Overall pattern of language impairments and preservations

VT had a severe reading impairment in the presence of preserved written and spoken language production. A deficit was identified at the level of abstract letter identification, as seen by poor letter recognition and an inability to match letters and words of varying fonts, in the presence of retained ability to perceive letter stimuli. She had access to the orthographic input lexicon as seen in her ability to recognise orally spelled real words and nonwords. She was unable, however, to read these words aloud but could do so when she copied the target word onto her hand – that is, visually tracing the words and supporting this with head movement. This suggested a difficulty getting from the visual stimulus to the orthographic lexical store. Once a word and sentence were traced on her hand, she was able to access the semantic system without error. Writing was unimpaired. Immediately post-trauma, VT had successfully learned to read Braille to a proficient level and had later received speech and language therapy for her dysarthria.

Time post-onset

VT was 14 months post-onset prior to a period of speech and language therapy. This study commenced on discharge from that therapy period (length of time not stated).

Therapy

Aims

1   To gain semantic access to a word through repeated exposure to the word.
2   To read a word following a motor cue (pretending to copy the written word) with and without colour highlighting in the spaces between words.

Therapy consisted of three phases, each involving a different task, which were conducted sequentially. The first phase of therapy targeting semantic access was conducted over six sessions; the time period was not stated. The second phase (i.e. motor cross-cueing without colour spacing) was conducted four times per week over 4½ weeks, with each session lasting one hour. The third phase (i.e. motor cross-cueing with colour spacing) was provided in six sessions spread over 2 weeks. A control task design was used to monitor efficacy.

Task	1. Implicit semantic access strategy Make a semantic judgement on a written word presented for approximately 1 second	2. Motor cross-cueing Trace each letter of a word onto a hard surface and say the word as quickly as possible	3. Colour spacing with motor cross-cueing Trace each letter of a word onto a hard surface and say the word as quickly as possible
Materials	Four categories of 10 written words. 20 words in each treatment session with 2–5 trials for each word	100 six-word sentences and 100 five-word sentences (from Yorkston & Beukelman, 1981). Organised into blocks of 10 sentences	Seven- and eight-word sentences organised into blocks of 10 sentences (from Yorkston & Beukelman, 1981). Spaces between words were highlighted by a colour
Hierarchy	None	None	None
Feedback	Immediate verbal feedback given on accuracy for 50% of items, with delayed verbal feedback (at end of block of items) for the other 50%	Feedback provided on reading speed of each response	Feedback provided on reading speed of each response

Outcome

Treatment response was measured by changes in reading speed, with some visual inspection of the data.

Following the first phase of therapy, VT made no improvement, remaining at chance in making semantic judgements. Following the second phase, VT's reading speed doubled, rising from approximately 20 words per minute (wpm) to 44.5 wpm. Generalisation was seen to non-treated sentences. Following the third task involving colour spacing, no additional gains were seen. Reading speed in Braille remained consistent throughout all phases.

Treatment benefits were, therefore, apparent following the motor cross-cueing strategy but not with the semantic strategy. These gains were not attributable simply to repeated practice, as seen by the generalisation to untreated items, or to generalised practice effects, as seen in the consistency of her performance reading Braille. The authors describe this strategy as a letter-by-letter strategy but with a motor element rather than a spoken naming one.

Reading speed remained slower than pre-morbid performance but VT had regained her ability to read so long as she used the motor cross-cueing and took sufficient time.

Other comments

Maher *et al.* provide a detailed discussion on the visual analysis system, identifying the component processes and the mechanisms underlying different deficits that may underpin pure alexia. The motor cross-cueing strategy was developed from an earlier study by Lott *et al.* (1994), in which the therapy involved copying the letters onto the palm of the hand and providing the client with tactile as well as motor feedback.

Study

Coltheart, M., & Byng, S. (1989). A treatment for surface dyslexia. In X. Seron & G. Deloche (Eds.), *Cognitive approaches in neuropsychological rehabilitation*. Hillsdale, NJ: Lawrence Erlbaum Associates.

Focus of therapy: Orthographic input lexicon (surface dyslexia).

Therapy approach: Reactivation.

Client details

General information

EE was a 40-year-old left-handed male postal worker who fell off a ladder. A CT scan showed an extensive haemorrhagic contusion of the right temporal lobe and a large subdural haematoma extending over the left temporal onto the left parietal lobe. A right temporoparietal craniotomy and evacuation of acute subdural haematoma and haemorrhagic contusions of the right temporal lobe was performed.

Overall pattern of language impairments and preservations

EE's spoken output was characterised by word-finding difficulties, with good auditory comprehension of single words. His reading of irregular words was significantly impaired compared with his reading of regular words, although the latter was impaired to some extent. His real word reading was characterised by regularisation errors. In a homophone matching task, EE showed a significant disadvantage for irregular words. Homophone confusions were also present in reading comprehension. The authors suggested that EE's pattern was consistent with surface dyslexia and that it reflected an impairment at the level of visual word recognition (the orthographic input lexicon).

Time post-onset

Therapy commenced when EE was 6 months post-trauma.

Therapy

Aim

To improve the reading of irregular words using a whole-word training approach. Therapy consisted of three phases, corresponding to three different tasks. Therapy in Phase 1 lasted for a total of 5 weeks. Each week the reading of the words without the mnemonic aids was tested. Therapy was carried out at home for 15 min each day, 2 weeks with Group 1 words and 2 weeks with Group 2 words. In Phase 2, therapy was carried out at home for a period of one week. Performance was re-tested immediately post-therapy and again at 4 weeks post-therapy. The duration of the third therapy phase was not stated. A multiple baseline therapy design was used to demonstrate the efficacy of treatment.

Task	Phase 1: Reading of irregular words	Phase 2: Reading of words	Phase 3: Reading of words
	Written word presented alongside a picture mnemonic representing meaning	Written word presented with mnemonic symbol	Written word presented with mnemonic symbol

Materials	24 words containing two vowels + 'gh' (e.g. 'cough'). Words divided into two groups of 12	54 words which EE misread during pre-test. Pre-test consisted of 485 most frequent words in Kučera and Francis (1967) frequency counts. Mnemonic symbols drawn on word chosen by EE. Words divided into two groups of 27. Only one group of words treated	101 words which EE misread during pre-test. Pre-test consisted of next 388 words in Kučera and Francis (1967) frequency counts. Mnemonic symbols drawn on word chosen by EE. Words divided into two groups. Only one group of words treated
Hierarchy	None	None	None
Feedback	Not specified. Progress chart kept each day	Not specified	Not specified

Outcome

A significant improvement for treated words followed Phase 1 of the therapy programme. Some improvement of untreated Group 2 words was seen following treatment of Group 1 words. Accurate performance for both groups of words was maintained one year post-therapy. As with the first phase, a significant improvement for both treated and untreated words followed Phases 2 and 3 of therapy, although reading of treated words was superior to that of untreated words.

In the second and third phases, EE's reading of the words was stable prior to treatment, leading the authors to suggest that improvement was not due to spontaneous recovery. There was significant improvement of treated words and improvement was maintained post-therapy, with some improvement of the reading of untreated words. The authors suggest that this non-specific treatment effect may be explained by a visual word recognition system based on distributed representations, as Hinton, McClelland and Rumelhart (1986) suggested.

Other comments

Coltheart and Byng provide a comprehensive discussion on the components of an item-specific model compared with a distributed-representation approach, emphasising the letter, word and semantic levels in the latter, and suggesting how a distributed-representation approach may underpin an explanation of the successful therapy reported here. EE's therapy is also summarised in Nickels (1995).

Study

Francis, D. R., Riddoch, M. J., & Humphreys, G. W. (2001b). Treating agnostic alexia complicated by additional impairments. *Neuropsychological Rehabilitation*, *11*, 113–145.

Focus of therapy: Orthographic-to-phonological conversion and the orthographic input lexicon.

Therapy approach: Relearning.

Client details

General information

MGM was a 19-year-old man who sustained a head injury at the age of 8. An MRI scan highlighted damage to the occipital, frontal and temporal lobes (temporal lobe damage more pronounced on the right-hand side). Before the trauma, reading acquisition was unimpaired. MGM had shown signs of being ambidextrous.

Overall pattern of language impairments and preservations

MGM's aphasic symptoms had resolved at the time of the reported study, with an almost total alexia remaining, coupled with a severe impairment in visual processing, which was not due to poor visual acuity or visual field defects. A severe visual agnosia was present as seen by his better performance on naming real objects than line drawings, his improved performance with tactile input (as opposed to visual input), and his better response to verbal information that relied on information other than visual information. A profound apperceptive agnosia was also present, together with an impairment of stored knowledge for words and reduced verbal memory.

Reading was characterised by a limited ability to perceive letter shapes, either visually or via tactile input, in the presence of largely intact phonological processing skills (i.e. use of his sub-lexical reading route). Good phonological processing was seen in good auditory discrimination of nonwords, auditory rhyme judgements and phoneme segmentation.

Time post-onset

MGM was 11 years post-onset at the time of the study.

Therapy

Aims

1   To teach identification of letters.
2   To re-teach letter-sound correspondences.
3   To resolve blending in words.
4   To teach irregular words using simultaneous oral spelling with the client's own phonetic reading.

Four separate interventions were carried out; the initial three addressed orthographic-to-phoneme conversion, while the final therapy targeted the orthographic input lexicon. The first therapy was given three times per week (4 hours a week) over a 9-month period. The second phase commenced approximately half way through the first therapy at around 5 months. The third intervention was only carried out for one session. The final therapy was carried out over 12 sessions, which took place twice a week over 6 weeks. A repeated multiple-baseline design was used.

Therapies 1–3: Targeting orthographic-to-phoneme conversion

Task	1. Identification of letters	2. Re-teaching letter–sound correspondences	3. Phoneme blending on final consonant clusters
	Reinforce the shape of letters and then name	Letter–sound association taught via relay. Client asked to: (a) Give the cue phrase for a letter and (b) Then provide the sound of a letter	Identify letters of a word and segment the final consonant blend
Materials	20 high-frequency letters used. For each correct letter, required: (a) Letter with part missing (b) A mirror image and second correct letter (c) A verbal mnemonic	Six letters consistently incorrect by client. Four letters given a lexical relay (residual word knowledge related to a letter). Two letters given a phrase linking letter name and sound	Two lists of words: (a) 22 final consonant blends (treated) (b) 22 initial consonant blends (control)

| Hierarchy | (a) Letter shape reinforcement via:
(i) correcting letters with part missing
(ii) verbally describing the shape of letters
(iii) discriminating letters from the mirror image
(iv) delayed copying
(b) Letter naming via mnemonics that incorporated a visual description and phonemic cue | | (a) Sound out letters in a word and blend to produce the word
(b) Repeat sounding out word but omitting the final consonant
(c) Add the final consonant and say the word |
| Feedback | Not specified | Not specified | Not specified |

Therapy 4: Targeting orthographic input lexicon

Methods 1 and 2 carried out simultaneously.

Task	**Method 1: Simultaneous oral spelling of irregular words** (based on Bryant & Bradley, 1985)	**Method 2: Simultaneous oral spelling of irregular words using client's own phonetic reading** (correct word and incorrect pronunciation or word placed in a rhyming/ alliterative phrase)
Materials	20 irregular words (high-frequency, often function words) divided into two sets for the two methods. For the second method, a rhyming or alliterative phrase containing the client's own phonetic reading of the word and the correct pronunciation was devised, e.g. if 'be' is pronounced as /bɛ/, then the phrase 'Ben BE good' might be generated to contrast /bɛ/ and /bi/	
Hierarchy	1 Client identifies a word which is written down 2 Client names the word 3 Client writes the word while simultaneously naming each letter 4 Client names the word again and then repeats the procedure with the same word	As for previous method but using the rhyming/alliterative phrase. The whole phrase is repeated instead of just the single name after the word is written down and then copied

Feedback on error	Not specified
Feedback if correct	Not specified

Outcome

Therapies 1–3

MGM's letter naming improved after the first stage. While this stage continued for 9 months, the authors reported marked improvement after 5 months of treatment, improving from near floor performance to 77–88% success. Only treated items improved. Generalisation was seen across fonts. MGM was also able to read words containing the treated letters, using a letter-by-letter strategy, despite no focus on words in therapy. After 6 weeks of the second therapy phase, MGM had learnt the first four letters using the relay strategy and went on to learn the remaining two letters by the end of the following 9 weeks. By the end of the first 9 months, MGM was reading short words and sentences. After only one session of the third stage of therapy, MGM's reading of final cluster words increased from 14% (41% with self-correction) to 68% (91% with self-correction). His ability to read untreated words (i.e. initial clusters) immediately, without self-correction, also improved significantly (from 38% to 71%); however, when self-correction was considered, the overall rate of success with untreated words did not change. MGM's reading pattern was, at this stage, characteristic of surface dyslexia where words were read through sounding out each letter.

Therapy 4

Those words treated by the second method, using the phrase, were successfully learnt, while those words using the initial method were not.

Francis *et al.* propose that the success of therapy was due to the fact that the methods used bypassed the underlying deficit (i.e. the visual processing impairment) and capitalised on intact abilities (e.g. phonological processing skills). They further suggest that the fourth intervention linked with the previous therapies – that is, 'the verbal description of the letter shape was linked, via rhyme or phonetic similarity, to its name' (p.140). This contrasts with other studies in which a whole-word approach was used over a phonetic strategy. They argue that a cognitive neuropsychological assessment directly influenced the selection of therapeutic methods despite being counter-intuitive.

Other comments

Francis *et al.* (2001) provide a discussion of the influences of cognitive neuropsychology on intervention into reading disorders, raising many issues related to *why* and *how* therapy works. Strategies, again, draw from the literature on reading acquisition.

Study

Scott, C. J., & Byng, S. (1989). Computer assisted remediation of a homophone comprehension disorder in surface dyslexia. *Aphasiology*, *3*, 301–320.

Focus of therapy: Orthographic input lexicon and access from the orthographic input lexicon to the semantic system (surface dyslexia).

Therapy approach: Reactivation.

Client details

General information

JB was a 24-year-old student nurse who suffered a head injury. A CT scan showed an infarct in the left temporal lobe.

Overall pattern of language impairments and preservations

JB's comprehension during conversation was good, although some difficulties were present in understanding both spoken complex commands and inference. On formal testing, severe word-finding difficulties were evident with the production of some semantic errors. Reading was slow and laboured, with reading of single words characterised by sub-vocal rehearsal. JB was able to extract the gist of sentences and paragraphs. She showed a non-significant trend for better reading of regular words relative to irregular words. Error responses were regularisations and words that were visually and phonologically related to the target word. She was able to read nonwords when these involved consonant and vowel units but experienced difficulties when vowel digraphs were present. In a homophone matching task, JB also showed a non-significant advantage for regular words. When asked to define homophones, she was inconsistent and showed a frequency effect, more often providing a definition for the most frequent homophone. The authors suggested that JB had impaired access to the orthographic input lexicon, with a partial dissociation of the orthographic input lexicon from the semantic system and the phonological output lexicon. Reading comprehension occurred via the phonological form rather than the orthographic form. Writing was characterised by word-finding difficulties and numerous spelling errors. On testing, JB was significantly impaired in her writing of irregular words relative to regular words, although some retrieval of irregular forms did occur. Error responses were regularisations. Spelling of homophones was impaired. The authors suggest some partial access to the orthographic output lexicon, but partial dissociation of the output lexicon from the semantic system and use of the sub-lexical route to aid spelling. They conclude that JB shows many of the features of surface dyslexia and surface dysgraphia.

Time post-onset

Therapy commenced 8 months post-trauma.

Therapy

Aim

To improve the comprehension of homophones by re-establishing the link from the orthographic input lexicon to the semantic system. Therapy consisted of 29 sessions over 10 weeks. A control task therapy design was used to demonstrate the efficacy of therapy.

Task	**Homotrain** Computer presented sentence completion task. Sentence presented on screen with missing homophonic word. Six word choices presented beneath
Materials	136 sentences containing 68 homophone pairs. Word choices: (a) Target (b) Homophone pair (c) Pseudohomophone (d) Three orthographically similar foils
Hierarchy	None
Feedback on error	Visual feedback – word in red Negative tune Required to make another selection
Feedback if correct	Visual feedback – word in blue Short, cheerful tune Sentence reproduced at foot of screen. Homophone to be typed in. Bad noise if inappropriate letters pressed

Outcome

JB made gradual and significant improvement during therapy. Comprehension of treated and untreated homophone sentences improved following therapy, although performance was superior for treated homophones. Significant improvement was seen in the ability to provide definitions for the treated and untreated homophones. No significant improvement was recorded in the ability to write homophones to dictation or in the ability to write irregular words to dictation.

Treatment resulted in significant improvement in homophone comprehension. There was no significant improvement in the writing of words, suggesting improvement was a consequence of treatment rather than spontaneous recovery. The authors suggested that significant improvement for treated items was a consequence of an item-specific improvement within the orthographic input lexicon. Improvement seen with the untreated homophones was considered to be a consequence of a general improvement in the functioning of the access route from the orthographic input lexicon to the semantic system. Generalisation to untreated items was only evident when sentence context was present. The lack of improvement in the ability to write even the treated homophones to dictation was thought to be a consequence of the word remaining on the screen during the therapy procedure, removing the need to encode the word in memory.

Other comments

JB's therapy is also described in Nickels (1995). Scott and Byng provide a discussion of their findings in relation to Behrmann's (1987) study of a person with surface dysgraphia, reviewed in Chapter 13.

Study

Byng, S. (1988). Sentence processing deficits: theory and therapy. *Cognitive Neuropsychology*, *5*, 629–676.

Focus of therapy: Semantic system – written comprehension of abstract words

Therapy approach: Reactivation.

Client details

General information

BRB was a 41-year-old man who had a left middle cerebral artery infarct. He had previously worked as a businessman.

Overall pattern of language impairments and preservations

BRB was initially diagnosed with moderate to severe expressive dysphasia and a mild receptive dysphasia characteristic of Broca's aphasia. Some articulatory difficulty was present on consonant clusters and polysyllabic words. At the time of the study, BRB had problems with the mapping of thematic roles in reversible and locative sentences (also treated), and was poor at spoken and written synonym judgements for abstract, but not concrete, words. He was unable to read nonwords, but could read function words and highly imageable words, making visual errors with low-imageability and low-frequency words. Reduced short-term memory matching span was also noted. Verbal output was characterised by few sentences and many single words, with a low proportion of closed-class items.

Time post-onset

This phase of therapy was begun 5–6 years post-onset, 6 months after a period of sentence therapy targeting mapping of thematic relations.

Therapy

Aim

To improve the comprehension of abstract words. The therapy was introduced by the therapist and then continued at home. Therapy consisted of 4 weeks of practice, one week per phase. A cross-over therapy design was used to monitor the efficacy of this therapy and the sentence therapy.

Task	1. Picture–written word matching task	2. Synonym generation task: 'dictionary therapy'
	Written word presented with 4 accompanying pictures: target, semantic distractor, 2 unrelated distractors. Select the picture to go with the written word	Using a dictionary to look at all the different meanings for each word, BRB made up his own one-word synonym or synonyms for each item 'to best encapsulate the range of meanings'
Materials	The 75 words of the Shallice and McGill picture–word matching test, with concrete and abstract words each divided into three groups: (i) correct in both auditory and visual pre-therapy testing; (ii) correct in one	The 75 words treated in the picture–word matching task

	modality; (iii) correct in neither modality. Each of these groups was then divided into two, to provide different items for treatment phases 1 and 2	
Hierarchy	None	None
Feedback	BRB had to check the response against an answer sheet (answers given as the number of the picture to prevent rote learning)	Not specified

Outcome

BRB's performance on task stimuli of the picture–word matching task increased to 100% correct. Improvement was item specific (treated items improved while untreated items did not) and task specific (performance on the same items in synonym judgements did not improve). Following the synonym generation task, performance on the synonym judgement task improved significantly. Improvement was, again, item specific but generalised to a word-to-picture matching task using the same items.

BRB, therefore, improved in his understanding of the treated written abstract words. The authors proposed that this improvement was a consequence of the 'restoration' of some lexical entries that had been 'lost'. This improvement was, however, task specific (i.e. comprehension of the same items from a picture–word matching task was not demonstrated in a synonym judgement task). The second type of treatment (dictionary method) provided a richer set of meanings than the picture–word matching method. The dictionary method, therefore, enabled BRB to learn a specific set of word meanings which he was able to generalise to a different task. Improvement can be attributed to therapy, as there was stable performance before therapy. Functional improvements were not stated.

Other comments

The design of this study was very robust in ensuring that change was attributable to therapy and also in addressing maintenance of therapy effects. Therapy with BRB is also summarised in Byng and Coltheart (1986).

Study

De Partz, M.-P. (1986). Re-education of a deep dyslexic patient: rationale of the method and results. *Cognitive Neuropsychology*, *3*, 149–177.

Focus of therapy: Orthographic-to-phonological conversion.

Therapy approach: Relearning.

Client details

General information

SP was a 31-year-old left-handed university-educated executive. He had a large intracerebral haematoma in the left parietotemporal lobe which was evacuated surgically. He was a native French speaker and therapy took place in this language. Before his illness, SP had read for at least 3 hours a day.

Overall pattern of language impairments and preservations

SP's spoken production was fluent and characterised by anomia, phonological and occasional semantic errors. He retained good repetition of letters and syllables, although some phonological difficulties were evident in word repetition. Auditory comprehension of single words was generally intact, although he had some difficulties in certain semantic fields (e.g. body parts). Reading performance was characterised by impaired reading of nonwords; content words were read more accurately than function words and nouns were better than verbs. Reading showed an effect of imageability but no effect of length, frequency or regularity. In written word-to-picture matching tests and odd-word-out tests, semantic, visual and derivational errors were produced. The authors considered SP's pattern to be consistent with deep dyslexia.

Time post-onset

Therapy commenced when SP was 3 months post-onset.

Therapy

Aim

To re-teach grapheme-to-phoneme correspondence. Therapy consisted of three stages. Stages 1 and 2 involved 9 months of intensive therapy. Stage 3 consisted of an additional 65 therapy sessions, with the overall period of therapy totalling approximately one year. A multiple-baseline therapy design was used to measure efficacy.

Stage 1: Simple grapheme reading reconstruction

Task	1. Generate code word for individual letters Letter of alphabet linked with lexical relay code word. Say code word in response to letter	2. Phoneme segmentation Segment initial phoneme from code words and say phoneme	3. Phoneme blending Sound out letters and blend to produce nonwords, then words
Materials	Code words generated by client	Code words as for (1)	Written words. Simple 3- or 4-letter monosyllabic nonwords and regular real words
Hierarchy	None	(a) Phoneme produced via code word (b) Phoneme produced in response to letter	Initial use of nonwords to prevent use of a semantic strategy
Feedback	Not applicable	If incorrect phoneme produced, return to code word	Not specified

Stage 2: Complex grapheme reading reconstruction

Therapy targeted groups of letters that corresponded to one phoneme in French or that presented few pronunciation ambiguities. The code words for this stage were content words that were homophones (or near homophones) or words which contained the targeted letter sequences. The steps of therapy were as above.

Stage 3: Learning grapheme contextual rules

Therapy involved the client being trained to apply three grapheme contextual rules. Error analysis had identified the three specific conversion rules sensitive to context that were causing most of his errors. Each of these rules was explained to the client and he was trained in their use in reading aloud and pointing out tasks. Nonwords and abstract words were used to prevent the use of a semantic strategy.

Outcome

At the end of Stages 1 and 2, SP was able to transcode letters into their corresponding phonemes. SP's reading aloud significantly improved and the discrepancy between words and nonwords was eliminated. The majority of the remaining reading errors were a consequence of the misapplication of grapheme-to-phoneme rules. Following the third stage of therapy, errors in reading aloud were reduced to 2%, while processing of letters and tasks involving reading comprehension were performed without error. Therapy resulted in SP being able to read aloud, albeit slowly. The authors propose that the improvement resulted from reorganisation of the impaired grapheme-to-phoneme process by using spared lexical knowledge as a relay between graphemes and their pronunciation.

Other comments

The author notes that the re-training of orthographic-to-phonological rules permitted the correct reading of only a relatively small proportion of the French lexicon, due to the many orthographical irregularities in French. De Partz suggests that this patient seems to be simultaneously using a combination of grapheme–phoneme codes and reading via direct access to meaning.

With respect to client suitability, the client reported here was fluent and able to repeat. This may limit the use of this therapy with non-fluent clients. The client further demonstrated a mnemonic capacity in memorising the different associations. The results also followed extensive therapeutic input that required high motivation and resource availability. His youthfulness may also have been a contributing factor in sustaining motivation.

A replication of this therapy procedure is discussed in Nickels (1992) and the therapy is summarised in Nickels (1995).

Study

Nickels, L. A. (1992). The autocue? Self-generated phonemic cues in the treatment of a disorder of reading and naming. *Cognitive Neuropsychology*, 9, 155–182.

Focus of therapy: Orthographic-to-phonological conversion to improve spoken naming.

Therapy approach: Relearning of orthographic-to-phonological conversion rules. Cognitive relay strategy to read aloud a visualised word to help spoken naming.

Client details

General information

TC was a right-handed male businessman. He had a left CVA when 43 years old, resulting in a global aphasia, right-sided weakness and right-sided sensory impairment. A CT scan showed a substantial left middle cerebral artery infarct. Five months post-onset, TC's perceptual, visuo-spatial and non-verbal reasoning skills were considered to be intact.

Overall pattern of language impairments and preservations

TC's speech was fluent with word-finding difficulties. He used a combination of speech, writing, drawing and gesturing of key words to communicate. He was able to write some high-imageability words. His auditory comprehension in conversation was functional, but on testing he made errors in single word and sentence comprehension. His written comprehension of single words and sentences was also impaired but better than that of his auditory comprehension. TC was unable to read or write nonwords. His reading aloud was characterised by semantic errors and showed an imageability effect. The author proposes that TC had deep dyslexia, with additional deficits in the sub-lexical writing route and in accessing semantics from the auditory input lexicon.

Time post-onset

TC was 16–18 months post-onset when therapy commenced.

Therapy

Aim

To teach grapheme-to-phoneme correspondence to improve reading aloud. As TC's written naming was superior to his spoken naming, it was hoped that he would be able to use 'visualised' written word forms to generate spoken forms. Therapy consisted of two 15–30 min sessions per week for 10 weeks. Some additional home exercises were carried out. A multiple baseline therapy design was used.

Task	1. Generate relay word (or code word) Letter of alphabet linked with relay word. Say relay word in response to letter	2. Phoneme segmentation Segment initial phoneme from relay words and say phoneme	3. Phoneme blending Sound out letters and blend to produce nonwords, then words

Materials	Relay words generated by TC. Relay words had the letter in its most frequent pronunciation	Relay words	Written words. Simple 3- or 4-letter monosyllabic nonwords and regular real words
Hierarchy	None	(a) Phoneme produced via relay word (b) Phoneme produced in response to letter	Initially nonwords; words introduced to reduce difficulty
Feedback	Not applicable	Not specified	Not specified

TC was unable to blend phonemes, which required the therapy programme to be changed. The final phase of therapy required TC to silently associate the initial letter of the target word with the relay word, sound out the initial phoneme and then produce the target word. If unable to produce the target word, TC was encouraged to think about the meaning of the word and to sound out additional letters. At this stage, it was discussed with TC that he could try and visualise words and then use this strategy to produce them in speech.

Outcome

A significant improvement was found in the reading of real words. Spoken naming also improved significantly and approximated to written naming performance. TC remained unable to read nonwords and there was no effect of regularity in reading or naming. Improvement in the reading of real words was maintained 5 months post-therapy.

TC's reading aloud and spoken naming therefore improved post-therapy. No other significant changes were evident. TC's improvement was considered to be a consequence of therapy. As TC remained unable to read nonwords, however, and there was no regularity effect in reading, these improvements cannot be a consequence of the use of grapheme-to-phoneme correspondences. The author hypothesised that TC visualised the initial letters and converted them to phonemes. These acted as self-generated phonemic cues.

Other comments

While this study drew on the therapy procedure described by De Partz (1986), reviewed earlier, Nickels highlights the different outcomes obtained for different clients. The client reported by Nickels was unable to blend phonemes together, a factor that would appear to be predictive of the success seen with client SP, reported by De Partz (1986). The treatment was nevertheless successful, showing how similar therapy protocols impact on different processes. TC's therapy is also summarised in Nickels (1995).

Study

Berndt, R. S., & Mitchum, C. C. (1994). Approaches to the rehabilitation of 'phonological assembly': elaborating the model of non-lexical reading. In G. Humphreys & M. J. Riddoch (Eds.), *Cognitive neuropsychology and cognitive rehabilitation*. London: Lawrence Erlbaum Associates.

Focus of therapy: Orthographic-to-phonological conversion.

Therapy approach: Relearning.

Client details

General information

LR was a 50-year-old female university professor who had a CVA, resulting in aphasia, dyslexia, dysgraphia and dyscalculia.

Overall pattern of language impairments and preservations

LR's overall pattern of language impairment was characterised by poor auditory comprehension, naming, repetition and sentence construction difficulties in spontaneous speech. She had retained non-linguistic cognitive abilities but impaired immediate verbal memory. On assessments of reading, LR showed poor nonword reading, better reading of high-imageability words than low-imageability words but no effect of regularity. Semantic errors in reading were evident. The authors suggested that LR's pattern was consistent with deep dyslexia. Pre-therapy assessment of the components of phonological assembly showed some problems in grapheme parsing, grapheme–phoneme association and blending. Although capable of parsing and blending lexical units, LR showed no appreciation that spoken words could be analysed into their component sounds.

Time post-onset

LR was 9 years post-onset when therapy commenced.

Therapy

Aim

To improve orthographic-to-phonological associations to place constraints on the lexical reading process, thereby reducing semantic and visual reading errors. Therapy did not aim to encourage LR to sound out every word. No details regarding the frequency or duration of therapy for the first and second tasks were given. A total of 17 hours was required to achieve production of an isolated phoneme in response to a written letter in the third task. Twelve sessions of therapy were reported for the final task. Task 3 of the therapy programme was modelled on De Partz (1986). A multiple-baseline therapy design was used to monitor efficacy.

Task	1. Phonological segmentation Sound segments produced. LR to manipulate colour tokens to represent sequence	2. Segmentation with written letters Precise details of task not specified	3. Grapheme–phoneme associations Produce phoneme in response to written letter	4. Phoneme blending Blending of two phoneme combinations
Materials	Colour-coded tokens Combinations of up to 3 sounds	Written words	18 consonant graphemes, 5 vowels	
Hierarchy	1 Discrete segments 2 Blended segments	None	1 See letter and generate code word 2 Segment first sound from code word 3 Learn to produce sound in response to letter	1 C + V combinations 2 V + C combinations
Feedback on error	Not specified	Not specified	Not specified	Not specified
Feedback if correct	Not specified	Not specified	Not specified	Not specified

Outcome

In Task 1, LR performed well when component phonemes were produced separately. The task was abandoned at the blending stage as LR resisted the idea that words could be decomposed. Despite this, following Task 1, LR's letter sounding had improved. Following the use of written words in Task 2, LR was able to segment the initial sounds from spoken words without difficulty. Following Task 3, LR was able to produce single phonemes in response to a presented grapheme. Although she was able to produce more of the component sounds of nonwords, she was not able to produce all three sound segments due to her inability to blend. Following blending therapy, LR was able to blend C + V, but she experienced increased difficulty with V + C, combinations. Voice onset time was a feature often implicated in errors. No improvement was seen in blending three-phoneme combinations. Following therapy, therefore, there was no significant improvement in LR's ability to read nonwords. There was, however, a significant improvement in the reading of high-imageability words. A non-significant improvement was noted in the reading of regular words with a corresponding decrease in the reading of irregular words. Semantic errors declined as predicted, but there was an increase in errors with visual and/or phonological similarity to the target. Therapy did not result in an improvement in nonword reading but did result in an improvement in the reading of high-imageability words. The authors suggested that LR was attempting to use sub-lexical information to support her reading. This had, however, more complicated effects on her reading than the authors had predicted. The effect on phoneme blending of deficits in phonetic control and short-term memory are discussed.

Other comments

This paper replicates the therapy procedure described in De Partz (1986). The authors elaborate on the processes involved in the non-lexical reading route and how these aspects can be assessed. They highlight the need to assess short-term memory deficits when considering this type of therapy.

Study

Conway, T. W., Heilman, P., Rothi, L. J. G., Alexander, A. W., Adair, J., Crosson, B. A., & Heilman, K. M. (1998). Treatment of a case of phonological alexia with agraphia using the Auditory Discrimination in Depth (ADD) program. *Journal of the International Neuropsychological Society, 4,* 608–620.

Focus of therapy: Orthographic-to-phoneme conversion.

Therapy approach: Reactivation of the non-lexical reading route via motor-articulatory feedback.

Client details

General information

GK was a 50-year-old ambidextrous man who worked as a systems analyst up until his CVA. An MRI scan showed an infarct of the posterior two-thirds of the temporal lobe, as well as parts of the inferior parietal and occipital lobes. This had resulted in aphasia, alexia, agraphia, limb apraxia and visual field problems.

Overall pattern of language impairments and preservations

At the time of the study, GK's pattern of aphasia was consistent with a conduction aphasia where auditory comprehension and lexical retrieval were within normal limits, repetition was impaired and phonological errors, with *conduite d'approche*, were evident in speech production. Reading difficulties also remained as reading was slow and there was a lexicality effect (nonwords were more difficult than real words) but no effect of regularity or semantic errors. This was consistent with a phonological dyslexia where problems arose from impairment in orthographic-to-phonological conversion. Spelling was impaired and also showed lexicality effects.

Time post-onset

GK was 15 months post-onset when therapy commenced.

Therapy

Aim

To improve phonological awareness to increase access to the sub-lexical route to reading and writing. The Auditory Discrimination in Depth (ADD) program (Lindamood & Lindamood, 1975) was adopted as set out in the manual. Four stages were carried out sequentially. The first stage required 15.75 treatment hours, the second stage 12.25 hours, the third stage 22.2 hours and the final stage a further 50.9 hours, giving a total of 101.1 hours. A multiple baseline across behaviours design with multiple probing was used to monitor treatment effects.

	1. Oral awareness training	2. Simple nonword training	3. Complex nonword–word training	4. Multisyllable nonword–word training
Task	Multisensory training in oral awareness	Repetition and identification of phonemes in simple nonwords	Repetition and identification of phonemes in complex nonwords	Repetition and identification of phonemes in multisyllable nonwords and text
Materials	Line drawings of the mouth and articulators (mouth pictures); phonemes, graphemes and verbal labels for 11 consonant groups and 4 vowel groups Mirror	Use of all materials from stage 1 Chains of 10 nonsense segments (e.g. /ip/, /apl/, /a/, /pap/) – V, VC, CV, CVC Coloured wooden blocks Plastic tiles of graphemes, handwritten spellings, printed words	As for stage 2 but using CCV, VCC, CVCC, CCVC, CCVCC nonwords, and simple phonic rules	As for stage 2 but using up to 5 syllable stimuli, passages, suffixes and prefixes
Hierarchy	1 Client to look at own mouth in mirror, produce a phoneme and decide main articulators involved, e.g. tongue, lips 2 Determine presence of voicing (noisy or quiet) through feeling throat	1 Stage 1 integrated 2 Client to repeat a nonword 3 Mouth pictures sequenced to indicate phonemes in nonword (hand mirror used) 4 Second new nonword introduced differing by one phoneme	1 As for stage 2 2 Selection of phonics rules introduced	1 As for stage 2 2 Selection of prefixes and suffixes introduced

	3 Verbal label attached 4 Client asked to identify phonemes contrasting in features, e.g. voice 5 Client shown 3 mouth pictures and asked to decide most appropriate for each phoneme	5 Client to repeat both while tapping each mouth picture in sequence of phonemes for each word 6 Original sequence of mouth pictures changed to reflect difference between 2 nonwords 7 When 90–100% accurate, mouth pictures replaced with blocks. Reading and spelling introduced at this stage	
Feedback on error	Not specified	Rigorous questioning approach used to get client to identify error	As for stage 2
Feedback if correct	Not specified	Not specified	Not specified

Outcome

GK improved following all treatment stages. Phonological awareness on single-syllable words improved, although this was not maintained 2 months later. He showed significant improvement in identifying phoneme changes on multisyllable nonwords, which was maintained. Reading of nonwords improved and was maintained, as did reading of real words, and other reading skills such as word attack (non-lexical reading). Some skills returned, however, to pre-therapy levels (e.g. passage comprehension). At follow-up, word identification had continued to improve. Spelling improved significantly and this was maintained.

The spelling of irregular words, used as a control measure, did not change over the study period.

This study used a phonological awareness approach (i.e. non-lexical) and resulted in changes to both non-lexical and lexical reading, and spelling. The improvement in real word reading was possibly linked to the gains made in word attack skills. Conway *et al.* propose that evidence for improvement being directly attributable to therapy is seen in the pattern of change with each therapy stage. While no direct evidence is offered to support the influence of the motor-articulatory training, the authors believed it to be a critical component of their therapy approach.

Other comments

Conway *et al.* acknowledge that GK had a mild phonological alexia and do not suggest that the case offers evidence for success in moderate or severe cases. Replicating this study with more severe cases than GK, as well as with other forms of dyslexia, is recommended by the authors.

Study

Kendall, D. L., McNeil, M. R., & Small, S. L. (1998). Rule-based treatment for acquired phonological dyslexia. *Aphasiology, 12,* 587–600.

Focus of therapy: Orthographic-to-phonological conversion.

Therapy approach: Relearning.

Client details

General information

WT was a 42-year-old right-handed nurse anaesthetist. She was struck by lightning at the age of 25 which resulted in a global aphasia. An MRI scan at age 39 showed involvement of the left middle cerebral artery, left frontotemporal cortex and left basal ganglia.

Overall pattern of language impairments and preservations

WT had mild auditory comprehension and spoken production deficits; her production was characterised by a reduced rate and lowered information content. Reading comprehension was lower for paragraphs than single words. More errors were seen in her reading aloud, where she omitted whole words and made both morphological errors (omitting and adding affixes) and errors with low-frequency words. Oral reading of nonwords was poor. Repetition of nonwords was higher but still impaired. Kendall *et al.* propose that WT has an impairment of the sub-lexical reading route (phonological dyslexia).

Time post-onset

Therapy commenced when WT was 18 years post-onset.

Therapy

Aim

To teach two of the seven grapheme-to-phoneme correspondence rules – the 'c-rule' and the 'g-rule'.[1] Six treatment sessions were given on the use of the 'c-rule' and then five on the 'g-rule' over a 6-week period. Extensive baseline and maintenance probing occurred. Sessions lasted approximately 2 hours; the first hour was used for assessment and probing, while treatment was provided during the second hour. A multiple-baseline across behaviours design was used alongside generalisation probes.

Task	Teaching 'c-rule' and 'g-rule' Presented with multiple examples of nonwords where each rule is applied and asked to say the word and then write it down (when picture removed). Instruction on pronunciation given
Materials	60 words per rule (four conditions): • 10 simple real words (one syllable, high concreteness, frequency, imagery and meaningfulness) • 20 simple nonwords • 10 difficult real words (2–3 syllable nouns, low concreteness, low imageability) • 20 difficult real words Each word was presented three times per session (total 180 items per session)
Hierarchy	None

Feedback on error	Feedback on verbal response: 1 Phonetic cue given 2 Real word (rhyming word) given ('it sounds like . . .') 3 Repetition of nonword Feedback on written response not specified
Feedback if correct	Not specified

Outcome

Following therapy for the 'c-rule', WT's performance increased 'beyond baseline levels and variability on magnitude and/or slope' on each of the four word lists. No statistics were reported. Generalisation occurred to the 'g-rule' during this phase. This was explained as WT applying a strategy to the 'g-rule' that had been derived from learning the 'c-rule'. Following treatment of the second rule, further improvement was present when ceiling performance had not already been reached. Generalised improvement was seen on other testing. Maintenance was present for both rules.

Kendall *et al.* hypothesise that WT had inefficient use of her sub-lexical route and that treatment was aimed at impaired grapheme–phoneme rule usage. Following therapy, Kendall *et al.* comment that it is unclear whether the deficit was to do with the actual rule and its efficient implementation or due to a processing resource allocation deficit, although they propose the former.

Other comments

A lack of statistical information raises some concerns about the robustness of the data.

Study

Friedman, R. B., & Lott, S. N. (2002). Successful blending in a phonological reading treatment for deep dyslexia. *Aphasiology*, *16*, 355–372.

Focus of therapy: Orthographic-to-phonological conversion.

Therapy approach: Cognitive relay strategy of learning a new method of decoding words.

Client details

Two clients were reported in this paper.

General information

LR was a 40-year-old man who had worked as a bus supervisor and a model prior to a CVA. A CT scan showed an infarct in the left frontotemporal region and compression of the lateral ventricle. KT was a 20-year-old right-handed woman who had a CVA following a motor vehicle accident at the age of 15. She had completed 9 years of education at this time. A CT scan showed an infarct in the territory of the left middle cerebral artery with some further frontal and lateral involvement.

Overall pattern of language impairments and preservations

LR had a mild-to-moderate non-fluent aphasia. Auditory comprehension was good for single words and up to four-stage commands, but was impaired beyond this level. Spoken production was only good for automatic sequences and impaired in all other output tasks. Length effects were seen in repetition. Oral reading was impaired at the single-word and sentence level, although comprehension was retained for single words. Writing was also impaired beyond short high-frequency words. Overall, LR's reading impairment was characterised by an inability to read or spell nonwords, semantic errors, and a trend for part-of-speech and concreteness effects, suggesting deep dyslexia.

KT also presented with a non-fluent aphasia but was able to produce longer phrases and sentences. Auditory comprehension was impaired only for complex information. Spoken production was characterised by impairment in confrontation naming, and semantic and phonological errors in repetition of three and more syllable words. Oral reading was impaired on all measures, while comprehension of single words was retained. Writing of single words was impaired. Like LR, KT's reading pattern was consistent with a diagnosis of deep dyslexia, as seen in her semantic errors, a part-of-speech trend, difficulties reading nonwords and a trend towards a concreteness effect.

Time post-onset

LR was 2 years post-onset at the time of the study and KT was 5 years post-onset.

Therapy

Aim

To teach bigraph–phoneme correspondences.[2] LR attended 355 treatment sessions over a 31-month period. KT attended therapy for 114 sessions over a 15-month period. Three one-hour sessions took place each week for both clients. A multiple-baseline design was used to monitor efficacy.

Task	Teaching bigraph–phoneme correspondence	
Materials	Three sets of stimuli, each containing CV and VC bigraphs for a group of phonemes and a set of training words. All bigraphs were paired with a relay word that began with the bigraph (e.g. 'it' with 'Italy'). Bigraphs were written on flashcards with the picture and the written name of the relay word on the back of the card. Words were written on one side of the card with the bigraphs on the reverse	
Hierarchy	*Training bigraphs* 1 Client learns relay word for each bigraph 2 Client produces only target sounds of relay word when shown bigraph 90% success criterion for two consecutive probe tests	*Training words* 1 Client produces CV bigraph 2 Client produces VC bigraph 3 Client combines these into the words by repeating them in rapid succession ('blending')
Feedback on error	An explicit response cueing hierarchy was applied: (a) Show relay word and picture (b) Sentence completion cue (c) Sentence completion plus visual articulatory placement cue (d) Sentence completion plus phonemic cue (e) The word is modelled (f) The target sound is modelled	An explicit response cueing hierarchy was applied: (a) Show bigraphs (b) Remind use of relay word (c) Remind of repeating in rapid succession (d) The bigraphs and 'blending' word are modelled (f) The word is modelled
Feedback if correct	Not specified	Not specified

Outcome

Both LR and KT learned the bigraphs; LR increased his success from 0% to 95%, while KT increased from 6% to 97%. No generalisation occurred from trained bigraphs to untrained bigraphs; this was an expected finding. Before the words were introduced, however, generalisation was seen to words containing those trained bigraphs. When words were introduced, LR's success with these increased from 1% to 82%, while KT improved from 8% to 84%. Generalisation was seen from trained to untrained words which contained the trained bigraphs, while no generalisation was seen to words containing untrained bigraphs.

The impact on reading, including functional activities, was recorded for LR; on self-report, improvement was noted on such activities as reading frequency, oral reading, and understanding newspapers and books. Reading speed was also reported to improve 'dramatically'. This information was not available for the second client.

While Friedman and Lott interpret their findings in relation to dual- and single-route models of reading, and an underlying impairment in phonological processing, they present the mechanism of training bigraph–phoneme (or bigraph–syllable) correspondences as 'creating specific pairings' that are memorised and stored separate to lexical information, and then activated on-line when required. While this is similar to grapheme–phoneme correspondences, the difference lies in the ease with which the bigraphs can be blended when combined into words for reading. Evidence of children's greater ease with syllable blending is used to motivate the therapeutic approach. The lowered co-articulatory demands of syllable blending and the requirement of only deleting a pause when blending bigraphs/syllables are reasons offered for why this approach provides an easier alternative to blending a series of isolated consonants.

The authors clearly state that the approach does not attempt to retrain normal or previous processes of reading or remediate the underlying phonological processing difficulties. Instead, it offers 'a new means of decoding words' that circumvents impaired processes.

Other comments

The length of intervention time, 335 and 114 sessions respectively for the two clients, was extensive, with probable implications for provision of services.

Study

Yampolsky, S., & Waters, G. (2002). Treatment of single word oral reading in an individual with deep dyslexia. *Aphasiology*, *16*, 455–471.

Focus of therapy: Orthographic-to-phonological conversion.

Therapy approach: Relearning.

Client details

General information

MO was a 23-year-old right-handed woman who had a left frontoparietal craniotomy for a ruptured arteriovenous malformation. Large tissue loss involved the frontal, parietal and temporal lobes. MO had recently graduated from high school at the time of the rupture and enjoyed reading.

Overall pattern of language impairments and preservations

MO had unimpaired visual analysis and functional access to semantic representations but impaired comprehension of abstract and derived words. A severe impairment was present in reading aloud single words and she was unable to apply orthographic-to-phonological conversion rules, blend unfamiliar letter strings or read nonwords, suggesting both an impaired lexical and sub-lexical route. Frequency and imageability effects were present, along with phonological and semantic errors. Yampolsky and Waters classified MO as having deep dyslexia.

Time post-onset

MO was 3 years post-onset at the time of the study.

Therapy

Aim

To establish sub-lexical reading ability by re-learning orthographic-to-phonological correspondences and blending using real words. Therapy was given three times per week over a 12-week period. Sessions were 2 hours in length. A multiple-baseline across behaviours design, with treatment and generalisation probes, was used.

Task	Phonological awareness and blending activities, including phoneme naming, manipulation of graphemes/phonemes in words and reading aloud
Material	The Wilson Reading Scheme (12 levels of increasing difficulty based on 6 syllable types of CVC words)
Hierarchy	Each session divided into four parts: 1 Client presented with cards of single letters and asked to say the corresponding phoneme 2 Presented with single-letter cards placed into CVC words, client asked to blend the sounds and say the words, tapping out each sound and dragging her finger under each letter while sounding out the words. Following correct response, CVC words are altered by changing one phoneme at a time

	3 Presented with cards with the full written CVC word, client asked to read aloud the words, again dragging her finger under each phoneme while sounding out the words 4 Client independently reads a list of 12 words using phonemes treated so far
Feedback on error	Clinician cues client by modelling correct phoneme with example word (e.g. /p/ as in *pig*)
Feedback if correct	Not specified. In word tasks, clinician manipulates phoneme when correct to alter CVC word

Outcome

MO's oral reading accuracy of treated words increased from baseline levels of as low as 30% to between 65 and 90% accuracy, suggesting that MO did re-acquire blending skills for CVC words. This is in contrast to other studies (e.g. Matthews, 1991; Mitchum & Berndt, 1991; Nickels, 1992). Generalisation to untreated words within the programme was seen. No improvement was seen on control items, suggesting item-specific improvement, or on other language tests, supporting improvement being due to therapy.

Yampolsky and Waters state that generalisation seen in the study may have been contributed to by the overlap of consonants across tasks. The lack of generalisation to control words may also be influenced by the fact that these words were not matched to the treated sets. Furthermore, while therapy only used real words, it may be argued that MO only used her lexical route. The authors argue, however, that her improved nonword reading is evidence of MO's use of her non-lexical route. Functional gains in reading were also reported.

MO also demonstrated a significant decrease in semantic errors in reading, leading Yampolsky and Waters to claim evidence in support of the 'summation hypothesis' account of word retrieval (Hillis & Caramazza, 1995) where phonological (sub-lexical) and lexical semantic information combine to produce a response in reading aloud. Naming also showed a non-significant improvement, suggesting that the phonological gains involved in using her GPC system may have assisted spoken production through increased phonological information.

Other comments

Yampolsky and Waters comment on MO's co-existing apraxia of speech, suggesting the need for therapy in this area but also highlighting the interaction with any future improvements in oral reading abilities.

Notes

1 The 'c-rule': when *c* comes just before *a*, *o* or *u*, it is produced as /k/; at other times, it is produced as /s/. The 'g-rule': when *g* comes at the end of words or just before *a*, *o* or *u*, it is produced as /g/; at other times, it is produced as /dʒ/.
2 To teach 'pat', the bigraphs 'pa'–/pæ/ and 'at'–/æt/ would be taught. This is in contrast to other grapheme–phoneme correspondence approaches, which have taught phonemes in isolation: 'p'–/pə/, 'a'–/æ/ and 't'–/tə/.

13 Therapy for writing

Summary of writing studies

If reading therapy has not fallen within the traditional domain of aphasia rehabilitation, writing has done so even less. Clinical priorities, resource constraints and possibly even expertise have meant that less attention has been directed to impairments of writing. Nevertheless, the last two decades have seen a number of studies reported in the literature where therapy has been shown to improve writing skills. Those studies reviewed here are listed in Table 13.1.

Therapy for writing comprises two main approaches: first, therapy targeting the lexical writing route and, secondly, therapy targeting the sub-lexical writing route. Decisions regarding which type of therapy is used are based on the relative sparing/impairment of each route, other retained abilities and the impact that remediation of a route would have on the client's spelling. For example, therapy that re-teaches phoneme-to-grapheme correspondences has a more beneficial impact for a regular language, such as Italian, than for English – a language with very irregular spelling. Writing therapy has been introduced following the recovery of spoken language (Luzzatti, Colombo, Frustaci, & Vitolo, 2000) and to provide clients who have minimal speech with an alternative means of communication (Robson, Pring, Marshall, Morrison, & Chiat, 1998).

Therapy for the lexical route has consisted of both reactivation techniques and the use of relay strategies. Reactivation techniques (e.g. Deloche, Dordan, & Kremin, 1993; Rapp & Kane, 2002) involve training clients to write words via repetitive practice. Words are copied or written to dictation via a number of different cues (e.g. anagrams, first letter cues). Therapy has generally resulted in item-specific learning, with improvements seen in the writing of the treated words but no improvement in the writing of untreated words. Improvement has been considered to result from changes within the orthographic output lexicon. In contrast, some generalisation to untreated words was seen in client RSB (Rapp & Kane, 2002), who had an additional impairment within the graphemic output buffer. This generalised improvement was considered to reflect changes to processes within the buffer, such as

Table 13.1 Summary of writing therapy studies reviewed here

Level of impairment	Therapy studies	Therapy tasks
Semantic system (deep dysgraphia)	Hatfield (1983) (see p. 230)	• Writing to dictation of function words via linking with homophonic or pseudohomophonic content word
Phonological-to-graphemic conversion (deep dysgraphia)	Hatfield (1983) (see p. 230) De Partz *et al.* (1992) (see p. 233)	• Teaching of spelling rules
Phonological-to-graphemic conversion (phonological dysgraphia)	Luzzatti *et al.* (2000) (see p. 236)	• Phonological segmentation of words • Teaching of phoneme-to-grapheme correspondence for single and syllabic phonemes • Identifying phonological contexts where words are likely to be irregular
	Hillis and Caramazza (1994) (see p. 151)	• Teaching of phonological-to-orthographic conversion (POC) rules • Teaching of orthographic-to-phonological conversion (OPC) rules
Access to orthographic output lexicon (surface dysgraphia)	Behrmann (1987) (see p. 240)	• Training of homophones via link with pictures depicting meaning • Written word-to-picture matching followed by writing of words
Orthographic output lexicon (surface dysgraphia)	Hatfield (1983) (see p. 230)	• Writing to dictation of words with different vowel spellings. Link group of words to a key word with the same spelling
	Hillis (1989) (see p. 157)	• Written naming using a cueing hierarchy
	De Partz *et al.* (1992) (see p. 233)	• Writing words using pictured object representing meaning which is presented alongside word/embedded within word
	Deloche *et al.* (1993) (see p. 243)	Computer-presented therapy • Orthographic cues to facilitate the writing of words • Anagram of written name • First syllable
	Robson *et al.* (1998) (see p. 245)	*Picture therapy phase* • Writing word form following: Identification of initial grapheme Anagram sorting Delayed copying

		Generalisation therapy • Writing words to convey information in picture description, list and communicative tasks *Message therapy* • Writing words to convey complex message in response to the presentation of everyday problems
	Beeson (2002) (see p. 250)	• Anagram sorting followed by repeated copying and recall of the word • Repeated copying followed by recall of the word • Writing treated words to convey information within a conversation
	Rapp and Kane (2002) (see p. 253)	• Writing to dictation – hear word, repeat it and attempt to spell it
Graphemic output buffer	Mortley *et al.* (2001) (see p. 255)	Computer-presented therapy to facilitate writing via good oral spelling • Writing words to dictation via letter-by-letter transcoding • Using a dictionary to find a word once the first few letters have been written • Writing sentences to dictation using letter-by-letter strategy • Adaptive word processor that provides choice of words with given letters
	Rapp and Kane (2002) (see p. 253)	Writing to dictation – hear word, repeat it and attempt to spell it

scanning speed or the speed of conversion between letters and their written shape.

Various relay strategies have been used to improve lexical spelling with different patterns of generalisation. In Hatfield's (1983) study, the clients were encouraged to link words that were difficult to spell with words they could spell. Therapy resulted in item-specific improvement. The spelling of irregular words in Behrmann's (1987) study was improved by linking the word's spelling with a pictorial image. Some generalisation was seen in the spelling of other words, possibly due to an increased ability to detect errors. Client MF (Mortley, Enderby, & Petheram, 2001) was taught to use his better oral spelling to aid his written spelling; this strategy enabled him to write all words and sentences.

Therapy for the sub-lexical writing route (De Partz, Seron, & Van der Linden, 1992; Luzzatti *et al.*, 2000) has involved the teaching of phoneme-to-grapheme correspondences enabling the writing of all regular words. Clients are then taught specific rules to enable the spelling of some irregular words.

In studies targeting both the sub-lexical and lexical writing routes, improvement has resulted from repetitive tasks carried out over a long period. As a consequence, direct therapy is often supported by self-directed work or work on a computer. When writing has improved in constrained tasks, there is some evidence that clients need to be encouraged to use their writing within conversation (Beeson, 2002) and will only use writing functionally if it can be done quickly (Mortley *et al.*, 2001).

EVALUATIONS OF THERAPY STUDIES

Study

Hatfield, F. (1983). Aspects of acquired dysgraphia and implications for re-education. In C. Code & D. J. Muller (Eds.). *Aphasia therapy*. London: Edward Arnold.

Focus of therapy: Semantic system (deep dysgraphia) and orthographic output lexicon (surface dysgraphia).

Therapy approach: Cognitive relay strategy to improve access to words within the semantic system. Reactivation within the orthographic output lexicon.

Client details

The study involved four clients.

General information

BB was a 43-year-old male grocery wholesaler. He had an embolic CVA resulting in a right hemiparesis. DE was a 26-year-old male assistant store keeper in a pharmaceutical firm. He had a traumatic neck injury (left internal carotid artery occlusion) resulting in left frontal and temporal damage and a right hemiparesis. PW was a 72-year-old male local government officer. A CVA resulted in a right hemiparesis with a CT scan showing damage to the frontal, parietal and temporal lobes. TP was a 51-year-old female senior radiographer who suffered a sub-arachnoid haemorrhage affecting the left temporo-occipital region. This resulted in a transient hemiparesis and a permanent right homonymous hemianopia. All four clients were reasonably proficient spellers before their cerebral incident.

Overall pattern of language impairments and preservations

BB, DE and PW all presented with Broca's type speech and a pattern of reading consistent with deep dyslexia. TP presented with a fluent aphasia with severe anomia and impaired comprehension. TP had received regular therapy for writing before the study. When assessed on their ability to write words to dictation, BB, PW and DE's performances were better when writing content words relative to function words and they were unable to write non-words. Their spelling of regular and irregular words did not differ significantly. They produced visual, semantic and derivational errors in writing. The author proposes that BB, DE and PW had a deep dysgraphia with a severe impairment of the sub-lexical spelling route (phoneme-to-grapheme conversion) and a partial sparing of the lexical semantic route. TP's writing was more preserved relative to the other clients. Her spelling of regular words was superior to her spelling of irregular words and she was able to write nonwords. TP's performance was characterised by the production of orthographically plausible errors, homophone errors and letter-by-letter writing. The author proposes that TP presented with surface dysgraphia.

Time post-onset

When therapy was commenced, BB was 2 years, DE was 10 years, PW was 15 years and TP was 1 year post-onset.

Therapy

Aims

1   *Semantic system*: to improve the ability to spell function words by linking them to homophonic (or pseudohomophonic) content words.
2   *Orthographic output lexicon*: to facilitate the acquisition of complex spelling rules and the spelling of homophones.

No information was given on the frequency or intensity of therapy. Sessions were supported by home practice consisting of sentence completion tasks. The paper discusses progress on the therapy task but no single case study design is used to demonstrate efficacy.

Task	Semantic system Writing to dictation of function words using homophonic content words	Orthographic output lexicon 1 Re-teaching of double consonant rule via explanation 2 Writing to dictation of words with different vowel spellings. Grouping of

		words in which vowels spelt in the same way. Groups linked to one key word which was reliably spelt by client
Materials	7 locational prepositions 6 auxiliaries 5 pronouns Function words paired with a homophonic content 'link' word which was selected by the client, e.g. 'on' paired with 'Don'	Three groups of words which involve different ways of spelling vowels. For example, /eɪ/ as in pain and pane; /i/ as in meat and meet
Hierarchy	(a) Association of link word with target word (b) Dictation of link word with picture support (c) Writing of link word (d) Dictation of sentence including function word (e) Writing of function word under link word (f) Dictation of sentence for the writing of the function word	Sorting words into groups. Memorising key word and group
Feedback on error	Not specified	Not specified
Feedback if correct	Not specified	Not specified

Outcome

Following three sessions, BB, PW and DE – the clients with deep dysgraphia – were able to use the prior writing of the link word to facilitate the correct spelling of the function word. By the end of the therapy programme, they were able to use the strategy silently to facilitate the spelling of function words. The author reported some improvement in the ability to write function words but reassessment data were difficult to interpret due to the omission of some words from the tests. Very limited reassessment data were available for TP following the therapy targeting the orthographic input lexicon.

Other comments

The author claimed a satisfactory outcome from the therapy for deep dysgraphia with some improvement in the ability to write function words. It is, however, difficult to determine the success of both therapies due to the limited reassessment data reported. Further information is necessary to evaluate the specific versus non-specific effects of treatment. The therapy protocol for deep dysgraphia is sufficiently detailed to allow replication, while the reporting of the therapy for surface dysgraphia does not permit replication.

Study

De Partz, M.-P., Seron, X., & Van der Linden, M. (1992). Re-education of a surface dysgraphia with a visual imagery strategy. *Cognitive Neuropsychology*, *9*, 369–401.

Focus of therapy: Phonological-to-graphemic conversion (orthographic output lexicon).

Therapy approach: Relearning of graphemic contextual rules to improve the non-lexical spelling route Cognitive relay strategy to improve the writing of irregular words via the orthographic output lexicon.

Client details

General information

LP was a 24-year-old right-handed male nursing student.[1] He contracted encephalitis which required a lobectomy of the left temporal point and suction of the lower left frontal lobe. Surgery resulted in a right hemiparesis and a mild right hemispatial neglect. LP presented with cognitive difficulties characteristic of frontal lobe damage and impaired visual and verbal memory.

Overall pattern of language impairments and preservations

LP presented with good functional comprehension, although he did make some semantic errors on single-word comprehension tasks. His speech was characterised by word-finding difficulties, circumlocutions and semantic errors. Repetition and automatic speech production were intact. Reading performance was characterised by relatively intact reading of nonwords, with no effect of frequency, length or regularity in the reading of words. LP was, however, impaired in his ability to understand homophones, his detection of regularisation errors and in visual lexical decision. The authors suggest that LP has a pre-semantic reading deficit in the orthographic input lexicon resulting in a reliance on the sub-lexical reading route. It was proposed that meaning was accessed via access to the phonological form and processing via the auditory route.

Writing performance was characterised by relatively well-preserved writing of nonwords. Writing of words showed a marked frequency effect, a trend for improved performance in the writing of regular words compared with irregular and ambiguous words and poor writing of homophones. The authors suggest that LP presents with a surface dysgraphia due to an impaired lexical route for writing alongside a relatively well-preserved sub-lexical route. Consistency of errors in the writing of irregular and ambiguous words was considered to reflect a loss of orthographic representations rather than an access difficulty.

Time post-onset

Therapy was commenced when LP was around 1 year post-onset.

Therapy

Aims

1 To maximise the use of the non-lexical writing route via the teaching of context-sensitive graphemic rules (Phase 1).
2 To improve the writing of irregular and ambiguous words using a visual imagery strategy (Phase 2).

A multiple baseline therapy design was used to examine the efficacy of therapy. Therapy consisted of two phases.

Phase 1

Phase 1 of therapy consisted of three sessions per week for 6 months.

Task	**Re-teaching of context-sensitive graphemic rules** Rules presented and explained. Use of rule in various written tasks, e.g. writing to dictation, sentence and text completion
Materials	Five rules frequently used in French selected for training following an analysis of LP's errors
Hierarchy	Each rule introduced and practised separately and then practised together
Feedback on error	Rule explained. Correct form presented to be read and copied
Feedback if correct	Not specified

Phase 2

Therapy for Phase 2 consisted of four stages corresponding to a different task. During Stage 1, the learning of imagery was carried out three times a week for 2 weeks. Stages 2 and 3 each involved three sessions per week for 3 months. The recall of spellings taught during stages 2 and 3 were assessed 1 day, 4 days and 15 days after the initial therapy session. Stage 4 also consisted of 3 months of therapy.

Task	1. Learning of imagery Generating images in response to pictures and words and drawing/describing those images	2. Learning of written words with embedded visual image Writing the word with its embedded image	3. Training of self-imagery Comparing the effects of therapist- or client-generated images	4. Transfer to spontaneous writing Detecting trained words and their derivations in spontaneous production and producing them with their drawings
Materials	240 words previously mis-spelt by LP Each treated word was given a semantically related image that was embedded within the part of the word which had been mis-spelt 120 words used in Stage (task) 2: 60 treated, 60 untreated words. Groups were matched for frequency 120 words used in Stage (task) 3: 30 untreated, 30 with patient image, 30 with therapist image, 30 trained using classic didactic verbal learning			
Hierarchy	(a) Direct visualisation – form an image with visual support (b) Indirect visualisation – form an image from name of object	(a) Copy the word with the embedded visual image (b) Delayed copying of word and image (10 sec) (c) Produce word and image in response to spoken word	As task 2	None
Feedback on error	Not applicable	If word produced incorrectly in (b) or (c), returned to copying	As task 2	Not specified
Feedback if correct	Not applicable	Not specified	Not specified	Not specified

Outcome

Following Phase 1, there was a reduction in the errors made on words requiring the taught rules. Some new errors also emerged as a consequence of the misapplication of those rules. There was no change in LP's ability to write irregular and ambiguous words following Phase 1. Following tasks 2 and 3 in Phase 2, LP's writing of the treated words using visual imagery improved. There was also some improvement in his writing of the untreated words. The writing of words treated using a traditional didactic verbal learning method did not improve. There was no significant difference between those words treated using therapist-generated images and those treated using patient-generated images. Performance was stable one year after therapy.

Both phases of therapy resulted in significant improvement in LP's writing ability, which the authors argued was not due to spontaneous recovery. LP's performance had been stable before therapy. Phase 1 resulted in no change in LP's ability to write irregular and ambiguous words. The improvements seen in Phase 2 were significantly greater for the treated words than the untreated words and no improvements were seen following didactic verbal learning. Improvements were maintained one year post-therapy.

Other comments

With rigorous initial assessment and reassessment data presented, this study permits a thorough evaluation of a therapy that resulted in significant and long-term gains.

Study

Luzzatti, C., Colombo, C., Frustaci, M., & Vitolo, F. (2000). Rehabilitation of spelling along the sub-word-level routine. *Neuropsychological Rehabilitation*, *10*, 249–278.

Focus of therapy: Phonological-to-graphemic conversion.

Therapy approach: Relearning.

Client details

Two clients are described in the study.

General information

RO was a 48-year-old man who had a cerebral abscess in the left hemisphere. He had 8 years of schooling and had worked as an administrator. DR was a 33-year-old man who worked as a dental technician. He had a cerebral haemorrhage following the rupture of an aneurysm of the left internal carotid artery.

Overall pattern of language impairments and preservations

RO had a Broca's aphasia. He presented with a moderate comprehension deficit and non-fluent agrammatic speech with word-finding difficulties. His reading was characteristic of phonological dyslexia. He was unable to write any words accurately and could only write about 60% of single letters. The authors suggest that RO had an impairment to the sub-lexical writing routine. He also had additional difficulties with acoustic-to-phonological conversion. DR also presented with a Broca's aphasia, with agrammatic speech and reading characteristic of phonological dyslexia. On formal assessment of his writing, he produced around 25% correct responses for regular words with particular difficulties with words requiring syllabic translation or containing voiced consonants or nasals. His writing of irregular words was less accurate than his writing of regular words. The authors suggest that DR has a mixed writing impairment involving both the lexical and non-lexical routes, with most accurate writing of regular words with one phoneme to one letter correspondence.

Time post-onset

RO was 3 years 9 months and DR was 10 years post-onset at the time of the study.

Therapy

Aim

To improve phonological segmentation and phonological-to-graphemic conversion. As Italian is predominantly a regular language, improvement to phoneme-to-grapheme conversion would permit the accurate writing of the majority of words. Following the learning of regular conversion rules, the clients were taught to identify phonological contexts where irregularities were likely to occur. The clients' writing was assessed before, at regular intervals during and after therapy. A multiple baseline therapy design was used. Clients had to reach 90% accurate performance at each therapy stage before proceeding to the next stage.

	1. Segmentation of words into syllables and syllables into phones (continuant phones)	2. Writing of single phonemes and words to dictation (continuant phones)	3. Segmentation of words into syllables and syllables into phones (plosive phones)	4. Writing of single phonemes and words to dictation (plosive phones)	5. Introduction of syllabic and complex conversion rules
Task	Presentation of words with prolongation of phones to aid segmentation	Client retrieves name of letter and then writes down	Presentation of words for segmentation	Client retrieves name of letter and then writes down	Introduce rules for the transcription of syllabic conversion and phonemes written via a single letter
Materials	Words containing continuant consonant phonemes /f v s z r l m n/ and 5 vowels	Words containing continuant consonant phonemes /f v s z r l m n/ and 5 vowels	Words containing the phonemes /p b t d/	Words containing the phonemes /p b t d/	Words containing the phonemes /k g ʃ tʃ dʒ kw ts dz/
Hierarchy	(a) Segmentation into syllables • Bisyllabic words with alternating consonants • Words with 3 or more syllables • Nonwords	(a) Bisyllabic words and nonwords with CV structure (b) Words with 3 syllables (c) Words with 4 syllables (d) Words with consonant clusters (e) Words with doubled consonants	(a) One-to-one phoneme-to-grapheme conversion (b) CV syllables with plosive onset	None	Not specified

	(b) Segmentation into phones • Words of increasing length • Words with clusters • Words with doubled consonants			
Feedback on error	Not specified	Reminds client of common word containing the letter	Not specified	Not specified	Not specified
Feedback if correct	Not specified	Not specified	Not specified	Not specified	Not specified

Following Phase 5 of therapy, the clients learned to identify phonological contexts when words were likely to be irregular so they could check the orthography.

Outcome

Both clients progressed through each stage of the programme, reaching the 90% accuracy criterion. At the end of therapy, RO showed appropriate use of one-to-one and syllabic phoneme-to-grapheme conversion. He was able to write 90% of regular words and 50% of irregular words; his errors writing irregular words were regularisation errors. The gains were mirrored in his reading performance, with improved reading of function words, abstract nouns and nonwords. His spontaneous speech remained unchanged. Writing performance was maintained 18 months after therapy. At the end of therapy, DR showed near-normal performance in writing, making errors only on words with non-univocal spellings. His writing performance was maintained 6 months after therapy.

Both clients showed significant gains in writing that can be attributed to therapy. The clients were a long time post-onset and showed improvements that were specific to the phase of therapy. Performance resulted in the improvement of all words and was maintained following the end of therapy. No information is given about whether the clients were using their new writing skills in functional settings.

Other comments

With rigorous initial assessment and reassessment data presented, this study permits a thorough evaluation of the therapy with the reported clients. The study considers the need to treat prerequisite phonological segmentation skills before direct teaching of phonological-to-graphemic rules. The outcomes of such a therapy technique in English would be more limited.

Study

Behrmann, M. (1987). The rites of righting writing: homophone remediation and acquired dysgraphia. *Cognitive Neuropsychology*, *4*, 365–384.

Focus of therapy: Access to orthographic output lexicon (surface dysgraphia).

Therapy approach: Reactivation.

Client details

General information

CCM was a 53-year-old high school educated woman who had an infarct in the middle cerebral artery in the left temperoparietal region. She had no hemiplegia or hemianopia. CCM was bilingual in English and Afrikaans.

Overall pattern of language impairments and preservations

CCM presented with a conduction aphasia. She had impaired repetition in the presence of fluent verbal output. Sentence comprehension was relatively preserved. Reading performance was characterised by intact lexical decision, well preserved nonword reading, and equivalent reading of regular and irregular words. Writing performance was characterised by well-preserved writing of nonwords and regular words but impaired writing of irregular words and homophones. Writing of irregular words involved the production of phonologically plausible errors. Neither imageability, word class or length affected performance in either writing or reading. The authors suggest that CCM has an impaired lexical writing route with a well-preserved sub-lexical route and therefore described her as having an acquired surface dysgraphia.

Time post-onset

Therapy commenced when CCM was 10 months post-onset.

Therapy

Aim

To retrain the lexical spelling route via the training of homophone pairs. Therapy consisted of weekly sessions over a period of 6 weeks, with additional home practice. A combination of an item-specific and control task design was used to investigate the efficacy of therapy.

Task	**Writing of homophone pairs** Writing of homophones paired with pictorial representation of meaning. Meaning used to promote correct spelling
Materials	50 homophone pairs of which either one or both homophones were written incorrectly in assessment. 8 pairs treated per session
Hierarchy	(a) Homophones introduced with pictorial representation (b) Written forms contrasted (c) Written word-to-picture matching (d) Writing of homophones with pictorial support (e) Writing of homophones to dictation
Feedback on error	Not specified
Feedback if correct	Not specified

Home practice consisted of forced choice word-to-picture matching, written homophone naming to pictures and sentence completion tasks.

Outcome

Significant improvement was recorded in the writing of treated homophones. This was maintained 8 weeks post-therapy. There was no significant improvement in the writing of untreated homophones, suggesting no generalisation. Significant improvement was also seen in the writing of irregular words. CCM's performance in sentence comprehension and in digit span did not change.

Therapy resulted in improvements in homophone and irregular word spelling. These were attributed to therapy, as CCM was not in the period of spontaneous recovery; a stable baseline in homophone writing was evident before therapy and no change in performance was recorded on control tasks. The authors proposed that the specific improvements in treated homophones and untreated irregular words were the consequence of a partial reinstatement of lexical spelling and the use of a visual check mechanism which detected spelling errors.

Other comments

A list of the homophones used in treatment are included in the paper. This study shows improvement in some of the observed characteristics of surface dysgraphia.

Study

Deloche, G., Dordan, M., & Kremin, H. (1993). Rehabilitation of confrontation naming in aphasia: relations between oral and written modalities. *Aphasiology*, 7, 201–216.

Focus of therapy: Access to the orthographic output lexicon (surface dysgraphia) in order to improve spoken naming.

Therapy approach: Reactivation.

Client details

Two clients were examined in the study.

General information

RB was a 28-year-old woman who had worked as a secretary before she had a meningeal haemorrhage resulting from a burst aneurysm of the left sylvian bifurcation. GC was a 50-year-old right-handed woman who had a meningeal haemorrhage due to disruption of an aneurysm of the left sylvian territory. A CT scan showed hypodensity in the posterior part of the insula and rolandic area extending to the frontal region.

Overall pattern of language impairments and preservations

RB presented with fluent, informative speech with occasional word-finding difficulties. Spoken and written comprehension was well preserved, along with oral reading and repetition. Writing to dictation was impaired, with errors consistent with surface dysgraphia. In assessments of confrontation naming, RB scored 79% correct in oral naming, with errors predominantly verbal paraphasias, and 73% correct in written naming. Errors in written naming were predominantly morpholexical errors or plausible transcriptions of phonological form. The authors suggest that RB was deriving written word forms from transcription of spoken word form by the application of phonological-to-graphemic conversion rules.

GC presented with a conduction aphasia. Spontaneous speech was characterised by word-finding difficulties with phonemic and semantic errors and circumlocutions. Written comprehension was preserved in the presence of impaired auditory comprehension. Oral reading of words was preserved, while impairment was seen in nonword reading. Repetition was also impaired. In assessments of confrontation naming, GC scored 42% correct in written naming and 35% correct in oral naming. Both oral and written naming were characterised by no responses and semantic and morpholexical errors. The authors suggest that oral naming may be derived from the orthographic word form, as GC often used a finger spelling strategy.

Time post-onset

Therapy was commenced when RB was 10 months post-onset and when GC was 12 years post-onset.

Therapy

Aim

To improve written naming and monitor the effects on spoken naming. Therapy consisted of 25 sessions over 6 weeks. Within each session, five blocks of 16 items were presented, one for each condition. Conditions were rotated across blocks in each session. A repeated baseline design was used to monitor changes in naming on three occasions before therapy, immediately after therapy and then one year later.

Task	**Presentation of a picture for written naming** Picture presented on computer (with a variety of different cues) and client types response
Materials	120 items from written naming were divided into two groups: 80 items for therapy and 40 used as control items. Groups were matched for number correct/incorrect **Five presentation conditions:** A. Cue presented on screen alongside picture 　　For RB: Open-ended sentence as semantic cue 　　For GC: Anagram of written name B. Cue presented on screen alongside picture 　　For RB: Anagram of written name 　　For GC: First syllable of written name A'. As A but with feedback (see below) B'. As B but with feedback (see below) C. No cue
Hierarchy	Not specified
Feedback on error	In A' and B', an auditory warning was given on first error. On second error, letter in error appeared on screen for copying
Feedback if correct	Not specified

Outcome

RB showed a significant facilitation of written naming with anagrams compared to when no cue was given. No significant facilitation occurred with semantic cues. Overall, a significant improvement was seen in written and oral naming of both treated and control items when compared with pre-therapy. Untreated oral naming improved significantly more than treated written naming. Written naming was characterised by a reduction in semantic, morphological and homophonic errors. Improvement was maintained one year post-therapy.

GC showed no difference between control cues, anagrams and first syllable cues. Overall, a significant improvement was present in oral and written naming of treated items. A significant improvement in written naming of control items was also seen, but no generalisation occurred to oral naming of untreated items. Improvements were maintained one year post-therapy.

The authors suggest that RB's improvement in oral naming was a consequence of increased speed of processing and the reduction of semantic errors. They further suggested that therapy also helped RB to relearn phoneme-to-grapheme conversion, resulting in improvements in both the treated and control items, and that the results provide evidence that RB was using phonemic information to support written naming.

GC's improvement was attributed to the use of morpholexical cues to aid written naming. It is not considered how the use of these cues facilitated the improvement in the writing of control items. The authors suggested that the lack of a significant improvement in the oral naming of untreated items was a consequence of GC failing to reach a threshold of performance in written naming. For both clients, improvements were unlikely to be a consequence of spontaneous recovery due to stable baseline performance pre-therapy and the time post-onset.

Other comments

Changes were seen in the written naming of both clients that can be attributed to therapy. The control items in presentation condition C were written in every session, so changes in the production of these may not necessarily indicate the use of a strategy.

Study

Robson, J., Pring, T., Marshall, J., Morrison, S., & Chiat, S. (1998). Written communication in undifferentiated jargon aphasia: a therapy study. *International Journal of Language and Communication Disorders, 33*, 305–328.

Focus of therapy: Orthographic output lexicon.

Therapy approach: Reactivation.

Client details

General information

RMM was a 75-year-old highly educated woman who had a left CVA, resulting in damage to the left temporoparietal region. She had initial right hemiplegia and right homonymous hemianopia.

Overall pattern of language impairment and preservations

RMM's speech was fluently produced, undifferentiated jargon. She had minimal awareness regarding spoken output and no signs of self-monitoring. Auditory comprehension was relatively well preserved. Writing was produced with considerable effort, and frequent attempts at single words suggested some evidence of monitoring written output. She was able to copy single words and sort anagrams. In a delayed copying task, she showed a significant advantage for words relative to nonwords (particularly for longer items). The authors proposed that this was a consequence of RMM having partial access to preserved orthographic information.

Time post-onset

Therapy was commenced when RMM was 18 months post-onset.

Therapy

Aim

To establish a small written word vocabulary and to transfer this to functional use. Therapy consisted of three phases with the following aims.

- Phase 1: to increase access to stored orthographic representations.
- Phase 2: to build on the success made in Phase 1 and encourage the functional use of the words.
- Phase 3: to enable RMM to associate single written words with complex messages.

In each session, tasks were selected depending on RMM's performance.

Phase 1: picture therapy

This phase of therapy consisted of fourteen 45-min sessions over a period of 5 weeks.

Task	1. Reflect on knowledge of word forms	2. Retrieval of lexical form Writing words in response to picture stimuli
Materials	74 words within 6 semantic categories. Words were paired by a semantic link. Pairs were split, resulting in two sets of 37 words Sets were matched for length and frequency. One set was treated, one set was untreated	
Hierarchy	(a) Identification of initial grapheme (b) Sorting pictures into those with long/short words	(a) Anagram sorting with letter tiles (b) Delayed copying (c) Writing words unaided
Feedback on error	Not specified	Provision of cues to aid production, e.g. first letter, number of letters Discussion of incorrect form Correct form presented
Feedback if correct	Not specified	Correct responses reinforced

Phase 2: Replication and generalisation therapy

This phase of therapy consisted of fifteen 45-min sessions. Three sessions were devoted to replication of Phase 1. Six sessions were devoted to generalisation therapy. Six sessions were split.

Task	1. Generalisation therapy Use of written words in response to a variety of cues. Production of written word communicatively	2. Replication therapy Tasks as in Phase 1
Materials	18 items from treated set in Phase 1 Items that were produced correctly either with no cue or with a first letter cue	18 items in untreated sets Semantic pair to items treated in generalisation therapy
Hierarchy	(a) Writing words to picture pairs (b) Complex picture description (c) Writing words to verbal description (d) Writing words to conversational cue	(a) Reflect on knowledge of words (b) Retrieval of word forms

	(e) Map task – writing in landmarks (f) Holiday list – writing items to be packed (g) Description of day out	
Feedback on error	Provision of cues as in Phase 1 Communicative attempts reinforced	Provision of cues to aid production, e.g. first letter, number of letters Discussion of incorrect Correct form presented
Feedback if correct	Correct responses reinforced	Correct responses reinforced

Phase 3: Message therapy phase, with revision of previous phases

This consisted of a total of 30 sessions. Five sessions were conducted with Set A items, 16 sessions with Set B items and nine sessions with Set C items.

Task	1. Replication therapy Tasks as in Phase 1	2. Message therapy Convey a variety of concepts and messages using single written words
Materials	Set A: 18 words from generalisation therapy in Phase 2 Three sets of new words from 5 semantic categories. Sets B and C both received picture therapy Set D was used as a control set	Set B: 18 new words initially treated using picture therapy
Hierarchy	(a) Reflect on knowledge of words (b) Retrieval of word forms	(a) Matching written synonyms and then copying the target (b) Selecting a written phrase and then copying the target (c) Selection of target from semantically related words (d) Written picture naming in response to message

		(e) Select written word from two messages and copy target (f) Select picture from two messages and write name (g) Write target word from two messages
Feedback on error	Provision of cues to aid production, e.g. first letter, number of letters Discussion of incorrect form Correct form presented	Provision of cues as in Phase 1 Communicative attempts reinforced
Feedback if correct	Correct responses reinforced	Correct responses reinforced

Outcome

Following Phase 1, written picture naming improved from 0 to 14/74 correct with an additional set of items that were produced correctly following an initial letter cue. A significant difference was seen between treated and untreated items. There was a decline in accuracy 6 weeks post-therapy but a significant improvement was still present compared with pre-therapy. There was no change in RMM's insight into her speech, and no functional use of writing.

Following Phase 2, RMM's written naming of treated items improved, and improvement was more rapid than in Phase 1. Generalisation therapy resulted in an increased use of written words demonstrated through a communicative questionnaire task. Improvement was noted in both the items treated in generalisation therapy and those treated only using picture therapy. RMM remained reluctant to use writing outside of therapy sessions.

As in previous phases, therapy resulted in improved picture naming for treated items, following Phase 3, with some decline 6 weeks post-therapy. Following message therapy, RMM's ability to write a word to convey a simple message improved. Improvement was seen in both the words treated using message therapy and those treated only using picture therapy. Friends reported RMM using treated written words within everyday communication. RMM was also attempting to use words not treated in therapy to communicate.

Therapy resulted in item-specific improvements in the writing of single words. The authors proposed that this improvement was a consequence of improved access to lexical orthographic representations of the words. As therapy progressed, the ease with which these representations were accessed improved. Functional use of writing did not emerge without specific targeting in therapy. Phase 3 seemed to result in functional writing as it showed that writing could be used to convey information not present in the original stimulus. Benefits of generalisation and message therapy were not item specific, with therapy resulting in communication at a functional level. The authors suggested that the functional use of writing was not a consequence of an improvement in RMM's self-monitoring but reflected the communicative value of the treated words.

Other comments

This comprehensive study provides a detailed account of how to treat writing in order to improve the communicative abilities of a client with limited speech. The stimuli used in the therapy study are included in the paper. Following specific improvements in the writing of single words, an explicit stage of therapy to encourage communicative use was required.

Study

Beeson, P. M. (2002). Treating acquired writing impairment: strengthening graphemic representations. *Aphasiology*, *13*, 767–785.

Focus of therapy: Orthographic output lexicon.

Therapy approach: Reactivation.

Client details

General information

ST was a 75-year-old man who had a large left temporo-occipital-parietal stroke following a left carotid endarterectomy. He had a mild right hemiparesis and right hemianopia. He was degree educated and was a retired toolmaker in the automotive industry. ST was multilingual, describing Polish and Yiddish as his first languages. He had learned German and English later but had been proficient in English for 40 years prior to the stroke.

Overall pattern of language impairments and preservations

ST presented with a Wernicke's aphasia. His spontaneous speech was characterised by fluent, stereotyped utterances lacking semantic content. His speech was supplemented by the use of gesture and drawing. He was unable to name pictures or to repeat or read words aloud. His comprehension of high-frequency nouns and simple commands was relatively intact but he had moderate to severe difficulties understanding phrases and complex sentences. He was unable to write words either in written naming or writing to dictation. His written naming was characterised by the production of the first letter. In writing to dictation, he mainly wrote phonologically implausible nonwords.

He was able to copy words accurately but only wrote the first few letters of the word following a delay. He also had difficulties transcoding letter across case. The author suggests that ST's writing impairment was a consequence of a significant degradation of orthographic representations in the lexicon with additional difficulties in the graphemic output buffer and with allographic conversion. He showed no evidence of using phonological-to-graphemic correspondences in writing.

Time post-onset

ST was 4 years post-onset at the start of the study.

Therapy

Aim

To improve ST's single-word writing and maximise the use of writing in daily communication. Therapy consisted of four phases: two phases of therapy accompanied by home practice and two home programmes. Phase 1 consisted of ten twice-weekly sessions supplemented by home practice. Phase 2 consisted of clinician-directed homework with the exchange of sheets each week. Phase 3 consisted of eight once-weekly sessions supplemented by home practice. Phase 4 consisted of 6 weeks of self-directed homework. A multiple-baseline design was used to monitor progress on the trained items. During the period of therapy, ST was also attending a weekly aphasia group.

Task	1. Anagram and copy treatment (ACT)	2. Copy and recall treatment (CART)	3. Conversational communicative writing	4. Self-directed home programme
	ACT used in therapy sessions. Arrange the letters of the word in the correct order, copy the word repeatedly and then write the word from memory. CART therapy used at home	Clinician-directed home programme. Look at picture and then repeatedly copy the word. Self-test pages to recall word without model	ACT therapy for new words and CART therapy for all treated words. Use of conversational exchanges to prompt the use of the trained words	Client chooses words from an illustrated dictionary. Words repeatedly copied

Materials	12 nouns and 5 verbs	10 nouns and 10 verbs	20 functionally useful nouns	40 self-directed words
Hierarchy	(a) Anagrams with target letters (b) Anagrams with target letters and two foils	None	None	None
Feedback on error	In anagram task, therapist arranged the letters. If errors in recall, returned to anagram tasks	Not specified	As in Phase 1	Not specified
Feedback if correct	Not specified	Not specified	Not specified	Not specified

Outcome

Following Phase 1, ST met the 80% criterion for the treated words. No improvement was seen in his spelling of untrained words. Following Phase 2, continued item-specific improvement was evident with the maintenance of the words trained in Phase 1 and learning of the words used in Phase 2. ST was not using the words in conversation. After Phase 3, ST continued to meet criterion for the trained words. Within conversational probes, he was able to provide some appropriate written words. An increased use of written single words and some multi-word responses was also noted at home and in the aphasia group. Following Phase 4, ST was able to make recognisable or correct responses for half of the self-selected words.

Overall, treatment resulted in significant item-specific learning in the production of the trained words. Improvement was maintained over a long period and resulted in the use of writing in conversation following the pragmatic training. No improvement was seen in the writing of untrained words or the spoken production of either trained or untrained words. Therapy was successful in enabling ST to learn a small number of words and use them to aid his communication. The authors suggest that therapy resulted in the strengthening of the orthographic representations of the trained words. The study stresses the importance of using home practice alongside and subsequent to clinician-directed therapy.

Other comments

Similar therapy procedures are used with four additional clients in a further study (Beeson, Rewega, Vail, & Rapcsak, 2000). The study shows the potential for self-directed therapy exercises that minimise clinician involvement. The client's writing shows improvement following therapy but it is not clear whether the anagram component is necessary (considering the gains seen in Phase 4). The study stresses the importance of using a small number of words in the treatment set.

Study

Rapp, B., & Kane, A. (2002). Remediation of deficits affecting different components of the spelling process. *Aphasiology*, *16*, 439–454.

Focus of therapy: Orthographic output lexicon and graphemic output buffer.

Therapy approach: Reactivation.

Client details

Two clients are described in the study.

General information

MMD was a right-handed woman who had a CVA at the age of 65. A CT scan showed left posteroparietal and temporal lesions. She was high-school educated and worked in a clerical position until retirement. Pre-morbidly, she was an avid reader and a good speller. RSB was a 58-year-old right-handed man. He had a CVA subsequent to an aortic valve replacement resulting in damage to the left anterior parietal region. He had a PhD and worked in toxicology research. He was bilingual in English and Spanish and had no pre-morbid spelling difficulties.

Overall pattern of language impairments and preservations

Both clients presented with retained single-word comprehension and good comprehension within conversation. They had mild to moderate naming difficulties. In writing, they were able to do cross-case transcoding, indicating an intact ability for retrieving and producing letter shapes. Both MMD and RSB presented with impaired writing to dictation. MMD's writing was characterised by a frequency effect and she produced a high percentage (44%) of phonologically plausible errors. RSB's writing was characterised by a length effect. His errors were phonologically implausible nonwords involving single-letter deletions and substitutions. The authors propose that MMD's writing reflected impairment to the orthographic output lexicon, whereas RSB's impairment was at the level of the graphemic buffer.

Time post-onset

MMD was 2½ years post-onset and RSB was 4 years post-onset at the time of the study.

Therapy

Aim

To improve single-word spelling and to monitor the effect of treatment on untreated words. Treatment was discontinued when the clients reached a stable performance of less than 5% of errors. MMD received 25 sessions of therapy (with a gap half way through) and RSB had a total of 16 sessions. No information was given on the frequency of sessions. An item-specific treatment design was used to contrast improvement on the trained words (those receiving therapy), repeated items (those written each session without feedback) and control items.

Task	**Writing to dictation** Hear word, repeat it and attempt to spell it
Materials	One set of 10 treated words matched for frequency/length with two other sets (the repeated and control items)
Hierarchy	None
Feedback on error	Shown correct spelling of word with therapist saying the letters aloud. Client studies word and then given another chance to spell the word correctly
Feedback if correct	Shown correct spelling of word with therapist saying the letters aloud. Client studies word

Outcome

For both clients, no difference was seen in the error rates across the three sets of words and across the two pre-therapy baselines. Following therapy, MMB showed more accurate writing of the treated words, as shown by a significant reduction in letter errors. Her writing of the treated words was significantly better than that of the repeated items, although also significantly improved. No change was seen in her writing of the control words. At follow-up (20 weeks post-therapy), the error rate for both the treated and repeated items increased but there was still a significant effect of therapy for the treated items. RSB showed significant improvement in his writing of the treated, repeated and control words. Improvement for the treated items was significantly greater than for the other sets. At follow-up, his error rate on all three sets remained unchanged.

Therapy resulted in significant improvement in the writing of the treated words for both clients, but different patterns of generalisation and maintenance were seen. MMB showed no generalised learning and gains were not maintained at follow-up. RSB showed generalisation to control items and writing of all items was maintained at post-therapy levels. No functional outcomes of therapy were discussed. The authors suggest that therapy for MMB resulted in a strengthening of word representation within the lexicon. For RSB, the authors suggest that there was a strengthening of the orthographic representation (making the representation more resistant to buffer damage) and improvement to the buffering process (e.g. scanning speed, speed of letter-to-shape conversion).

Other comments

The number of items within the word sets is small. Despite this, many sessions were required to improve the spelling of the treated words. Although significant improvement was seen on reassessment, the evaluation of efficacy and measuring generalisation was limited due to the small number of items in the treated, repeated and control sets.

Study

Mortley, J., Enderby, P., & Petheram, B. (2001). Using a computer to improve functional writing in a patient with severe dysgraphia. *Aphasiology*, *15*, 443–461.

Focus of therapy: Graphemic output buffer.

Therapy approach: Cognitive relay.

Client details

General information

MF was a 67-year-old man who was a retired civil servant. He had a left CVA resulting in multiple infarcts.

Overall pattern of language impairments and preservations

MF had retained auditory and written comprehension. His spontaneous speech was characterised by high-level word-finding problems. He presented with severe writing difficulties and was unable to use a dictionary or word processor to compensate for these difficulties. On formal testing, he was able to do mirror reversal and cross-case matching but had some problems with letter naming, letter sounding and matching spoken to written letters. He was unable to write either words or nonwords to dictation or write words within written naming. His errors consisted of a random array of letters. He was aware of his errors but was unable to correct them. His oral spelling of words was superior to his written spelling. The authors propose that MF had intact lexical knowledge for shorter words at least but that his writing may reflect a multi-level impairment involving the graphemic output buffer.

Time post-onset

MF was 18 months post-onset when writing therapy began.

Therapy

Aim

To use MF's good oral spelling to aid his written spelling by encouraging him to say the word, spell the word orally letter by letter and then write the word letter by letter. Therapy ran for a period of 6 months with the use of a computer to administer the tasks. Therapist input was restricted to an hour a week for the first month and then one session every 2–3 weeks. No information was given regarding the amount of time MF spent on the computer. A control task design was used. Before the introduction of the strategy, therapy was carried out to develop prerequisite skills: writing single letters to dictation, increasing his awareness of his ability to orally spell words and knowledge of the computer keyboard.

Task	1. Writing words to dictation	2. Introduction of dictionary	3. Sentence-based writing tasks	4. Functional writing tasks
	Hear word, spell the word aloud and then write down each letter	Start writing the words and then use the dictionary to find the rest of the word	Using the strategy to write sentences	Use of an adaptive word processor which provides a list of possible words

Materials	Various words of increasing length	Various words	Various sentences of increasing length	
Hierarchy	(a) Write down two-letter word spoken by therapist (b) Write down three-letter words spoken by therapist (c) Write down four-letter words on computer (d) Write down five-letter words on computer (e) Write down words of 6 or more letters on computer	(a) Written picture naming (b) Solving of definitions	(a) Identification of the individual words within a sentence (b) Write sentences spoken by therapist (c) Sentence copying on computer (d) Writing sentences on computer to describe a composite picture	(a) Write a diary (b) Encourage regular correspond-ence using computer
Feedback on error	Therapist gives next letter or computer gives a choice of letter	Not specified	Not specified	Not specified
Feedback if correct	Not stated	Not specified	Not specified	Not specified

Outcome

During the period of therapy, MF demonstrated the ability to write single words of increasing length, write sentences of increasing length and use these newly acquired writing skills in functional tasks. He also learned to use a dictionary and an adaptive word processor to aid his spelling of longer words. When reassessed using pen and paper, he showed significant improvement in all written tasks. No changes were seen in tasks unrelated to therapy (e.g. digit span, sentence comprehension and letter sounding). Eight weeks after therapy, MF's written spelling performance was maintained and continued to improve. Only following the introduction of the adaptive word processor did writing become quick and easy enough to be of functional benefit.

The introduction of the therapy strategy which encouraged MF's reliance on his oral spelling resulted in a significant improvement in the writing of treated and untreated words in isolation, sentences and connected writing. Improvement was likely to be a consequence of therapy, as no change was seen on control tasks.

Other comments

The therapy tasks used in the study was similar to that reported in a study by Pound (1996). The computer allowed intensive work with minimal input from the therapist, with significant and impressive gains in the client's writing ability. The paper discusses the relationship between oral and written spelling.

Note

1 Although two clients were examined in the study, only one is discussed here.

Epilogue

The outcome of therapy is affected by a variety of factors; some – but not all – of these are illustrated in Figure E.1. This book has concentrated on just two of these. In Part 2, we described how a cognitive neuropsychological model can be used to identify the nature of the impairments and the retained abilities in single-word processing of people with aphasia. The different kinds of therapy that have been shown to be effective in reasonably well-designed studies that use a cognitive neuropsychological perspective in designing and evaluating therapy for specific disorders were described in Part 3. We make no claims to this being an exhaustive review of the literature. Nor have we reported only perfect therapy designs. Many of the studies that have been reviewed did not meet all the desired criteria. The coverage of these studies in the literature is also patchy. For instance, there are many studies of therapy for disorders of word retrieval and, as we have seen, there is now real sophistication in the accounts of how therapy in this area might work and the levels of deficit for which particular approaches might be suitable (Nickels, 2002b). In contrast, there is a disappointingly small number of studies of therapy for difficulties in language comprehension – possibly, as we noted, because such difficulties are not often seen to be the most disabling aspect of chronic aphasia.

While we believe that the studies reviewed in Part 3 provide the best current evidence base for developing and designing therapy in clinical practice, there is no guarantee that the therapy approaches we have described are the best possible methods; new methods and new understanding will come. Our understanding of aphasic language impairments, of specific therapy techniques, and of the ways in which therapies work has improved immeasurably over the last 20 years; however, this knowledge is still often sketchy and fragmentary. But as clinicians, we have an obligation to do what we can with the knowledge available to us. Basso (2003) emphasises: 'What is done should always be the best that can be done with reference to current knowledge. The more knowledge we have, the better we should do, but we cannot wait for the ultimate truth to act' (p. 263).

As Figure E.1 indicates, there are many other factors that may affect the outcome of therapy. These include:

- The nature of the interplay between client and therapist during treatment. The process of therapy cannot, ultimately, be reduced to any mechanistic listing, but involves subtle and probably important interactions at many different levels (Byng & Black, 1995). Just as therapists differ immensely in their therapy 'style', we suspect that there are some therapists who are better at making their clients better, as accounts of aphasia and its therapy often attest (see, for example, Hale, 2002).

- How much therapy – in terms of total hours or intensity of treatment – the client has (e.g. Bhogal, Teasell, & Speechley, 2003). As Somerville (1974) pointed out, far too many treatment studies involve therapy given in 'homeopathic doses'. We would only anticipate significant improvement with enough therapy, but often very little treatment is available to people with aphasia both in the UK and in other countries (Enderby & Petheram, 2002; Katz *et al.*, 2000). However, some of the studies reviewed in Part 3 do show specific targeted improvements with relatively little intervention (in terms of therapist time), giving some grounds for optimism.

- Therapy can be 'delivered' in many different ways: in one-to-one sessions with a trained therapist, in groups, as home practice, with a computer, by working with a friend, family member or volunteer, or remotely by telephone, or even, perhaps, over the internet. Each of these has different advantages and drawbacks, but the variety of methods, used creatively,

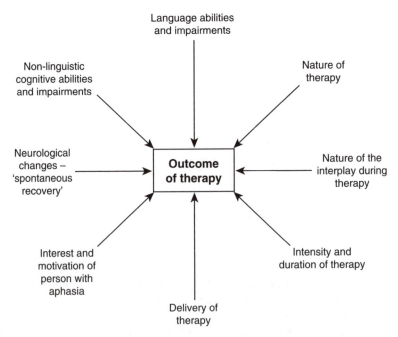

Figure E.1 Some of the factors affecting the outcome of therapy.

offer some means of ensuring that people with aphasia can get a reasonable amount of treatment.

- Therapy will probably be most effective – and certainly most useful – if the person with aphasia is involved as a motivated, active participant, aiming towards goals that make sense in their real lives (e.g. Hillis, 1998). As a corollary of this, therapy usually needs to have 'face validity'; it needs to appear to be directed towards real-life goals. So, for example, although De Partz (1986) may be correct to emphasise that relearning grapheme-to-phoneme correspondences for reading should first be practised with nonwords, some people with aphasia may reject this approach because their aim is to relearn how to read real words.

- Neurological changes in the early periods of spontaneous recovery are important determinants of outcome. The early period of having aphasia is a time of rapid and confusing change, of multiple therapies and of huge social adjustment to a changed social role. Therapy during this period may have to be rather differently organised to build upon and enhance the neurological changes (Huber, Springer, & Willmes, 1993; Robey, 1998). It is no accident that most of the studies reviewed in Part 3 are from clients in the post-acute stage (with the notable exception of Grayson *et al.*, 1997). Practically, it is much easier to demonstrate specific therapy effects when the results are not clouded by rapid changes in many domains, but this is also a period when people with aphasia may be ready to put substantial effort into systematic language therapy.

- Non-linguistic cognitive abilities and disabilities may be important determinants of therapy outcomes (Helm-Estabrooks, 2002). These potentially include semantic and episodic memory (Swinburn, Porter, & Howard, 2004), non-verbal reasoning ability (Bailey, Powell, & Clark, 1981), attention (Lapointe & Erickson, 1991; Laures, Odell, & Coe, 2003) and ability to learn (Ferguson, 1999; Fillingham, Hodgson, Sage, & Lambon Ralph, 2003). In addition, many people with aphasia are (not surprisingly) depressed following a stroke (Huff, Ruhrmann, & Sitzer, 2001; Kauhanen *et al.*, 2000) and this may affect their ability to benefit from treatment. Current knowledge of the impact of these factors is fragmentary (see Basso, 2003) and they have been curiously neglected, but it seems likely that they are important.

There are, clearly, multiple factors affecting therapy outcomes which almost certainly interact. Teasing them apart and determining their importance will be a complex process, but a process that is essential for deciding on the right (i.e. optimally effective in addressing their real-life goals) therapy methods for individual people with aphasia, and for deciding how services should be organised.

Leaving aside these other important factors affecting the outcomes of therapy, there are, we believe, some very important advantages in adopting a cognitive neuropsychological approach to treatment. Of primary importance is that, when based on good assessment, this approach is framed by know-ledge of the client's strengths and weaknesses in processing terms. This gives the therapist the specific knowledge to allow him or her to develop therapy that builds upon and develops the strengths, and that addresses (or avoids) the impaired processes.

Secondly, development of therapy for single clients, or for a small series of clients, means that the content and form of the therapy needs to be described very precisely. This has meant that the content of therapy, as well as its aims and intended mechanisms of change, can be brought into the realm of enquiry. This is in radical contrast to the large-scale group studies of aphasia therapy where a variety of different techniques (never described in any detail – because it would be impossible to do so) are used with a very heterogeneous group of people with aphasia. The problem here is that, even where the therapy is found to be effective, it is impossible for anyone else to use the same (effective) therapy because it is not described in any detail (Howard, 1986). It is only when therapy is described in, using Coltheart's (1983) term, 'cook-book detail' that we can build from studies that show therapy to be effective.

Furthermore, cognitive neuropsychological studies invariably, by the nature of the approach, use *targeted* therapy to cause improvement in *specific* language functions. The result is that outcome measures can assess improve-ment in just those tasks (or just those items) where therapy is intended to produce an effect; they may, as we have seen, be contrasted with tasks or items where effects of treatment are not anticipated. The result is that therapy can be given a 'fair' test: did it result in improvement in just those tasks (or items) where improvement was anticipated?

Finally, these studies allow us to begin to think about *why* therapy works – what is the underlying mechanism resulting in behavioural change? In most cases, therapy studies clearly state why it is that the therapy tasks *should* result in the changes anticipated. It is much rarer though to find clear and specific evidence that these truly *are* the mechanisms; even where a therapy can be shown to be effective, it is not always clear that it is effective for the reasons supposed. To take one example: with word retrieval impairments, 'semantic therapy' has been seen as improving semantic representations, and lexical/phonological therapy as improving access to lexical representations for output. This is because these correspond to the clients' identified underlying deficits, and they were what were targeted in therapy. However, Howard (2000) argued that the available evidence supported the view that both sets of therapy methods, despite their superficial differences, were effective for the same reason: they paired semantic and phonological word representations and strengthened the links between them. Which of these perspectives is correct is unclear; importantly, though, adopting a cognitive neuropsychological perspective makes debates about such issues possible.

In more practical terms, adopting a cognitive neuropsychological approach requires the therapist to think clearly about two things. First, on the basis of the assessment results, the clinician must identify why performance in language tasks is breaking down. Secondly, in the process of treatment, the therapist needs to be clear *why* doing a particular task should result in change. In short, it provides the therapist with the theoretical and practical framework to be able to live up to Schuell, Jenkins and Jimenez-Pabon's (1964) exhortation that 'A good therapist should never be taken unawares by the question, "Why are you doing this?" ' (p. 333).

At the neurological level, how and why therapy might work is an important issue (e.g. Musso *et al.*, 1999). It is now clear that behavioural change and neurological change are related; functional changes are reflected at a structural level (Rijntjes & Weiller, 2002). Research on brain imaging of recovery from aphasia and the effects of therapy is only just beginning. As far as we are aware, there are no findings to date that constrain or inform the practice of aphasia therapy.

There are two ways in which we think studies of aphasia therapy should develop over the next few years. First, there is a need to refine and develop our knowledge of how the effectiveness of particular therapy methods relates to the client's pattern of aphasia. Over the last 20 years, we have made enormous strides in our ability to identify levels of breakdown within motivated and theoretically explicit models of language processing. The result is a much improved ability to identify both impaired processes and intact processes.

Then, how do we decide what therapy approach to adopt with a client? There are, crudely, two possible approaches. The first approach is to base the decision on some theoretical or logical understanding of how the therapy works and who it is appropriate for. There are a number of examples of this. For instance, Nickels' 'autocue' therapy (self-generated phonemic cues for word retrieval) is, she argues, appropriate for clients who (i) benefit from phonemic cues and (ii) know about the initial letter of words that they cannot produce in written form. Similarly, Miceli, Armitrano, Capasso and Caramazza (1996) believe that their 'lexical therapy' is appropriate for clients with post-semantic impairments in word retrieval.

The difficulty here is that these beliefs about how specific therapies work may turn out to be wrong. For example, Howard (2000) argues that the evidence suggests that both 'semantic' and 'lexical' (or 'phonological') therapies for word retrieval may work in the same way and for the same types of clients – by, essentially, pairing meanings with phonological forms. Whether this argument is correct is, for the moment, immaterial. The point is that how therapies operate can only really be determined empirically by proper hypothesis testing. In particular, it requires applying a therapy both to those for whom it is believed to be appropriate and those for whom it is not (as Nettleton and Lesser, 1991, tried to do).

The most productive approach to this, however, is probably to conduct studies that compare the degree of improvement for different kinds of clients with one kind of treatment. If a case series approach is adopted, each participant can be analysed as a single case, and then it is possible to use homogeneity tests to examine if there are significant differences among the participants in the size of the treatment effects (Howard, 2003). Where there are differences, these can be related to the forms of deficit (see Best *et al.*, 2002, for an example). Furthermore, we need studies that compare the effectiveness of different therapies for one client. Most of the studies we have reviewed consider only one treatment approach. When the participant shows improvement, this is obviously a gratifying result, but we do not know if another approach might not have been more effective. Studies of this kind can, therefore, provide critical information about the optimum therapy methods. Moreover, the comparison of different therapy methods can, in the light of knowledge of the participant's underlying deficits, provide critical information about how the treatments are having their effects. To date, a few studies that have adopted this kind of approach (see, for example, Hickin *et al.*, 2002; Hillis & Caramazza, 1994; Howard, 2000; Springer, Glindemann, Huber, & Willmes, 1991) have shown that this can be productive.

We consider it axiomatic that the aim of all therapies with people with aphasia is to improve their functioning in the real, social world, to enable them to cope with barriers to participation and fulfilment. In that sense, the therapy methods are embedded in a 'social model' (Byng, Pound, & Parr, 2000). These aims can often be best addressed through improving language abilities, and it is to this end that the studies in this book are addressed. There is no contradiction between functional, social aims and therapy directed at reducing impairments. In music, one practises scales not because a performance consists of playing scales, but because doing this develops skills that result in better performance. The same applies to 'impairment-oriented' therapy.

There is, however, a real issue. How does one ensure that skills learned in therapy have an impact on the real-life, day-to-day communication of a person with aphasia? Is it the case that only skills learned in 'real-life situations' result in real-life improvement? This claim has sometimes been made, but, as far as we are aware, there is no supporting evidence. Many of the therapies described in this book, particularly those aimed at word retrieval and at spelling, have item-specific effects (i.e. only the items worked on in therapy improve). Where this is the case, selection of target items with the client so that the words are those most likely to be useful in their day-to-day communication is clearly essential. Hillis (1998), for example, describes therapy with a woman returning to work as a librarian, where the therapy targets were specifically chosen by client and therapist together to be words likely to be useful in her work.

As Basso (2003) argues, we, as therapists, have a responsibility to use the best available knowledge about aphasia and about aphasia therapy in our treatment with people with aphasia. Like Basso, we have argued that the best existing knowledge base is drawn from our understanding of the cognitive neuropsychology of language, and so it is from that field that we have drawn our principles. As Oliver Zangwill (1947) wrote, almost 60 years ago, 'No method of treatment is better than the principles on which it is based, and the search for principles should concern us no less than the immediate clinical situation' (p. 7).

Glossary

Allographic realisation   spatial representations of letters in their different allographic forms (e.g. upper and lower case)

Allographs   a variant form of a grapheme (e.g. 'a' or 'A')

Anomia   delays and failures in word retrieval

Articulatory programming   the conversion of phonemes into neuromuscular commands

Auditory phonological analysis   identifies speech sounds by analysing the string of sounds heard

Brain reorganisation strategies   strategies that aim to encourage alternative parts of the brain to take over the impaired language function

Circumlocution   error responses that indicate access to some intact semantic information in the absence of a phonological representation, e.g. NAIL → 'you bang it into wood'

Cognitive relay strategies   strategies that seek an alternative route or means of performing the language function; that is, use intact components of the language system to achieve the impaired function through indirect means

Compensation strategies   strategies that attempt to maximise the use of retained language and communication behaviours, without focusing on the impaired functions

Conduite d'approche   repeated phonological errors produced during spoken word production; repeated attempts often result in a closer approximation to the target word. Often present due to difficulties with phonological assembly

CT   computerised tomography (also known as computerised axial tomography, or a CAT scan) is a sophisticated radiographic diagnostic technique that produces computerised images of the brain (or body), enabling areas of damage to be identified

CVA   cerebrovascular accident, or stroke, which occurs when there is a rupture or occlusion of a blood vessel in the brain resulting in damage to the surrounding tissue

Direct lexical route for reading   the route involved in reading aloud via a lexical but not semantic route

Direct lexical route for writing the route involved in writing to dictation via a lexical but not semantic route

Graphemic output buffer storage of abstract graphemic representations (i.e. case not specified)

Graphemic output lexicon a store of the spelling of familiar words or written word forms

Graphic-to-motor realisation translation of allographs to motor patterns

Homophones words with same phonology but a different meaning (e.g. sail–sale, two–too–to)

Morphological errors error responses that share at least the root morpheme with the target word but have errors in addition, deletion or substitution of prefixed or suffixed morphemes (e.g. DISCORD → 'concorde', UNREALITY → 'real')

MRI magnetic resonance imaging scan is a diagnostic technique that uses magnetic fields and computer technology to produce detailed images of the brain (or body); it is more detailed than computerised tomography

Neologisms nonword error responses that do not share sufficient phonemes to be classified as phonological errors

Orthographic input lexicon a store of visual word recognition units; accesses written word forms by recognising the word as a familiar one

Orthographic output lexicon a store of the spelling of familiar words or written word forms

Orthographic-to-phonological conversion (non-lexical reading route) reading aloud via sub-word level orthographic-to-phonological correspondences. It involves the 'sounding out' of graphemes

Phoneme-to-grapheme conversion (non-lexical writing route) writing via the segmentation of a word into phonemes and then translation of the phonemes into graphemes

Phonemic cueing provision of a phonological cue to facilitate production of a word, either by providing a single phoneme (usually the initial) or progressively more phonological information

Phonological assembly the generation of a metrically specified phoneme string for production

Phonological errors error responses that are similar to the target in phonological form. A common criterion for phonological similarity is that at least 50% of the phonemes in the stimulus occur in the error response in approximately the same order

Phonological input lexicon a store of auditory word recognition units; accesses auditory word forms by recognising the word as a familiar one

Phonologically plausible errors errors in reading or writing that are an appropriate production for the phonology of the word

Phonological output lexicon a store of spoken word forms; provides access to spoken word forms

Reactivation approaches therapy that aims to reactivate access to impaired language and processing

Relearning approaches therapy that aims to re-teach impaired language procedures or knowledge

Semantic cueing provision of semantic information to facilitate production of a word

Semantic errors error responses that are semantically related to the target (e.g. NAIL → 'screw')

Semantic lexical route for reading the route involved in the reading aloud of words via access to their meaning

Semantic lexical route for writing the route involved in the writing of words via access to their meaning

Semantic system a store of word meanings

Substitution strategies strategies that encourage the adoption of an external prosthesis to promote communication

Visual errors reading errors that are similar to the target in orthographic form

Visual orthographic analysis identifies letters and codes the position of letters within a word. May be involved in the parsing of letters into graphemes

Visual and semantic errors errors that are both visually and semantically related to the target

Word form deafness a deficit in the phonological input lexicon

Word meaning deafness a deficit in accessing the semantic system from the phonological input lexicon

Word sound deafness a deficit in auditory phonological analysis

References

Albert, M., Sparks, R., & Helm, N. A. (1973). Melodic intonation therapy for aphasia. *Archives of Neurology, 29*, 130–131.

Albert, M. L., Goodglass, H., Helm, N. A., Rubens, A. B., & Alexander, M. P. (1981). *Clinical aspects of dysphasia*. Vienna: Springer-Verlag.

Allport, D. A. (1985). Distributed memory, modular subsystems and dysphasia. In S. K. Newman & R. Epstein (Eds.), *Current perspectives in dysphasia*. Edinburgh: Churchill Livingstone.

Allport, D. A., & Funnell, E. (1981). Components of the mental lexicon. *Philosophical Transactions of the Royal Society of London, B295*, 397–410.

Baayen, R., Piepenbrock, R., & Gulikers, L. (1995). *The CELEX Lexical Database (Release 2) [CD-ROM]*. Philadelphia, PA: Linguistic Data Consortium, University of Pennsylvania.

Bachy-Langedock, N., & De Partz, M. P. (1989). Co-ordination of two re-organization therapies in a deep dyslexic patient with oral naming disorders. In X. Seron & G. Deloche (Eds.), *Cognitive approaches in neuropsychological rehabilitation*. Hillsdale, NJ: Lawrence Erlbaum Associates.

Badecker, W., Hillis, A. E., & Caramazza, A. (1990). Lexical morphology and its role in the writing process: evidence from a case of acquired dysgraphia. *Cognition, 35*, 205–244.

Bailey, S., Powell, G. E., & Clark, E. (1981). A note on intelligence and recovery from aphasia: the relationship between Raven's matrices scores and change on the Schuell aphasia test. *British Journal of Disorders of Communication, 16*, 193–203.

Barry, C., Morrison, C. M., & Ellis, A. W. (1997). Naming the Snodgrass and Vanderwart pictures: effects of age of acquisition, frequency and name agreement. *Quarterly Journal of Experimental Psychology: Human Experimental Psychology, 50*, 560–585.

Basso, A. (1989). Spontaneous recovery and language rehabilitation. In X. Seron & G. Deloche (Eds.), *Cognitive approaches in neuropsychological rehabilitation*. Hillsdale, NJ: Lawrence Erlbaum Associates.

Basso, A. (2003). *Aphasia and its therapy*. Oxford: Oxford University Press.

Basso, A., & Marangolo, P. (2000). Cognitive neuropsychological rehabilitation: the emperor's new clothes? *Neuropsychological Rehabilitation, 10*, 219–229.

Bastiaanse, R., Bosje, M., & Franssen, M. (1996). Deficit-oriented treatment of word-finding problems; another replication. *Aphasiology, 10*, 363–383.

Bastiaanse, R., Nijober, S., & Taconis, M. (1993). The Auditory Language

Comprehension Programme: a description and case study. *European Journal of Disorders of Communication, 12*, 415–433.

Baxter, D. M., & Warrington, E. K. (1986). Ideational agraphia: a single case study. *Journal of Neurology, Neurosurgery and Psychiatry, 49*, 369–374.

Beauvois, M. F., & Derouesne, J. (1981). Lexical or orthographic agraphia. *Brain, 104*, 21–49.

Beeson, P. M. (2002). Treating acquired writing impairment: strengthening graphemic representations. *Aphasiology, 13*, 767–785.

Beeson, P. M., Rewega, M. A., Vail, S., & Rapcsak, S. Z. (2000). Problem-solving approach to agraphia treatment: interactive use of lexical and sublexical spelling routes. *Aphasiology, 14*, 551–565.

Behrmann, M. (1987). The rites of righting writing: homophone remediation and acquired dysgraphia. *Cognitive Neuropsychology, 4*, 365–384.

Behrmann, M., & Bub, D. (1992). Surface dyslexia and dysgraphia – dual routes, single lexicon. *Cognitive Neuropsychology, 9*, 209–251.

Behrmann, M., & Lieberthal, T. (1989). Category-specific treatment of a lexical-semantic deficit: a single case study of global aphasia. *British Journal of Disorders of Communication, 24*, 281–299.

Belin, P., Van Eeckhout, P., Zilbovicius, M., Remy, P., Francois, C., Guillaume, S., Chain, F., Rancurel, G., & Samson, Y. (1996). Recovery from nonfluent aphasia after melodic intonation therapy: a PET study. *Neurology, 47*, 1504–1511.

Berndt, R. S., Haendiges, A. N., Burton, M. W., & Mitchum, C. C. (2002). Grammatical class and imageability in aphasic word production: their effects are independent. *Journal of Neurolinguistics, 15*, 353–371.

Berndt, R. S., & Mitchum, C. C. (1994). Approaches to the rehabilitation of 'phonological assembly': elaborating the model of non-lexical reading. In M. J. Riddoch & G. W. Humphreys (Eds.), *Cognitive neuropsychology and cognitive rehabilitation*. London: Lawrence Erlbaum Associates.

Best, W. (1995). A reverse length effect in dysphasic naming: when elephant is easier than ant. *Cortex, 31*, 637–652.

Best, W., Herbert, R., Hickin, J., Osborne, F., & Howard, D. (2002). Phonological and orthographic facilitation of word-retrieval in aphasia: immediate and delayed effects. *Aphasiology, 16*, 151–168.

Bhogal, S. K., Teasell, R., & Speechley, M. (2003). Intensity of aphasia therapy, impact on recovery. *Stroke, 34*, 987–992.

Bigland, S., & Speake, J. (1992). *Semantic links*. Northumberland: STASS Publications.

Bird, H., Franklin, S., & Howard, D. (2002). 'Little words' – not really: function and content words in normal and aphasic speech. *Journal of Neurolinguistics, 15*, 209–237.

Bird, H., Howard, D., & Franklin, S. (2000). Why is a verb like an inanimate object? Grammatical category and semantic category deficits. *Brain and Language, 72*, 246–309.

Booth, S., & Perkins, L. (1999). The use of conversation analysis to guide individualised advice to carers and evaluate change in aphasia; a case study. *Aphasiology, 13*, 283–303.

Booth, S., & Swabey, D. (1999). Group training in communication skills for carers of adults with aphasia. *International Journal of Language and Communication Disorders, 34*, 291–309.

Boyle, M., & Coelho, C. A. (1995). Application of semantic feature analysis as a treatment for aphasic dysnomia. *American Journal of Speech and Language Pathology, 4*, 94–98.

Breedin, S. D., Saffran, E. M., & Coslett, H. B. (1994). Reversal of the concreteness effect in a patient with semantic dementia. *Cognitive Neuropsychology, 11*, 617–660.

Bruce, C., & Howard, D. (1987). Computer generated phonemic cueing: an effective aid for naming in aphasia. *British Journal of Disorders of Communication, 22*, 191–201.

Brumfitt, S. (1993). Losing your sense of self: what aphasia can do. *Aphasiology, 7*, 569–575.

Bryant, P. E., & Bradley, L. (1985). *Children's reading problems: Psychology and education*. Oxford: Blackwell.

Bub, D., Cancelliere, A., & Kertesz, A. (1985). Whole-word and analytic translation of spelling to sound in a non-semantic reader. In K. E. Patterson, J. C. Marshall, & M. Coltheart (Eds.), *Surface dyslexia: Neuropsychological and cognitive studies of phonological reading*. London: Lawrence Erlbaum Associates.

Bub, D., & Kertesz, A. (1982). Deep agraphia. *Brain and Language, 17*, 146–165.

Byng, S. (1988). Sentence processing deficits: theory and therapy. *Cognitive Neuropsychology, 5*, 629–676.

Byng, S., & Black, M. (1995). What makes a therapy? Some parameters of therapeutic intervention in aphasia. *European Journal of Disorders of Communication, 30*, 303–316.

Byng, S., & Coltheart, M. (1986). Aphasia therapy research: methodological requirements and illustrative results. In R. Hjelmquist & L. B. Nilsson (Eds.), *Communication and handicap*. Amsterdam: Elsevier.

Byng, S., Pound, C., & Parr, S. (2000). Living with aphasia: a framework for therapy interventions. In I. Papathanasiou (Ed.), *Acquired neurological communication disorders: A clinical perspective*. London: Whurr Publishers.

Capitani, E., Laiacona, M., Mahon, B., & Caramazza, A. (2003). What are the facts of semantic category-specific deficits? A critical review of the clinical evidence. *Cognitive Neuropsychology, 20*, 213–261.

Caplan, D., Vanier, M., & Baker, C. (1986). A case study of reproduction conduction aphasia. I: Word production. *Cognitive Neuropsychology, 3*, 99–128.

Caramazza, A. (1986). On drawing inferences about the structure of normal cognitive systems from the analysis of patterns of impaired performance: the case for single-patient studies. *Brain and Cognition, 5*, 41–66.

Caramazza, A. (1989). Cognitive neuropsychology and rehabilitation: an unfulfilled promise? In X. Seron & G. Deloche (Eds.), *Cognitive approaches in neuro-psychological rehabilitation*. Hillsdale, NJ: Lawrence Erlbaum Associates.

Caramazza, A., & Hillis, A. E. (1989). The disruption of sentence production: some dissociations. *Brain and Language, 36*, 625–650.

Caramazza, A., & Hillis, A. E. (1990). Where do semantic errors come from? *Cortex, 26*, 95–122.

Caramazza, A., & Mahon, B. Z. (2003). The organization of conceptual knowledge: the evidence from category-specific semantic deficits. *Trends in Cognitive Sciences, 7*, 354–361.

Chall, J. S. (1983). *Stages of reading development*. New York: McGraw-Hill.

Chapey, R. (Ed.) (1981). *Language intervention strategies in adult aphasia*. Baltimore, MD: Williams & Wilkins.

Clark, E. (1993). *The lexicon in acquisition*. Cambridge: Cambridge University Press.

Coelho, C. A., McHugh, R. E., & Boyle, M. (2000). Semantic feature analysis as a treatment for aphasic dysnomia. *Aphasiology, 14*, 133–142.

Cole-Virtue, J., & Nickels, L. A. (2004). Why cabbage and not carrot? An investigation of factors affecting performance on spoken word to picture matching. *Aphasiology, 18*, 153–179.

Coltheart, M. (1980). Deep dyslexia: a right hemisphere hypothesis. In M. Coltheart, K. E. Patterson, & J. C. Marshall (Eds.), *Deep dyslexia*. London: Routledge & Kegan Paul.

Coltheart, M. (1981). The MRC psycholinguistic database. *Quarterly Journal of Experimental Psychology, 33A*, 497–505.

Coltheart, M. (1983). Aphasia therapy research: a single-case study approach. In C. Code & D. Muller (Eds.), *Aphasia therapy*. London: Edward Arnold.

Coltheart, M. (2001). Assumptions and methods in cognitive neuropsychology. In B. Rapp (Ed.), *The handbook of cognitive neuropsychology*. Philadelphia, PA: Psychology Press.

Coltheart, M., & Byng, S. (1989). A treatment for surface dyslexia. In X. Seron & G. Deloche (Eds.), *Cognitive approaches in neuropsychological rehabilitation*. Hillsdale, NJ: Lawrence Erlbaum Associates.

Coltheart, M., Curtis, B., Atkins, P., & Haller, M. (1993). Models of reading aloud – dual-route and parallel-distributed-processing approaches. *Psychological Review, 100*, 589–608.

Coltheart, M., Langdon, R., & Haller, M. (1996). Computational cognitive neuro-psychology and reading. In B. Dodd, L. Worrall, & R. Campbell (Eds.), *Models of language: Illuminations from impairment*. London: Whurr Publishers.

Coltheart, M., Rastle, K., Perry, C., Langdon, R., & Ziegler, J. (2001). DRC: a dual route cascaded model of visual word recognition and reading aloud. *Psychological Review, 108*, 204–256.

Conway, T. W., Heilman, P., Rothi, L. J. G., Alexander, A. W., Adair, J., Crosson, B. A., & Heilman, K. M. (1998). Treatment of a case of phonological alexia with agraphia using the Auditory Discrimination in Depth (ADD) program. *Journal of the International Neuropsychological Society, 4*, 608–620.

Cubelli, R., Foresti, A., & Consolini, T. (1988). Re-education strategies in conduction aphasia. *Journal of Communication Disorders, 21*, 239–249.

Cutler, A. (1981). The reliability of speech error data. *Linguistics, 19*, 561–582.

De Haan, E. H. F. (2001). Face perception and recognition. In B. Rapp (Ed.), *The handbook of cognitive neuropsychology: What deficits reveal about the human mind*. Philadelphia, PA: Psychology Press.

De Partz, M.-P. (1986). Re-education of a deep dyslexic patient: rationale of the method and results. *Cognitive Neuropsychology, 3*, 149–177.

De Partz, M.-P., Seron, X., & Van der Linden, M. (1992). Re-education of a surface dysgraphia with a visual imagery strategy. *Cognitive Neuropsychology, 9*, 369–401.

Dell, G. S., Schwartz, M. F., Martin, N., Saffran, E. M., & Gagnon, D. A. (1997). Lexical access in aphasic and nonaphasic speakers. *Psychological Review, 104*, 801–838.

Deloche, G., Dordan, M., & Kremin, H. (1993). Rehabilitation of confrontation naming in aphasia: relations between oral and written modalities. *Aphasiology, 7*, 201–216.

Destreri, N. D., Farina, E., Alberoni, M., Pomati, S., Nichelli, P., & Mariani, C.

(2000). Selective uppercase dysgraphia with loss of visual imagery of letter forms: a window on the organization of graphomotor patterns. *Brain and Language, 71*, 353–372.

Ellis, A. W., Flude, B. M., & Young, A. W. (1987). 'Neglect dyslexia' and the early visual processing of letters in words. *Cognitive Neuropsychology, 4*, 439–464.

Ellis, A. W., & Morrison, C. M. (1998). Real age-of-acquisition effects in lexical retrieval. *Journal of Experimental Psychology: Learning, Memory and Cognition, 24*, 515–523.

Enderby, P., & Petheram, B. (2002). Has aphasia therapy been swallowed up? *Clinical Rehabilitation, 16*, 604–608.

Farah, M. J. (1990). *Visual agnosia: Disorders of object recognition and what they tell us about normal vision.* Cambridge, MA: MIT Press.

Ferguson, A. (1999). Learning in aphasia therapy: it's not so much what you do, but how you do it! *Aphasiology, 13*, 125–132.

Fillingham, J. K., Hodgson, C., Sage, K., & Lambon Ralph, M. A. (2003). The application of errorless learning to aphasic disorders: a review of theory and practice. *Neuropsychological Rehabilitation, 13*, 337–363.

Foygel, D., & Dell, G. S. (2000). Models of impaired lexical access in speech production. *Journal of Memory and Language, 43*, 182–216.

Francis, D. R., Clark, N., & Humphreys, G. W. (2002). Circumlocution-induced naming (CIN): a treatment for effecting generalisation in anomia? *Aphasiology, 16*, 243–259.

Francis, D. R., Riddoch, M. J., & Humphreys, G. W. (2001a). Cognitive rehabilitation of word meaning deafness. *Aphasiology, 15*, 749–766.

Francis, D. R., Riddoch, M. J., & Humphreys, G. W. (2001b). Treating agnostic alexia complicated by additional impairments. *Neuropsychological Rehabilitation, 11*, 113–145.

Franklin, S. (1989). Dissociations in auditory word comprehension – evidence from nine fluent aphasic patients. *Aphasiology, 3*, 189–207.

Franklin, S. (1997). Designing single case treatment studies for aphasic patients. *Neuropsychological Rehabilitation, 7*, 401–418.

Franklin, S., Buerk, F., & Howard, D. (2002). Generalised improvement in speech production for a subject with reproduction conduction aphasia. *Aphasiology, 16*, 1087–1114.

Franklin, S., Howard, D., & Patterson, K. (1994). Abstract word meaning deafness. *Cognitive Neuropsychology, 11*, 1–34.

Franklin, S., Howard, D., & Patterson, K. (1995). Abstract word anomia. *Cognitive Neuropsychology, 12*, 549–566.

Franklin, S., Turner, J. E., & Ellis, A. W. (1992). *The ADA Comprehension Battery.* London: Action for Dysphasic Adults.

Franklin, S., Turner, J. E., Lambon Ralph, M. A., Morris, J., & Bailey, P. J. (1996). A distinctive case of word meaning deafness? *Cognitive Neuropsychology, 13*, 1139–1162.

Friedman, R. B., & Lott, S. N. (2002). Successful blending in a phonological reading treatment for deep alexia. *Aphasiology, 16*, 355–372.

Frith, U. (1986). A developmental framework for developmental dyslexia. *Annals of Dyslexia, 36*, 69–81.

Funnell, E. (1983). Phonological processes in reading: new evidence from acquired dyslexia. *British Journal of Psychology, 74*, 159–180.

Funnell, E. (1987). Morphological errors in acquired dyslexia – a case of mistaken identity. *Quarterly Journal of Experimental Psychology: Human Experimental Psychology, 39*, 497–539.

Garrard, P., & Hodges, J. R. (1999). Semantic dementia: implications for the neural basis of language and meaning. *Aphasiology, 13*, 609–623.

Gernsbacher, M. A. (1984). Resolving 20 years of inconsistent interactions between lexical familiarity and orthography, concreteness, and polysemy. *Journal of Experimental Psychology: General, 113*, 256.

Gielewski, E. J. (1989). Acoustic analysis and auditory retraining in the remediation of sensory aphasia. In C. Code & D. Muller (Eds.), *Aphasia therapy* (2nd edn.). London: Whurr Publishers.

Goodglass, H., Kaplan, E., & Barresi, B. (2001). *Boston Diagnostic Aphasia Examination* (3rd edn.). Philadelphia, PA: Lippincott, Williams & Wilkins.

Goodglass, H., Kaplan, E., & Weintraub, S. (2001). *The Boston Naming Test.* Philadelphia, PA: Lippincott, Williams & Wilkins.

Gough, P. B. (1996). How children learn to read and why they fail. *Annals of Dyslexia, 46*, 3–20.

Grayson, E., Hilton, R., & Franklin, S. E. (1997). Early intervention in a case of jargon aphasia: efficacy of language comprehension therapy. *European Journal of Disorders of Communication, 32*, 257–276.

Greenwald, M. L., Raymer, A. M., Richardson, M. E., & Rothi, L. J. G. (1995). Contrasting treatments for severe impairments of picture naming. *Neuropsychological Rehabilitation, 5*, 17–49.

Greenwald, M. L., & Rothi, L. J. G. (1998). Lexical access via letter naming in a profoundly alexic and anomic patient: a treatment study. *Journal of the International Neuropsychological Society, 4*, 595–607.

Hale, S. (2002). *The man who lost his language.* London: Allen Lane.

Hall, D. A., & Riddoch, M. J. (1997). Word meaning deafness: spelling words that are not understood. *Cognitive Neuropsychology, 14*, 1131–1164.

Hatfield, F. M. (1983). Aspects of acquired dysgraphia and implications for re-education. In C. Code & D. J. Muller (Eds.), *Aphasia therapy*. London: Edward Arnold.

Hatfield, F. M., & Patterson, K. (1983). Phonological spelling. *Quarterly Journal of Experimental Psychology, 35A*, 451–468.

Hatfield, F. M., & Shewell, C. (1983). Some applications of linguistics to aphasia therapy. In C. Code & D. J. Muller (Eds.), *Aphasia therapy*. London: Edward Arnold.

Helm-Estabrooks, N. (2002). Cognition and aphasia: a discussion and a study. *Journal of Communication Disorders, 35*, 171–186.

Helm-Estabrooks, N., Fitzpatrick, P. M. R., & Barresi, B. (1982). Visual action therapy for global aphasics. *Journal of Speech and Hearing Disorders, 47*, 385–389.

Hickin, J., Best, W., Herbert, R., Howard, D., & Osborne, F. (2002). Phonological therapy for word-finding difficulties: a re-evaluation. *Aphasiology, 16*, 981–999.

Hillis, A. E. (1989). Efficacy and generalisation of treatment for aphasic naming errors. *Archives of Physical Medicine and Rehabilitation, 70*, 632–636.

Hillis, A. E. (1993). The role of models of language processing in rehabilitation of language impairments. *Aphasiology, 7*, 5–26.

Hillis, A. E. (1998). Treatment of naming disorders: new issues regarding old therapies. *Journal of the International Neuropsychological Society, 4*, 648–660.

Hillis, A. E., & Caramazza, A. (1994). Theories of lexical processing and rehabilitation of lexical deficits. In M. J. Riddoch & G. W. Humphreys (Eds.), *Cognitive neuropsychology and cognitive rehabilitation*. London: Lawrence Erlbaum Associates.

Hillis, A. E., & Caramazza, A. (1995). Converging evidence for the interaction of semantic and sublexical phonological information in accessing lexical representations for spoken output. *Cognitive Neuropsychology, 12*, 187–227.

Hillis, A. E., Rapp, B., Romani, C., & Caramazza, A. (1990). Selective impairment of semantics in lexical processing. *Cognitive Neuropsychology, 7*, 191–243.

Hinton, G. E., McClelland, J. L., & Rumelhart, D. E. (1986). Distributed representations. In D. E. Rumelhart & J. L. McClelland (Eds.), *Parallel distributed processing*. London: Bradford Books.

Hodges, J. R., Patterson, K., Oxbury, S., & Funnell, E. (1992). Semantic dementia – progressive fluent aphasia with temporal lobe atrophy. *Brain, 115*, 1783–1806.

Holland, A. L. (1982). Observing functional communication of aphasic adults. *Journal of Speech and Hearing Disorders, 47*, 50–56.

Howard, D. (1985). *The semantic organisation of the lexicon: evidence from aphasia*. Unpublished PhD thesis, University of London.

Howard, D. (1986). Beyond randomised controlled trials: the case for effective case studies of the effects of treatment in aphasia. *British Journal of Communication Disorders, 21*, 89–102.

Howard, D. (1995). Lexical anomia: or the case of the missing lexical entries. *Quarterly Journal of Experimental Psychology, 48*, 999–1023.

Howard, D. (2000). Cognitive neuropsychology and aphasia therapy: the case of word retrieval. In I. Papathanasiou (Ed.), *Acquired neurogenic communication disorders*. London: Whurr Publishers.

Howard, D. (2003). Single cases, group studies and case series in aphasia therapy. In I. Papathanasiou & R. De Bleser (Eds.), *The sciences of aphasia: From therapy to theory*. Oxford: Pergamon Press.

Howard, D., & Franklin, S. (1988). *Missing the meaning?* Cambridge, MA: MIT Press.

Howard, D., & Harding, D. (1998). Self-cueing of word retrieval by a woman with aphasia: why a letter board works. *Aphasiology, 12*, 399–420.

Howard, D., & Hatfield, F. M. (1987). *Aphasia therapy: Historical and contemporary issues*. London: Lawrence Erlbaum Associates.

Howard, D., & Nickels, L. A. (2005). Separating input and output phonology: semantic, phonological and orthographic effects in short-term memory impairment. *Cognitive Neuropsychology, 22*, 42–77.

Howard, D., & Orchard-Lisle, V. M. (1984). On the origin of semantic errors in naming: evidence from a case of global aphasia. *Cognitive Neuropsychology, 1*, 163–190.

Howard, D., & Patterson, K. E. (1989). Models for therapy. In X. Seron & G. Deloche (Eds.), *Cognitive approaches in neuropsychological rehabilitation*. Hillsdale, NJ: Lawrence Erlbaum Associates.

Howard, D., & Patterson, K. E. (1992). *The Pyramids and Palm Trees Test*. Bury St. Edmunds, UK: Thames Valley Test Corporation.

Howard, D., Patterson, K. E., Franklin, S., Orchard-Lisle, V., & Morton, J. (1985). Treatment of word retrieval deficits in aphasia: a comparison of two therapy methods. *Brain, 108*, 817–829.

Huber, W., Springer, L., & Willmes, K. (1993). Approaches to aphasia therapy in

Aachen. In A. Holland & F. Forbes (Eds.), *Aphasia treatment: World perspectives*. San Diego, CA: Singular Publishing Group.

Huff, W., Ruhrmann, S., & Sitzer, M. (2001). Post-stroke depression: diagnosis and therapy. *Fortschritte der Neurologie Psychiatrie, 69*, 581–591.

Humphreys, G. W., & Riddoch, M. J. (1987). *To see but not to see: A case study of visual agnosia*. London: Lawrence Erlbaum Associates.

Jones, E. V. (1989). A year in the life of EVJ and PC. Paper presented at the *Summer Conference of the British Aphasiology Society*, Cambridge.

Kaplan, E., Goodglass, H., & Weintraub, S. (2001). *The Boston Naming Test*. Philadelphia, PA: Lippincott, Williams & Wilkins.

Katz, R. C., Hallowell, B., Code, C., Armstrong, E., Roberts, P., Pound, C., & Katz, L. (2000). A multinational comparison of aphasia management practices. *International Journal of Language and Communication Disorders, 35*, 303–314.

Kauhanen, M. L., Korpelainen, J. T., Hiltunen, P., Maatta, R., Mononen, H., Brusin, E., Sotaniemi, K. A., & Myllyla, V. V. (2000). Aphasia, depression, and non-verbal cognitive impairment in ischaemic stroke. *Cerebrovascular Diseases, 10*, 455–461.

Kay, J., & Ellis, A. W. (1987). A cognitive neuropsychological case study of anomia: implications for psychological models of word retrieval. *Brain, 110*, 613–629.

Kay, J., Lesser, R., & Coltheart, M. (1992). *PALPA: Psycholinguistic Assessments of Language Processing in Aphasia*. London: Lawrence Erlbaum Associates.

Kendall, D. L., McNeil, M. R., & Small, S. L. (1998). Rule-based treatment for acquired phonological dyslexia. *Aphasiology, 12*, 587–600.

Kučera, H., & Francis, W. N. (1967). *A computational analysis of present day American English*. Providence, RI: Brown University Press.

Lambon Ralph, M. A., Graham, K. S., Ellis, A. W., & Hodges, J. R. (1998). Naming in semantic dementia – what matters? *Neuropsychologia, 36*, 775–784.

Lambon Ralph, M. A., & Howard, D. (2000). Gogi aphasia or semantic dementia? Simulating and assessing poor verbal comprehension in a case of progressive fluent aphasia. *Cognitive Neuropsychology, 17*, 437–465.

Lapointe, L. L., & Erickson, R. J. (1991). Auditory vigilance during divided task attention in aphasic individuals. *Aphasiology, 5*, 511–520.

Laures, J., Odell, K., & Coe, C. (2003). Arousal and auditory vigilance in individuals with aphasia during a linguistic and nonlinguistic task. *Aphasiology, 17*, 1133–1152.

Le Dorze, G., Boulay, N., Gaudreau, J., & Brassard, C. (1994). The contrasting effects of a semantic versus a formal-semantic technique for the facilitation of naming in a case of anomia. *Aphasiology, 8*, 127–141.

Lesser, R. (1990). Superior oral to written spelling – evidence for separate buffers. *Cognitive Neuropsychology, 7*, 347–366.

Lesser, R., & Milroy, L. (1993). *Linguistics and aphasia: Psycholinguistic and pragmatic aspects of intervention*. London: Longman.

Lesser, R., & Perkins, L. (1999). *Cognitive neuropsychology and conversation analysis in aphasia: An introductory case-book*. London: Whurr Publishers.

Levelt, W. J. M., Roelofs, A., & Meyer, A. S. (1999). A theory of lexical access in speech production. *Behavioral and Brain Sciences, 22*, 1–45.

Lindamood, C. H., & Lindamood, P. C. (1975). *Auditory discrimination in depth*. Allen, TX: DLM/Teaching Resources.

Lomas, J., Pickard, L., Bester, S., Elbard, H., Finlayson, A., & Zoghaib, C. (1989). The communicative effectiveness index: development and psychometric evaluation of a functional communication measure for adult aphasia. *Journal of Speech and Hearing Disorders, 54*, 113–124.

Lott, S. N., Friedman, R. B., & Linebaugh, C. W. (1994). Rationale and efficacy of a tactile-kinesthetic treatment for alexia. *Aphasiology, 8*, 181–195.

Lowell, S., Beeson, P. M., & Holland, A. L. (1995). The efficacy of a semantic cueing procedure on naming performance of adults with aphasia. *American Journal of Speech-Language Pathology, 4*, 109–114.

Luce, P. A., & Large, N. R. (2001). Phonotactics, density, and entropy in spoken word recognition. *Language and Cognitive Processes, 16*, 565–581.

Luce, P. A., Pisoni, D. B., & Goldinger, S. D. (1990). Similarity neighborhoods of spoken words. In G. T. M. Altmann (Ed.), *Cognitive models of speech processing: Psycholinguistic and computational perspectives*. Cambridge, MA: MIT Press.

Luria, A. R. (1970). *Traumatic aphasia*. The Hague: Mouton.

Luzzatti, C., Colombo, C., Frustaci, M., & Vitolo, F. (2000). Rehabilitation of spelling along the sub-word-level routine. *Neuropsychological Rehabilitation, 10*, 249–278.

Maher, L. M., Clayton, M. C., Barrett, A. M., Schober-Peterson, D., & Rothi, L. J. G. (1998). Rehabilitation of a case of pure alexia: exploiting residual abilities. *Journal of the International Neuropsychological Society, 4*, 636–647.

Marcel, A. J., & Patterson, K. E. (1978). Word recognition and production: reciprocity in clinical and normal studies. In J. Requin (Ed.), *Attention and performance VII*. Hillsdale, NJ: Lawrence Erlbaum Associates.

Marshall, J., Chiat, S., Robson, J., & Pring, T. (1996). Calling a salad a federation: an investigation of semantic jargon. 2: Verbs. *Journal of Neurolinguistics, 9*, 251–260.

Marshall, J., Pound, C., White-Thomson, M., & Pring, T. (1990). The use of picture/word matching to assist word retrieval in aphasic patients. *Aphasiology, 4*, 167–184.

Marshall, J. C., & Newcombe, F. (1966). Syntactic and semantic errors in paralexia. *Neuropsychologia, 4*, 169–176.

Marshall, J. C., & Newcombe, F. (1973). Patterns of paralexia: a psycholinguistic approach. *Journal of Psycholinguistic Research, 2*, 175–199.

Marslen-Wilson, W. D. (1987). Functional parallelism in spoken word-recognition. *Cognition, 25*, 71–102.

Martin, N., Dell, G. S., Saffran, E. M., & Schwartz, M. F. (1994). Origins of paraphasias in deep dysphasia – testing the consequences of a decay impairment to an interactive spreading activation model of lexical retrieval. *Brain and Language, 47*, 609–660.

Matthews, C. (1991). Serial processing and the 'phonetic route': lessons learned in the functional reorganization of deep dyslexia. *Journal of Communication Disorders, 24*, 21–39.

McCann, R. S., & Besner, D. (1987). Reading pseudohomophones – implications for models of pronunciation assembly and the locus of word-frequency effects in naming. *Journal of Experimental Psychology: Human Perception and Performance, 13*, 14–24.

McCann, R. S., Besner, D., & Davelaar, E. (1988). Word recognition and identification – do word frequency effects reflect lexical access? *Journal of Experimental Psychology: Human Perception and Performance, 14*, 693–706.

McKenna, P. J., & Warrington, E. K. (1983). *The Graded Naming Test*. Windsor, UK: NFER-Nelson.

McKenna, P. J. (1998). *The Category-Specific Names Test*. Hove, UK: Psychology Press.

Metsala, J., & Ehri, L. (1998). *Word recognition in beginning reading.* Hillsdale, NJ: Lawrence Erlbaum Associates.

Miceli, G., Amitrano, A., Capasso, R., & Caramazza, A. (1996). The treatment of anomia resulting from output lexical damage; analysis of two cases. *Brain and Language, 52,* 150–174.

Miceli, G., Silveri, M. C., & Caramazza, A. (1985). Cognitive analysis of a case of pure dysgraphia. *Brain and Language, 25,* 187–212.

Miceli, G., Silveri, M. C., & Caramazza, A. (1987). The role of the phoneme-to-grapheme conversion system and of the graphemic output buffer in writing. In M. Coltheart, G. Sartori, & R. Job (Eds.), *The cognitive neuropsychology of language.* London: Lawrence Erlbaum Associates.

Mitchum, C. C., & Berndt, R. S. (1991). Diagnosis and treatment of the non-lexical route in acquired dyslexia: an illustration of the cognitive neuropsychological approach. *Journal of Neurolinguistics, 6,* 103–137.

Monsell, S. (1987). On the relation between lexical input and output pathways. In D. Allport, D. MacKay, W. Prinz, & E. Scheerer (Eds.), *Language perception and production: Common processes in listening, speaking, reading and writing.* London: Academic Press.

Morris, J., & Franklin, S. (1995). Assessment and remediation of a speech discrimination deficit in a dysphasic patient. In M. Perkins & S. Howard (Eds.), *Case studies in clinical linguistics.* London: Whurr Publishers.

Morris, J., Franklin, S., Ellis, A. W., Turner, J. E., & Bailey, P. J. (1996). Remediating a speech perception deficit in an aphasic patient. *Aphasiology, 10,* 137–158.

Mortley, J., Enderby, P., & Petheram, B. (2001). Using a computer to improve functional writing in a patient with severe dysgraphia. *Aphasiology, 15,* 443–461.

Morton, J. (1969). The interaction of information in word recognition. *Psychological Review, 76,* 165–178.

Morton, J. (1979a). Facilitation in word recognition: experiments causing change in the logogen model. In P. Kolers, M. Wrolstad, & H. Bouma (Eds.), *Processing of visible language* (Vol. 1). New York: Plenum Press.

Morton, J. (1979b). Word recognition. In J. Morton & J. C. Marshall (Eds.), *Psycholinguistics* (Vol. 2). London: Elek.

Morton, J., & Patterson, K. E. (1980). A new attempt at an interpretation, or an attempt at a new interpretation. In M. Coltheart, K. E. Patterson, & J. C. Marshall (Eds.), *Deep dyslexia.* London: Routledge & Kegan Paul.

Murray, L. L., & Karcher, L. (2000). A treatment for written verb retrieval and sentence construction skills. *Aphasiology, 14,* 585–602.

Musso, M., Weiller, C., Kiebel, S., Muller, S. P., Bulau, P., & Rijntjes, M. (1999). Training-induced brain plasticity in aphasia. *Brain, 122,* 1781–1790.

Nettleton, J., & Lesser, R. (1991). Therapy for naming difficulties in aphasia: application of a cognitive neuropsychological model. *Journal of Neurolinguistics, 6,* 139–157.

Newcombe, F., & Marshall, J. C. (1980). Response monitoring and response blocking in deep dyslexia. In M. Coltheart, K. E. Patterson, & J. C. Marshall (Eds.), *Deep dyslexia.* London: Routledge & Kegan Paul.

Newcombe, F., Oldfield, R. C., Ratcliff, G. G., & Wingfield, A. (1971). Recognition and naming of object-drawings by men with focal brain wounds. *Journal of Neurology, Neurosurgery and Psychiatry, 34,* 329–340.

Nicholas, L. E., & Brookshire, R. H. (1993). A system of quantifying the informativeness and efficiency of the connected speech of adults with aphasia. *Journal of Speech and Hearing Research, 36*, 338–350.

Nickels, L. A. (1992). The autocue? Self-generated phonemic cues in the treatment of a disorder of reading and naming. *Cognitive Neuropsychology, 9*, 155–182.

Nickels, L. A. (1995). Reading too little into reading – strategies in the rehabilitation of acquired dyslexia. *European Journal of Disorders of Communication, 30*, 37–50.

Nickels, L. A. (2001). Spoken word production. In B. Rapp (Ed.), *The handbook of cognitive neuropsychology: What deficits reveal about the human mind*. Philadelphia, PA: Psychology Press.

Nickels, L. A. (2002a). Improving word finding: practice makes (closer to) perfect? *Aphasiology, 16*, 1047–1060.

Nickels, L. A. (2002b). Therapy for naming disorders: revisiting, revising and reviewing. *Aphasiology, 16*, 935–980.

Nickels, L. A., & Howard, D. (1994). A frequent occurrence? Factors affecting the production of semantic errors in aphasic naming. *Cognitive Neuropsychology, 11*, 289–320.

Nickels, L. A., & Howard, D. (1995a). Aphasic naming – what matters? *Neuropsychologia, 33*, 1281–1303.

Nickels, L. A., & Howard, D. (1995b). Phonological errors in aphasic naming – comprehension, monitoring and lexicality. *Cortex, 31*, 209–237.

Nickels, L. A., & Howard, D. (2000). When the words won't come: relating impairments and models of spoken word production. In L. R. Wheeldon (Ed.), *Aspects of language production*. Hove, UK: Psychology Press.

Nickels, L. A., & Howard, D. (2004). Dissociating effects of number of phonemes, number of syllables, and syllabic complexity on word production in aphasia: it's the number of phonemes that counts. *Cognitive Neuropsychology, 21*, 57–78.

Parkin, A. J. (2001). The structure and mechanisms of memory. In B. Rapp (Ed.), *The handbook of cognitive neuropsychology: What deficits reveal about the human mind*. Philadelphia, PA: Psychology Press.

Patterson, K. E. (1978). Phonemic dyslexia: errors of meaning and the meaning of errors. *Quarterly Journal of Experimental Psychology, 30*, 587–601.

Patterson, K. E. (1979). What is right with 'deep' dyslexic patients. *Brain and Language, 8*, 111–129.

Patterson, K. E., & Kay, J. (1982). Letter-by-letter reading: psychological descriptions of a neurological syndrome. *Quarterly Journal of Experimental Psychology, 34A*, 411–441.

Patterson, K. E., & Marcel, A. J. (1977). Aphasia, dyslexia and the phonological coding of written words. *Quarterly Journal of Experimental Psychology, 29*, 307–318.

Patterson, K. E., & Shewell, C. (1987). Speak and spell: dissociations and word-class effects. In M. Coltheart, R. Job, & G. Sartori (Eds.), *The cognitive neuropsychology of language*. Hillsdale, NJ: Lawrence Erlbaum.

Patterson, K. E., & Wilson, B. A. (1990). A rose is a rose or a nose – a deficit in initial letter identification. *Cognitive Neuropsychology, 7*, 447–477.

Patterson, K. E., & Wing, A. M. (1989). Processes in handwriting – a case for case. *Cognitive Neuropsychology, 6*, 1–23.

Plaut, D. C. (1999). A connectionist approach to word reading and acquired dyslexia: extension to sequential processing. *Cognitive Science, 23*, 543–568.

Plaut, D. C., McClelland, J. L., Seidenberg, M. S., & Patterson, K. (1996). Understanding normal and impaired word reading: computational principles in quasi-regular domains. *Psychological Review, 103*, 56–115.

Plaut, D. C., & Shallice, T. (1993). Deep dyslexia: a case study in connectionist neuropsychology. *Cognitive Neuropsychology, 10*, 377–500.

Pound, C. (1996). Writing remediation using preserved oral spelling: a case for separate output buffers. *Aphasiology, 10*, 283–296.

Pound, C., Parr, S., Lindsay, J., & Woolf, C. (2000). *Beyond aphasia: Therapies for living with communication disability*. Oxford: Speechmark Publishing.

Price, C. J. (2001). Functional-imaging studies of the 19(th) century neurological model of language. *Revue Neurologique, 157*, 833–836.

Price, C. J., Gorno-Tempini, M. L., Graham, K. S., Biggio, N., Mechelli, A., Patterson, K., & Noppeney, U. (2003). Normal and pathological reading: converging data from lesion and imaging studies. *NeuroImage, 20*, S30–S41.

Pring, T., Hamilton, A., Harwood, A., & Macbride, L. (1993). Generalisation of naming after picture/word matching tasks: only items appearing in therapy benefit. *Aphasiology, 7*, 383–394.

Rapp, B., & Goldrick, M. (2000). Discreteness and interactivity in spoken word production. *Psychological Review, 107*, 460–499.

Rapp, B., & Kane, A. (2002). Remediation of deficits affecting different components of the spelling process. *Aphasiology, 16*, 439–454.

Raymer, A. M., & Ellsworth, T. A. (2002). Response to contrasting verb retrieval treatments: a case study. *Aphasiology, 16*, 1031–1045.

Riddoch, M. J., & Humphreys, G. W. (1986). Neurological impairments of object constancy: the effects of orientation and size disparities. *Cognitive Neuropsychology, 3*, 207–224.

Riddoch, M. J., & Humphreys, G. W. (1993). *BORB – Birmingham Object Recognition Battery*. Hove, UK: Psychology Press.

Riddoch, M. J., & Humphreys, G. W. (2001). Object recognition. In B. Rapp (Ed.), *The handbook of cognitive neuropsychology: What deficits reveal about the human mind*. Philadelphia, PA: Psychology Press.

Rijntjes, M., & Weiller, C. (2002). Recovery of motor and language abilities after stroke: the contribution of functional imaging. *Progress in Neurobiology, 66*, 109–122.

Robey, R. R. (1998). A meta-analysis of clinical outcomes in the treatment of aphasia. *Journal of Speech, Language and Hearing Research, 41*, 172–187.

Robson, J., Pring, T., Marshall, J., Morrison, S., & Chiat, S. (1998). Written communication in undifferentiated jargon aphasia: a therapy study. *International Journal of Language and Communication Disorders, 33*, 305–328.

Romani, C., & Calabrese, A. (1998). Syllabic constraints in the phonological errors of an aphasic patient. *Brain and Language, 64*, 83–121.

Ruml, W., & Caramazza, A. (2000). An evaluation of a computational model of lexical access: comment on Dell *et al.* (1997). *Psychological Review, 107*, 609–634.

Schuell, H. M., Jenkins, J. J., & Jimenez-Pabon, E. (1964). *Aphasia in adults: Diagnosis, prognosis and treatment*. New York: Harper & Row.

Schwartz, M. F., Dell, G. S., Martin, N., & Saffran, E. M. (1994). Normal and aphasic naming in an interactive spreading activation model. *Brain and Language, 47*, 391–394.

Schwartz, M. F., Saffran, E. M., & Marin, O. S. M. (1980). Fractionating the reading process in dementia: evidence for word-specific print-to-sound associations. In M. Coltheart, K. E. Patterson, & J. C. Marshall (Eds.), *Deep dyslexia*. London: Routledge & Kegan Paul.

Scott, C. J., & Byng, S. (1989). Computer assisted remediation of a homophone comprehension disorder in surface dyslexia. *Aphasiology, 3*, 301–320.

Seidenberg, M. S., & McClelland, J. L. (1989). A distributed, developmental model of word recognition and naming. *Psychological Review, 96*, 523–568.

Seron, X. (1984). Reeducation strategies in neuropsychology: cognitive and pragmatic approaches. In F. Rose (Ed.), *Advances in neurology, Vol. 442: Progress in aphasiology*. New York: Raven Press.

Shallice, T. (1981). Phonological agraphia and the lexical route in writing. *Brain, 104*, 413–429.

Shallice, T. (1988). *From neuropsychology to mental structure*. Cambridge: Cambridge University Press.

Shallice, T., & Warrington, E. K. (1977a). Auditory-verbal short term memory and conduction aphasia. *Brain and Language, 4*, 479–491.

Shallice, T., & Warrington, E. K. (1977b). The possible role of selective attention in acquired dyslexia. *Neuropsychologia, 15*, 31–41.

Shankweiler, D., & Liberman, I. Y. (1989). *Phonology and reading disability: Solving the reading puzzle*. Ann Arbor, MI: University of Michigan Press.

Share, D. L., & Stanovich, K. E. (1995). Cognitive processes in early reading development: a model of acquisition and individual differences. *Issues in Education: Contributions from Educational Psychology, 1*, 1–57.

Snodgrass, J. G., & Vanderwart, M. (1980). A standardised set of 260 pictures: norms for name agreement, image agreement, familiarity and visual complexity. *Journal of Experimental Psychology: Human Learning and Memory, 6*, 174–215.

Somerville, J. G. (1974). Rebuilding the stroke patient's life. *Nursing Mirror, 139*, 57–58.

Spencer, K. A., Doyle, P. J., McNeil, M. R., Wambaugh, J. L., Park, G., & Carroll, B. (2000). Examining the facilitative effects of rhyme in a patient with output lexicon damage. *Aphasiology, 14*, 567–584.

Spreen, O., & Benton, A. L. (1977). *Neurosensory Center Comprehensive Examination for Aphasia (NCCEA)*. Victoria, BC: University of Victoria, Neuropsychology Laboratory.

Springer, L., Glindemann, R., Huber, W., & Willmes, K. (1991). How efficacious is PACE-therapy when language systematic training is incorporated? *Aphasiology, 5*, 391–399.

Swinburn, K., Porter, G., & Howard, D. (2004). *The Comprehensive Aphasia Test*. Hove, UK: Psychology Press.

Tyler, L. K., Moss, H. E., Durrant-Peatfield, M. R., & Levy, J. P. (2000). Conceptual structure and the structure of concepts: a distributed account of category-specific deficits. *Brain and Language, 75*, 195–231.

Vallar, G., & Shallice, T. (1992). *Neuropsychological impairments of short term memory*. Oxford: Oxford University Press.

Warrington, E. K. (1975). The selective impairment of semantic memory. *Quarterly Journal of Experimental Psychology, 27*, 635–657.

Warrington, E. K. (1981). Concrete word dyslexia. *Brain, 103*, 99–112.

Warrington, E. K., & James, M. (1991). *Visual Object and Space Perception Battery (VOSP)*. Bury St Edmunds, UK: Thames Valley Test Company.

Warrington, E. K., & Shallice, T. (1980). Word-form dyslexia. *Brain, 30*, 99–112.

Weekes, B., Davies, R., Parris, B., & Robinson, G. (2003). Age of acquisition effects on spelling in surface dysgraphia. *Aphasiology, 17*, 563–584.

Whitworth, A. B. (1994). *Thematic role assignment in word retrieval deficits in aphasia.* Unpublished PhD thesis, University of Newcastle-upon-Tyne.

Willmes, K. (1990). Statistical methods for a single case study approach to aphasia therapy research. *Aphasiology, 4*, 415–436.

Wilson, B. A., Cockburn, J., & Halligan, P. W. (1987). *Behavioural Inattention Test (BIT).* Bury St Edmunds, UK: Thames Valley Test Company.

Wilson, B. A., & Patterson, K. E. (1990). Rehabilitation for cognitive impairment: does cognitive psychology apply? *Applied Cognitive Psychology, 4*, 247–260.

Yampolsky, S., & Waters, G. (2002). Treatment of single word oral reading in an individual with deep dyslexia. *Aphasiology, 16*, 455–471.

Yorkston, K. M., & Beukelman, D. R. (1981). *The Assessment of Intelligibility of Dysarthric Speech.* Austin, TX: Pro-Ed.

Zangwill, O. L. (1947). Psychology, speech therapy and rehabilitation. *Speech, 11*, 4–8.

Author index

Adair, J., 188, 214–218
Alberoni, M., 85
Albert, M. L., 107, 110
Alexander, A. W., 188, 214–218
Alexander, M. P., 107
Allport, D. A., 8, 9, 18
Amitrano, A., 135, 137, 140, 141, 169–172, 263
Armstrong, E., 260
Atkins, P., 13

Baayen, R., 14
Bachy-Langedock, N., 140, 174
Badecker, W., 89
Bailey, P. J., 15, 16, 32, 34, 35, 40, 115, 116, 120–121
Bailey, S., 261
Baker, C., 8
Barresi, B., 132, 144
Barrett, A. M., 187, 188, 192–195
Barry, C., 57
Basso, A., 108, 109, 259, 261, 264
Bastiaanse, R., 115, 117, 131–134, 140, 174
Baxter, D. M., 85
Beauvois, M. F., 83
Beeson, P. M., 137, 167–169, 229, 230, 250–253, 253
Behrmann, M., 8, 17, 115, 117, 129–131, 204, 228, 229, 240–242
Belin, P., 110
Benton, A. L., 51
Berndt, R. S., 18, 188, 189, 212–214, 225
Besner, D., 14, 57
Best, W., 16, 110, 135, 138, 177–179, 264
Bester, S., 166

Beukelman, D. R., 194
Bhogal, S. K., 260
Biggio, N., 4
Bigland, S., 42
Bird, H., 18
Black, M., 109, 111, 260
Booth, S., 108
Bosje, M., 140, 174
Boulay, N., 135, 137, 140, 157, 162–164
Boyle, M., 137, 140, 164–167
Bradley, L., 200
Brassard, C., 135, 137, 140, 157, 162–164
Breedin, S. D., 15
Brookshire, R. H., 166, 183
Bruce, C., 136, 159–162
Brumfitt, S., 108
Brusin, E., 261
Bryant, P. E., 200
Bub, D., 8, 17, 74, 83, 90
Buerk, F., 8, 56, 138, 140, 184–186
Bulau, P., 263
Burton, M. W., 18
Byng, S., 109, 111, 188, 189, 195–198, 202–206, 260, 264

Calabrese, A., 16
Cancelliere, A., 74
Capasso, R., 135, 137, 140, 141, 169–172, 263
Capitani, E., 99
Caplan, D., 8
Caramazza, A., 6, 8, 19, 22, 43, 48, 53, 89, 93, 94, 99, 108, 135, 136, 137, 140, 141, 151–157, 169–172, 225, 228, 263, 264
Carroll, B., 138, 140, 181–184

Chain, F., 110
Chall, J. S., 187
Chapey, R., 42, 51
Chiat, S., 15, 28, 227, 245–250
Clayton, M. C., 187, 188, 192–195
Clark, E., 10, 261
Clark, N., 137, 175–177
Cockburn, J., 67, 100
Code, C., 260
Coe, C., 261
Coelho, C. A., 137, 140, 164–167
Cole-Virtue, J., 139
Colombo, C., 227, 228, 229, 236–240
Coltheart, M., xi, 5, 6, 12, 13, 22, 35, 188,
    195–198, 206, 262
Consolini, T., 140
Conway, T. W., 188, 214–218
Coslett, H. B., 15
Crosson, B. A., 188, 214–218
Cubelli, R., 140
Curtis, B., 13
Cutler, A., 19

Davelaar, E., 14, 57
Davies, R., 17
De Haan, E. H. F., 98
De Partz, M.-P., 138, 140, 174, 188, 189,
    206–209, 211, 212, 213, 214, 228, 229,
    233–236, 261
Dell, G. S., 7, 8, 9, 19, 22
Deloche, G., 228, 243–245
Derouesne, J., 83
Destreri, N. D., 85
Dordan, M., 228, 243–245
Doyle, P. J., 138, 140, 181–184
Durrant-Peatfield, M. R., 7

Ehri, L., 187
Elbard, H., 166
Ellis, A. W., xi, 14, 15, 35, 48, 57, 63, 115,
    116, 120–121
Ellsworth, T. A., 139
Enderby, P., 228, 229, 230, 255–258,
    260
Erickson, R. J., 261

Farah, M. J., 98
Farina, E., 85
Ferguson, A., 261

Fillingham, J. K., 261
Finlayson, A., 166
Fitzpatrick, P. M. R., 132
Flude, B. M., 63
Foresti, A., 140
Foygel, D., 7, 9, 22
Francis, D. R., 115, 116, 126–129, 137,
    175–177, 188, 198–202
Francis, W. N., 14
Francois, C., 110
Franklin, S., xi, 8, 10, 15, 16, 18, 19, 20,
    21, 30, 31, 32, 34, 35, 36, 37, 38, 40, 54,
    55, 56, 111, 115, 116, 120–126, 135,
    136, 138, 140, 144–146, 164, 166–167,
    181, 184–186, 261
Franssen, M., 140, 174
Friedman, R. B., 187, 188, 189, 190, 195,
    220–223
Frith, U., 187
Frustaci, M., 227, 228, 229, 236–240
Funnell, E., 8, 9, 18, 57, 78

Gagnon, D. A., 8, 22
Garrard, P., 31
Gaudreau, J., 135, 137, 140, 157,
    162–164
Gernsbacher, M. A., 14
Gielewski, E. J., 115, 116, 117–120
Glindemann, R., 264
Goldinger, S. D., 31
Goldrick, M., 7
Goodglass, H., 51, 107, 141, 144
Gorno-Tempini, M. L., 4
Gough, P. B., 187
Graham, K. S., 4, 15
Grayson, E., 115, 116, 121–126, 261
Greenwald, M. L., 187, 188, 190–192
Guillaume, S., 110
Gulikers, L., 14

Haendiges, A. N., 18
Hale, S., 260
Hall, D. A., 129
Haller, M., 13, 13
Halligan, P. W., 67, 100
Hallowell, B., 260
Hamilton, A., 136, 149–151
Harding, D., 137, 172–175
Harwood, A., 136, 149–151

Hatfield, F. M., xi, 92, 107, 108, 109, 228, 229, 230–233
Heilman, K. M., 188, 214–218
Heilman, P., 188, 214–218
Helm, N. A., 107, 110
Helm-Estabrooks, N., 132, 261
Herbert, R., 110, 135, 138, 177–179, 264
Hickin, J., 110, 135, 138, 177–179, 264
Hillis, A. E., 19, 22, 43, 48, 53, 89, 108, 109, 136, 137, 140, 151–159, 166, 225, 228, 261, 264
Hilton, R., 115, 116, 121–126, 261
Hiltunen, P., 261
Hinton, G. E., 197
Hodges, J. R., 15, 31, 57
Hodgson, C., 261
Holland, A. L., 108, 137, 167–169
Howard, D., 7, 8, 10, 11, 13, 15, 16, 18, 19, 22, 31, 33, 34, 37, 38, 40, 42, 48, 51, 54, 55, 56, 57, 88, 104, 107, 108, 109, 110, 111, 127, 135, 136, 137, 138, 139, 140, 144–146, 147, 159–162, 164, 166–167, 172–175, 177–179, 181, 184–186, 261, 262, 263, 264
Huber, W., 261, 264
Huff, W., 261
Humphreys, G. W., 98, 100, 101, 115, 116, 126–129, 137, 175–177, 188, 198–202

James, M., 101
Jenkins, J. J., 263
Jimenez-Pabon, E., 263
Jones, E. V., 126

Kane, A., 228, 229, 253–255
Kaplan, E., 51, 141, 144
Karcher, L., 139
Katz, L., 260
Katz, R. C., 260
Kauhanen, M. L., 261
Kay, J., xi, 35, 48, 63, 64, 70
Kendall, D. L., 188, 218–220
Kertesz, A., 74, 83, 90
Kiebel, S., 263
Korpelainen, J. T., 261
Kremin, H., 228, 243–245
Kučera, H., 14

Laiacona, M., 99
Lambon Ralph, M. A., 15, 16, 32, 34, 40, 261
Langdon, R., 5, 13
Lapointe, L. L., 261
Large, N. R., 31
Laures, J., 261
Le Dorze, G., 135, 137, 140, 157, 162–164
Lesser, R., xi, 14, 35, 96, 108, 109, 110, 135, 136, 138, 139, 140, 141–144, 263
Levelt, W. J. M., 7, 57
Levy, J. P., 7
Liberman, I. Y., 187
Lieberthal, T., 115, 117, 129–131
Lindamood, C. H., 215
Lindamood, P. C., 215
Lindsay, J., 107, 108
Linebaugh, C. W., 187, 195
Lomas, J., 166
Lott, S. N., 187, 188, 189, 190, 195, 220–223
Lowell, S., 137, 167–169
Luce, P. A., 31
Luria, A. R., 110, 115
Luzzatti, C., 227, 228, 229, 236–240

Maatta, R., 261
MacBride, L., 136, 149–151
Maher, L. M., 187, 188, 192–195
Mahon, B. Z., 99
Marangolo, P., 109
Marcel, A. J., 12, 15
Mariani, C., 85
Marin, O. S. M., 61, 62
Marshall, J., 15, 28, 136, 146–149, 157, 227, 245–250
Marshall, J. C., 3, 63, 64, 76
Marslen-Wilson, W. D., 7
Martin, N., 8, 19, 22
Matthews, C., 225
McCann, R. S., 14, 57
McClelland, J. L., 9, 197
McHugh, R. E., 167
McKenna, P. J., 51, 104
McNeil, M. R., 138, 140, 181–184, 188, 218–220
Mechelli, A., 4
Metsala, J., 187
Meyer, A. S., 7, 57

Miceli, G., 93, 94, 135, 137, 140, 141,
    169–172, 263
Milroy, L., 14, 108, 109
Mitchum, C. C., 18, 188, 189, 212–214,
    225
Mononen, H., 261
Monsell, S., 8
Morris, J., 15, 16, 32, 34, 35, 40, 115, 116,
    120–121
Morrison, C. M., 14, 57
Morrison, S., 28, 227, 245–250
Mortley, J., 228, 229, 230, 255–258
Morton, J., 4, 5, 8, 12, 13, 14, 19, 68, 135,
    136, 138, 140, 144–146, 164, 166–167,
    181
Moss, H. E., 7
Muller, S. P., 263
Murray, L. L., 139
Musso, M., 263
Myllyla, V. V., 261

Nettleton, J., 110, 135, 136, 138, 139, 140,
    141–144, 263
Newcombe, F., 3, 63, 64, 76
Nichelli, P., 85
Nicholas, L. E., 166, 183
Nickels, L. A., 7, 8, 11, 16, 19, 33, 51, 57,
    88, 135, 138, 139, 140, 155, 157,
    179–181, 188, 189, 198, 204, 209–212,
    225, 259, 263
Nijober, S., 115, 117, 131–134
Noppeney, U., 4

Odell, K., 261
Oldfield, R. C., 76
Orchard-Lisle, V. M., 22, 48, 135, 136,
    138, 140, 144–146, 164, 166–167, 181
Osborne, F., 110, 135, 138, 177–179, 264
Oxbury, S., 57

Park, G., 138, 140, 181–184
Parkin, A. J., 98
Parr, S., 107, 108, 264
Parris, B., 17
Patterson, K. E., 4, 5, 9, 12, 15, 19, 33,
    40, 42, 54, 57, 63, 64, 68, 69, 70, 85, 92,
    104, 108, 127, 135, 136, 138, 140,
    144–146, 147, 164, 166–167, 181
Perkins, L., 108

Perry, C., 5, 13
Petheram, B., 228, 229, 230, 255–258, 260
Pickard, L., 166
Piepenbrock, R., 14
Pisoni, D. B., 31
Plaut, D. C., 9, 15
Pomati, S., 85
Porter, G., 261
Pound, C., 96, 107, 108, 136, 146–149,
    157, 258, 260, 264
Powell, G. E., 261
Price, C. J., 4
Pring, T., 15, 28, 136, 146–151, 157, 227,
    245–250

Rancurel, G., 110
Rapcsak, S. Z., 253
Rapp, B., 7, 22, 43, 157, 228, 229,
    253–255
Rastle, K., 5, 13
Ratcliff, G. G., 76
Raymer, A. M., 139, 192
Remy, P., 110
Rewega, M. A., 253
Richardson, M. E., 192
Riddoch, M. J., 98, 100, 101, 115, 116,
    126–129, 188, 198–202
Rijntjes, M., 263
Roberts, P., 260
Robey, R. R., 261
Robinson, G., 17
Robson, J., 15, 28, 227, 245–250
Roelofs, A., 7, 57
Romani, C., 16, 22, 43, 157
Rothi, L. J. G., 187, 188, 192–195,
    214–218
Rubens, A. B., 107
Ruhrmann, S., 261
Rumelhart, D. E., 197
Ruml, W., 8

Saffran, E. M., 8, 15, 19, 22, 61, 62
Sage, K., 261
Samson, Y., 110
Schober-Peterson, D., 187, 188, 192–195
Schuell, H. M., 263
Schwartz, M. F., 8, 19, 22, 61, 62
Scott, C. J., 188, 189, 202–204
Seidenberg, M. S., 9

Seron, X., 107, 228, 229, 233–236
Shallice, T., 3, 6, 9, 10, 11, 15, 57, 63, 83, 96
Shankweiler, D., 187
Share, D. L., 187
Shewell, C., xi, 5
Silveri, M. C., 93, 94
Sitzer, M., 261
Small, S. L., 188, 218–220
Snodgrass, J. G., 22, 51, 165
Somerville, J. G., 260
Sotaniemi, K. A., 261
Sparks, R., 110
Speake, J., 42
Speechley, M., 260
Spencer, K. A., 138, 140, 181–184
Spreen, O., 51
Springer, L., 261, 264
Stanovich, K. E., 187
Swabey, D., 108
Swinburn, K., 261

Taconis, M., 115, 117, 131–134
Teasell, R., 260
Turner, J. E., xi, 15, 16, 32, 34, 35, 40, 115, 116, 120–121
Tyler, L. K., 7

Vail, S., 253

Vallar, G., 57
Van Der Linden, M., 228, 229, 233–236
Van Eeckhout, P., 110
Vanderwart, M., 22, 51, 165
Vanier, M., 8
Vitolo, F., 227, 228, 229, 236–240

Wamburgh, J. L., 138, 140, 181–184
Warrington, E. K., 15, 51, 57, 63, 85, 101
Waters, G., 188, 223–225
Weekes, B., 17
Weiller, C., 263
Weintraub, S., 51, 141
White-Thompson, M., 136, 146–149, 157
Whitworth, A. B., 109
Willmes, K., 111, 261, 264
Wilson, B. A., 67, 69, 85, 100, 108
Wing, A. M., 85
Wingfield, A., 76
Woolf, C., 107, 108

Yampolsky, S., 188, 223–225
Yorkston, K. M., 194
Young, A. W., 63

Zangwill, O. L., vii, 264
Ziegler, J., 5, 13
Zilbovicius, M., 110
Zoghaib, C., 166

Subject index

Achromotopsia, 98, 100
Age of acquisition/age of acquisition
  effects, 14
Akinetopsia, 98
Allographic realisation, 79–85, 265
  assessment of, 94
Apperceptive visual agnosia, 99–100, 198
Articulatory programming, 45, 49, 265
Associative agnosia, 99–100, 198
Attentional dyslexia, 62, **63**
Auditory phonological analysis, 20, **21**,
  29–30, 36, 123, 265
  assessment of, 34–36
  therapy for, 115, **116**, 117–122

Brain reorganisation therapy
  approaches, 109, **110**, 265

Case series designs, 4, 110, 263
Category specific semantic disorders,
  32–33, 99, 103–104, 175
Circumlocutions, 265
  clients who produce, 55, 76–77, 142,
  150, 170, 175, 231, 243
  in diagnosis, 48, 51, 53
  in therapy, 175–177
Cognitive relay therapy approaches, 109,
  110, 172–175, 190–195, 209–212,
  220–223, 227, 229–236, 255–258, 265
Compensation therapy approaches, 109,
  110, 126–129, 159–162, 265
Computational interactive activation
  model, 8
Conduite d'approche, 265
  clients who produce, 56, 184, 215
  in diagnosis, 48, 55

Control task designs, **112**, 120–122,
  129–131, 192–195, 202–204, 240–242
Critical variables, 11–18, 27
Cross-over designs, **112**, 121–129,
  167–169, 204–206

Deep dysgraphia, 82, **83**, 84–85, 90
  assessment of, 88–96
  therapy for, 227, **228–229**, 230,
  233–240
Deep dyslexia, 5, 12, **64–65**, 66, 76, 173,
  231
  assessment of, 72–77
  therapy for, **188**, 189, 206–226
Direct lexical route for reading aloud,
  61–63, **64–65**, 66, 68–76, 90, 266
Direct lexical route for writing to
  dictation, 81–85, 266

Facilitation studies, 135–141, 144–146,
  162–164, 177–179
Familiarity/familiarity effects, 14, 55
Frequency/frequency effects, 14–15
  clients who show, 74, 175, 202, 219,
  234
  in diagnosis, 31, 38, 48, 50, 53, 70,
  83–84, 86–87, 91
Function words, 18, **64–65**, 76, **83**, 89, 96,
  152, 207, 231

Grammatical class/grammatical class
  effects, 18, 90
  in diagnosis, **64–65**, 76, 83, 89
Graphemic output buffer, 79–85, 94, 266
  assessment of, 92–93
  therapy for, 227, **229**, 253–258

Graphic to motor programming, 79–85, 266
assessment of, 95

Homophones, 21, 66, 70–72, **83**, 91, 92, 196, 202–203, 231, 233, 241, 266
Hypothesis-testing, 25

Imageability/imageability effects, 15, 18
clients who show, 90, 205, 207, 210, 212
in diagnosis, 32, 34, 38, 42–43, 47–48, 50, **64–65**, 66, 67, 75–76, **83**, 86, 89–90
Item-specific designs, **112**, 126–129, 144–151, 159–164, 169–172, 179–183, 240–242, 253–255

Length/length effects, 15–16
clients who show, 93, 182, 221
in diagnosis, 49–50, 55–56, 64, 86–87, 93
Letter by letter reading, 62, **63**, 70, 187–189, 190–192
Lexicality effects, 17, 215
in diagnosis, 34, 36, 64–65, 67
Logogen model, 4–5, 8, 174

Melodic intonation therapy, 110
Morphological errors, **64–65**, 68, **83**
clients who produce, 152, 219
Multiple baseline designs, **112**, 141–144, 151–159, 164–166, 175–179, 181–186, 190–192, 195–202, 206–225, 233–240, 250–253

Neglect dyslexia, 62, **63**
Neologisms, 48, 51, 266
clients who produce, 123, 182, 184

Object concepts, 98–99
assessment of, 103–104
Object recognition, 97–104
model of, **5**, 97–98
Orthographic (letter) cues
in therapy, 157–159, 172–175, 177–179, 227, 245–250
Orthographic input lexicon, 8, 59–62, **63–65**, 66, 79–84, 266
assessment of, 70–73

therapy for, **188**, 189, 195–204
Orthographic output lexicon, 8, 266
assessment of, 90–92
therapy for, **228–229**, 230–236, 240–255
Orthographic-to-phonological conversion (sub-lexical reading route), 17, 60–62, **63–65**, 66, 71–78, 266
assessment of, 77
therapy for, 137–140, 151–157, **188**, 189, 206–226

Phonemic cues
in diagnosis, 49, 52, 53–54, 147
in therapy, 140, 144–146, 151–162, 169–172, 177–179
Phonemic miscues, 48, 52, 53, 142
Phonological assembly, 7, 29, 45–49, 56, 141–146, 266
assessment of, 55–56
therapy for, **138**, 139–140, 184–186
Phonological dysgraphia, 82, **83**, 84–85
assessment of, 88–96
therapy for, 227, **228–229**, 233–240
Phonological dyslexia, **65**, 66, 78, 237
assessment of, 72–77
therapy for, **188**, 189, 206–226
Phonological errors, 18–19, 21, 266
clients who produce, 56, 70, 92, 142, 147, 170, 173, 182, 184, 207, 215, 221, 243
in diagnosis, 48, 50, 53, 55–56, 68
Phonological input lexicon, 8, 20, **21**, 29–32, 266
assessment of, 36–40
therapy for, 115, **116**, 121, 123–129
Phonological input-to-output conversion, 29, 56, **83**
Phonological neighbours, 16, 31
Phonological output lexicon, 8, 45–48, 54, 266
assessment of, 53–54
therapy for, 135, **136–138**, 139–184
Phonological-to-graphemic conversion (sub-lexical route for writing), 17, 81–82, **83**, 84–85, 88–96
assessment of, 95–96
therapy for, 137–140, 151–157, 227, **228–229**, 230, 233–240

Prospagnosia, 98

Reactivation therapy approaches, 109, **110**, 117–134, 141–159, 162–172, 175–186, 192–198, 202–206, 214–218, 227, 230–233, 240–255, 266
Reading aloud, 46–50, 52, 55–56, 59–78
model of, **5**, **47**, **60**
Regularisation errors, 3
clients who produce, 74, 196, 203
in diagnosis, **64**, 68, **83**, 91
Regularity effects, 16–17, 74
in diagnosis, **64–65**, 67, 70–72, 83, 86–87, 91
Relearning therapy approaches, 109, **110**, 198–202, 206–214, 218–220, 223–225, 233–240
Repeated baseline designs, **112**, 120–122, 164–166, 198–202, 243–245
Repetition, 29–43, 46–50, 52, 55–56
model of, **5**, **47**
Reverse imageability effects, 15, 32, 48
Reverse length effects, 16, 31, 34

Semantic cues
in diagnosis, 49, 52
in therapy, 129–131, 140, 167–169, 181–184
Semantic errors, 3, 12, 18–19, 267
clients who produce, 76, 90, 120, 142, 147, 150, 152, 162, 202, 207, 210, 212, 221, 231, 233, 243
in diagnosis, 43, 48, 50, 53, 64, 68, **83**, 89–90
Semantic lexical route for reading aloud, 60–62, **63–65**, 66, 68–76, 267
Semantic lexical route for writing to dictation, 80–85, 88–89, 227–230, 267
Semantic system, 20, **21**, 29, 32–33, 43, 45–48, 59–62, **63–65**, 66, 79–84, 90, 98
assessment of, 40–43, 52–55, 73–76, 88–90
therapy for, 115, **116–117**, 126–134, 135, **136–138**, 157, 162–169, 175–177, 188–189, 202–206, **228**,
Single case study designs, 4, 111–112, 262

Spoken word production, 26, 45–50
assessment of, 49–56
model of, **5**, 45, **46–47**
therapy for, 135–186
Spoken word comprehension, 20–21, 26, 29–43
assessment of, 33–43
model of, **5**, 29, **30**
therapy for, 115–134
Substitution therapy approaches, 109, **110**, 267
Surface dysgraphia, 54, 82, **83**, 84–85, 92, 127
assessment of, 90–91
therapy for, **228–229**, 230–236, 240–255
Surface dyslexia, 3, 54, **64–65**, 66, 74, 196, 203
assessment of, 70–73
therapy for, **188**, 189, 195–204
Structural descriptions, 97–99
assessment of, 103

Therapy approaches, 107–109, **110**
Triangle model, 9

Visual dyslexia, 3, 62, **63**
Visual neglect, 66, 86, 102
Visual errors, 3, 12, 18, 267
clients who produce, 70, 92, 170, 205, 231
in diagnosis, 43, **63–65**, 68
Visual and semantic errors, **64**, 68, 267
Visual then semantic errors, **64**, 68
Visual orthographic analysis, 59–62, **63**, 64–65, 267
assessment of, 68–70
therapy for, 187, **188**, 189–195
Visual perceptual analysis, 97–98
assessment of, 100–102

Word form deafness, 30, 38, 267
assessment of, 36–40
Word meaning deafness, 32, 40, 267
assessment of, 39–40
therapy for, 126–129
Word sound deafness, 30, 36, 267
assessment of, 36–40

therapy for, 120–122
Written word comprehension, 59–78
    assessment of, 67–86
    model of, **5**, 59, **60**

Written word production, 79–85
    assessment of, 86–96
    model of, **5**, 79, **80–82**
    therapy for, 227–258